Other Titles in the Jossey-Bass Nonprofit and Public Management Series:

# THE COLLABORATIVE LEADERSHIP FIELDBOOK

## A Guide for Citizens and Civic Leaders

David D. Chrislip

Foreword by John Parr

JOSSEY-BASS
A Wiley Company
www.josseybass.com

Published by

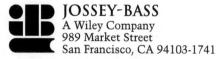

**JOSSEY-BASS**
A Wiley Company
989 Market Street
San Francisco, CA 94103-1741

www.josseybass.com

Copyright © 2002 by John Wiley & Sons, Inc.
Jossey-Bass is a registered trademark of John Wiley & Sons, Inc.

Jossey-Bass books and products are available through most bookstores. To contact Jossey-Bass directly, call (888) 378-2537, fax to (800) 605-2665, or visit our website at www.josseybass.com.

Substantial discounts on bulk quantities of Jossey-Bass books are available to corporations, professional associations, and other organizations. For details and discount information, contact the special sales department at Jossey-Bass.

We at Jossey-Bass strive to use the most environmentally sensitive paper stocks available to us. Our publications are printed on acid-free recycled stock whenever possible, and our paper always meets or exceeds minimum GPO and EPA requirements.

Jossey-Bass also publishes its books in a variety of electronic formats. Some content that appears in print may not be available in electronic books.

**Library of Congress Cataloging-in-Publication Data**

Chrislip, David D.
   The collaborative leadership fieldbook : a guide for citizens and
civic leaders / David D. Chrislip ; foreword by John Parr..
         p. cm. — (The Jossey-Bass nonprofit and public management
series)
Includes bibliographical references and index.
   ISBN 0-7879-5719-4 (alk. paper)
   1. Municipal government—United States—Citizen participation.
2. Community leadership—United States.   I. Title.   II. Series.
   JS323 .C48 2002
      303.3'4—dc21                                                           2002004443

FIRST EDITION
*HB Printing*   10 9 8 7 6 5 4 3 2

The Jossey-Bass Nonprofit and
Public Management Series

To John Gardner (1913–2002),
civic entrepreneur and public philosopher,
who envisioned a more inclusive
and democratic society through collaboration

# CONTENTS

Foreword   xi
   John Parr

Preface   xiii

Acknowledgments   xxi

The Author   xxiii

The Contributors   xxv

Introduction: The Power of Collaboration   1

**PART ONE: META: THE IMPORTANCE OF COLLABORATION   5**

   1   America's Civic Challenges   7

   2   Civil Society, Democracy, and Collaboration   20

   3   Building the Civic Community   29

**PART TWO: MACRO: PREMISES AND PRINCIPLES
OF SUCCESSFUL COLLABORATION  39**

   4  Essential Concepts of Collaboration   41

   5  A Framework for Collaboration   49

**PART THREE: MICRO: PRACTICES OF SUCCESSFUL COLLABORATION  61**

   6  Getting Started   63

   7  Setting Up for Success   71

   8  Working Together   93

   9  Moving to Action   113

   10  Developing Networks of Responsibility   120

**PART FOUR: STORIES AND EXAMPLES OF SUCCESSFUL
COLLABORATION AND CIVIC LEADERSHIP DEVELOPMENT  131**

   11  Joint Venture Silicon Valley   133
       Christopher Wilson

   12  Transforming Civic Culture: Sitka, Alaska 1999–2001   159
       David D. Chrislip

   13  Neighborhood Action Initiative: Engaging Citizens
       in Real Change   170
       William R. Potapchuk

   14  Equal Partners, Shared Vision: The Colorado
       Partnership for Educational Renewal   187
       Carol A. Wilson

   15  Scenarios: Catalysts for Civic Change   200
       David D. Chrislip, James Butcher, Adam Kahane

   16  Building Civic Leadership in Portland, Maine   218
       Thomas J. Rice

17  Building Leadership Capacity in a Socially
    Emerging Community   230

    Allan Wallis

Appendix A: Learning from Research and Experience   246

Appendix B: Institute for Civic Leadership Curriculum and Agenda   258

References   263

Index   269

# FOREWORD

## John Parr

*Collaborative Leadership* (Chrislip and Larson, 1994) broke new ground when it was published by outlining the collaborative premise that "if you bring the appropriate people together in constructive ways with good information, they will create authentic visions and strategies for addressing the shared concerns of the organization or community" (p. 14). That premise emerged from extensive research on successful efforts to deal with tough community issues. At that time, few people had any experience with collaboration; still others were skeptical of the concept.

Since then, neighborhood activists, business leaders, local government officials, foundation staff members, and many others have used collaborative techniques to make dramatic improvements on issues facing their communities and regions. Despite a long history of successful collaborative efforts, many other community processes that were called "collaborative" failed to accomplish anything. These experiences—both successes and failures—have helped many people working on specific issues to become skilled at using collaborative tools and techniques. The field of collaborative problem solving, however, clearly needed more in-depth analysis of what techniques work and why.

Because of David Chrislip's early research and his long experience in collaborative problem solving and leadership development, several of us encouraged him to write a book that would help people understand the principles and practices that make collaboration such a useful approach. He has written a book that will be useful to a wide variety of readers. It can help a city council member,

neighborhood activist, or chamber of commerce board member understand
and then apply this new approach to dealing with complex issues. The book will
also be useful to local government or civic organization professionals charged with
developing and implementing a process in which a diverse group of people come
together to work on a problem. The melding of a how-to guide with rich case studies makes this a book that you will return to often for advice and inspiration.

The book provides a guide for thinking about, designing, initiating, and facilitating a collaborative process from conception to implementation. The tools
and concepts can be applied to informal and lightly structured collaborative initiatives as well as to large-scale, extended, and highly structured ones.

Leaders focused on seeing that problems get solved rather than that their
solution gets adopted are key to the success of any collaborative effort. As challenges become more complex and interrelated, it becomes increasingly important
to find new solutions that can be addressed at the local and regional levels through
new partnerships between all sectors. These collaborative efforts take a different
kind of leadership. This book provides concepts and tools for developing collaborative leaders in communities and regions. It provides a plethora of stories about
citizens and civic leaders who successfully used collaborative processes without
looking to higher levels of government for solutions.

Although the book is titled *The Collaborative Leadership Fieldbook,* it is ultimately
not about process but about dealing directly and effectively with the toughest problems facing communities. After you become comfortable using the techniques described in the book, you too will trust the collaborative premise and understand
that collaboration is not an end in itself but simply the most effective means of
dealing with the complex issues facing society.

*Denver, Colorado*
*November 2001*

# PREFACE

The sudden emergence of Charlotte, North Carolina, as an international financial center fueled population growth and urban sprawl that were inconceivable just ten years ago. As a result, battles between rural and urban interests threaten the integrity of the region. Citizens search for the common ground that will support future development without destroying civility and the region's high quality of life. The relative impotence of traditional ways of addressing regional issues spurs this search for common ground.

Charlotte can trace its interest in finding its way through this thicket of problems to the increasingly obvious negative impacts of growth and sprawl. Traffic-clogged freeways, a shortage of trained workers, and serious environmental damage outpaced the economic benefits of the boom. A region made up of fourteen counties and dozens of jurisdictions with competing needs and interests challenged the capacity of civic leaders to address these issues. Neil Peirce's analysis of these problems in 1995 led him to recommend the formation of a regional citizen-based collaborative to address regional challenges. (Peirce is a nationally known journalist writing about regional and urban issues.)

Following Peirce's recommendation, four influential regional organizations—the Foundation for the Carolinas, *Charlotte Observer*, Carolina's Partnership, and the Urban Institute at the University of North Carolina in Charlotte—created a new organization, Voices & Choices, to help the region escape the paralysis of parochialism and develop a vision of a sustainable future. In 1998, Voices &

Choices used scenarios describing possible futures as a starting point for creating visions and strategies. More than five hundred people from throughout the area participated. Action teams formed around six key areas to build partnerships and develop specific action plans. These teams took their plans to decision makers across the region in January 2000. The plan identified 150 action steps necessary to achieve the vision and established a process for implementation over the next two to three years. Complementing the work of Voices & Choices, a civic leadership development program established in 2000 helps build a critical mass of citizens with the skills for collaborative action.

Charlotte's experience highlights several emerging lessons about how communities address public problems in constructive ways. Each community must begin by identifying and acknowledging the challenges it faces. Obscuring real challenges hinders future action. (Charlotte's use of scenarios helped expose future challenges.) Citizens need to take the time to learn about alternative approaches to public problems and learn new roles for supporting them. (Charlotte's civic leadership development efforts help citizens learn to work together.) Because each place faces different challenges and has its own political dynamics, no one model or process fits every community or region. General principles of collaboration shape each of these processes while tailoring them to meet particular needs. (Voices & Choices designed an extended process to address Charlotte's specific regional challenges.) Stakeholder groups must build linkages to the wider community and to organizations that will implement the work. (Voices & Choices has created a network of new partnerships to engage citizens and implementing organizations.)

Collaborative efforts like Charlotte's demand a new form of leadership that transforms the notion of leadership itself. Collaborative leaders are insistent yet not domineering, compelling but not heroic, credible rather than powerful (in the traditional sense), concerned with process as much as content, and much more behind the scenes than on center stage. Civic leaders must learn new behaviors and practices to support this form of leadership: how to get people to the table and keep them there, how to subsume individual desires for a specific outcome or solution and trust the work of the group, how to encourage and support the participation of others, how to help others solve problems without having to know or provide the answer, how to acknowledge and celebrate the successes of others without taking credit, how to lead as peer rather than as superior. Exemplifying this form of leadership poses far more difficulties than the heroic practices of the past, where the leader provided direction and the others simply followed.

This is not, as some think, leadership without vision. Rather, it is leadership with a vision of a different kind: a more deeply democratic and constructive way of making public decisions. When this kind of leadership works, it leads to tangible and sustainable results, heals divisions among competing interests, engages citizens deeply in addressing the problems that concern them, and builds the capacity to negotiate future conflicts. The experience of working together creates the networks, norms, and social trust that facilitate communication and cooperation for mutual benefit; it builds social capital rather than destroys it.

## Purpose and Scope of the Book

In 1994, Carl Larson and I published *Collaborative Leadership: How Citizens and Civic Leaders Can Make a Difference* (Jossey-Bass). Based on extensive research into more than fifty examples from America's communities and regions, that book described the premise, principles, and leadership characteristics of successful collaboration. The lessons set out in that book continue to provide a useful framework for working together. On the other hand, the book offered few tools for applying these lessons in practical ways. *The Collaborative Leadership Fieldbook* fills this need by bridging the gap between theory and practice.

This book provides a pragmatic guide for citizens, civic leaders, public officials, and professional facilitators to help communities and regions address complex public issues in collaborative ways. It presents concepts and tools applicable to a wide variety of circumstances that require the engagement of numerous stakeholders: problems of racial and ethnic diversity, polarized public concerns that leave communities and regions divided, local and regional issues involving many governmental jurisdictions, issues of governance where citizens and public officials must work together, and others.

The book is both an extended argument about the importance of collaboration and a comprehensive reference work. It can help readers in five ways:

1. By providing a meta view of the importance of collaboration in a democratic society
2. By providing a macro view of the premise and principles of successful collaboration in communities and regions
3. By describing in detail—a micro view—a wide range of concepts and tools that can help achieve meaningful results
4. By describing how to establish effective civic leadership development programs to support collaborative efforts and revitalize civic culture
5. By providing stories and examples to illustrate concepts and tools

It will help citizens, civic leaders, and public officials learn to apply this knowledge to contemporary political challenges. Citizens and civic leaders can learn how to convene, catalyze, facilitate, and sustain collaborative initiatives to address public concerns. Elected, appointed, and professional public officials can learn new leadership capacities to work as partners with citizens. Grassroots leaders can learn more constructive ways of interacting with other stakeholders rather than relying on confrontation. Professional consultants, facilitators, and process experts will have a guide for designing and facilitating collaborative initiatives to address complex, multistakeholder public issues. Those using this book will find the concepts and tools to help them in a variety of ways:

- Making the case for collaboration rather than confrontation with the citizens and government leaders they work with
- Understanding the premises, principles, and lessons of experience about successful collaboration in America's communities and regions
- Working with others in their communities and regions to design and initiate collaborative processes to address shared concerns
- Using a wide variety of tools and techniques to help address the specific needs of their communities and regions
- Guiding and facilitating extended multistakeholder collaborative engagements that lead to meaningful agreements and effective implementation
- Initiating civic leadership development programs to revitalize the civic culture of their communities and regions

The book is designed to help readers find what they need for their situations quickly and easily. It presents tools and concepts in a clear and concise way, with specific guidance for practitioners. The book provides a comprehensive guide to collaboration from conception to implementation, and it incorporates the insights and experiences of scholars and practitioners.

## Overview of the Contents

The book is organized in four parts. Part One explores the deeper importance of collaboration—the meta aspects. Collaboration is not just another strategy or tactic for addressing public concerns; it also provides a means for building social capital, sustaining a democratic society, and transforming the civic culture of a community or region.

Chapter One analyzes America's current civic challenges and demonstrates the importance of collaborative strategies as an alternative to more traditional and polarizing approaches to public issues. It introduces a new set of standards for addressing public issues in ways that build social capital and enhance civic culture.

Chapter Two provides a broader conceptual framework connecting the ideas of social capital, civil society, democracy, and collaboration.

Chapter Three examines what is known about building social capital and enhancing civic culture. It demonstrates how collaboration can play an essential role in redefining democracy in America.

Part Two examines the macro aspects of collaboration: essential concepts, working premises, and an organizing framework for collaboration.

Chapter Four defines collaboration and the underlying assumptions inherent in the idea of working together. It describes four basic concepts that inform the practice of collaboration: the idea of adaptive work, the notion of a holding environment to contain the stresses of collaboration, the use of facilitation to make collaboration easier, and the use of consensus-based decision making.

Chapter Five establishes an organizing framework for collaboration that draws on research and experience. It describes how a community or region gets to the point where collaboration becomes possible, the key elements and critical roles for successful collaboration, and the phases and stages of a collaborative process.

Part Three covers the micro aspects of working together, that is, the practical tools that support successful collaboration. Each stage of a collaborative effort uses specific tools to accomplish tasks that lead to agreement and action. This part describes a broad selection of tools, including commentary on how to choose them as well as how to use them.

Chapter Six describes how to begin thinking about a collaborative process. It provides tools for analyzing the context for collaboration, determining the feasibility of collaboration, and defining the purpose, scope, and focus of an intervention.

Chapter Seven defines the tasks of initiating a collaborative process. Tools include choosing an appropriate approach to an issue, identifying stakeholders in the process, designing the process, defining critical roles, defining information needs, and finding the resources to support the initiative.

Chapter Eight describes tools for building the capacity of stakeholders to work together, informing their work, and deciding what needs to be done.

Collaborative action requires a continuous effort to build a broader constituency by reaching out to the community or region and linking agreements to legislative and implementing organizations. Chapter Nine describes tools for moving agreements reached through collaboration to action.

The continuous development of civic leadership with the skills to work together supports collaboration and helps transform the civic culture of a community or region. Chapter Ten describes how communities and regions can establish successful civic leadership development programs.

Part Four provides stories and examples to illustrate the concepts and tools of collaboration covered in the book. A range of examples reflects different geographical regions, rural and urban perspectives, and a variety of social, environmental, education, and economic issues.

Appendix A provides a summary of the research for *Collaborative Leadership: How Citizens and Civic Leaders Can Make a Difference,* incorporating new findings from scholars and practitioners and outlines an agenda for future research. Appendix B describes the curriculum for an exemplary civic leadership development program.

## A Reality Check

My interest in collaboration grew out of twenty years of experience as a group leader with the Colorado Outward Bound School and the National Outdoor Leadership School. Day after day, I found myself with a diverse group of people in challenging situations. My role as an instructor was to teach the skills necessary for safe travel in the wilderness and help the group learn to work together and make sound decisions in potentially risky situations. Rather than guiding participants through these experiences, I helped the group develop the skills and capacities to meet the challenges they would face on their own.

Over the years, I began to work with groups of civic leaders from different communities or regions. As I watched these groups transform themselves from a motley collection of diverse individuals to tightly knit teams, I began to realize the power of community building as a means for transforming civic culture. As a result, I began to shift my work from the wilderness to the communities themselves. I spent several years learning new skills and gaining more understanding of civic needs.

Reflecting on twenty years of experience as a consultant, trainer, and facilitator working with the idea of collaboration, I see several evolutionary stages. At first, I enthusiastically encouraged others to work together. New skills came easily as I gained experience. Over time, I began to see collaboration as the necessary civic art for our times. While community organizing, political campaigns, and protests—all the familiar means—may, in certain situations, offer better ways to make progress, if we cannot learn to work together, civic life will remain divisive and frustrating. With experience, I learned that few collaborative efforts were well conceived and well executed, including some that I had facilitated. I had become, by this time, a realistic advocate of collaboration. I understood through experience what conditions support collaboration and what it takes to make it work.

Early in this evolutionary process, I believed that deep, enduring universal values permeate and inform human experience. Collaboration, I thought, provided a tool for drawing on this deeper, more unified, and harmonious understanding of what it means to be human. Experience has a way of undermining cherished beliefs. Working with very diverse people with profoundly different stories and experiences led me to a different view. The British philosopher Isaiah Berlin (1998) observes that different societies hold different values and that some of these values may ultimately be incompatible with the values of other societies. Similarly, the anthropologist Clifford Geertz (2000) is profoundly skeptical of the idea that any useful universal characteristics or values of human societies can be discerned. If pluralism of values and beliefs characterizes the human situation, then what is needed is tolerance, respect, and skillful means for living together, not the pursuit of unrealistic hopes for universal harmony.

Collaboration, although not a panacea, offers the possibility of reconciling these incompatibilities in more constructive ways than politics by other means. It has proven its usefulness. Done correctly, it can and does work. With the increasing complexity of public issues and the wide diversity of stakeholders, it has emerged as the best strategy for addressing most public concerns and has earned a prominent place in the repertoire of skills and capacities that communities and regions need.

*Boulder, Colorado*                                                                David D. Chrislip
*May 2002*

# ACKNOWLEDGMENTS

S ince *Collaborative Leadership*, which I wrote with Carl Larson, was published in 1994, my work has deepened my commitment to collaboration and to the need to make appropriate concepts and tools available to a broader audience. Although I am the sole author of Parts One through Three, much of the material evolved from workshops on collaboration and so has the benefit of insight from both fellow practitioners and a multitude of participants from communities and regions throughout the country.

The book reflects a collaborative dimension in another sense. Part Four includes stories and examples of successful collaboration contributed by highly skilled and experienced practitioners or observers of collaboration. Each of these stories offers powerful insights and guidance for future efforts. I thank each of the chapter authors for bearing with me through the trials of rewriting early drafts and accommodating themselves to the demands of a publishing schedule. The book is far richer because of their contributions. They bring life to collaboration in ways that no explanation of concepts and tools ever could.

A number of colleagues reviewed the book and provided guidance. Stephen McCormick, a consultant with the Open Society Institute, and Sarah Van de Wetering, associate editor of the *Chronicle of Community*, read an early and very rough draft. Their thorough critique of the book's content helped clarify and refine a number of points, and their comments sharpened the focus of the book's argument and presentation of concepts. I thank them for staying with it despite the shortcomings in my writing style.

Debra Banks, Ron Bogle, Richard Couto, Mark Gerzon, Gary Holthaus, David Kahane, Carl Larson, Dorik Mechau, Carolyn Servid, Catherine Sweeney, and John Zola read various parts of the manuscript. Their comments helped improve the book by making it more complete, accurate, and useful.

My longtime colleagues and mentors, David Straus and John Parr, continue to provide guidance. Without their persistent encouragement and support, I would never have gained the experience in collaboration necessary to attempt this endeavor.

Dorothy Hearst of Jossey-Bass gave me early encouragement when I first presented an outline of the book. Associate editor Ocean Howell of Jossey-Bass gave me invaluable advice about how to make the book more readable and accessible. My parents, Dean and Mildred Chrislip, never wavered in their belief in my capacity to make this contribution. My partner in life, Carol Wilson, contributed much to the book through her deep understanding of democracy and education. Her experience and advice helped me understand the synergistic relationship of collaboration to a civil and democratic society.

I thank all of you for your very special encouragement and support.

*—D.D.C.*

# THE AUTHOR

**David D. Chrislip,** principal of Skillful Means, has spent twenty-five years help-ing people develop their leadership capacities and create visions and strategies for their organizations and communities. The broader purpose of his work, which fo-cuses on civic leadership development, collaboratively addressing complex commu-nity issues, and organizational strategy and development, is to build civil society. His roles include research, writing, process design, capacity building, leadership coach-ing and consulting, and facilitation. He has served as senior associate of the National Civic League and as vice president of research and development for American Lead-ership Forum. He is the cofounder of the Denver Community Leadership Forum. He has taught graduate courses in leadership and ethics at the University of Den-ver and at the University of Colorado at Denver. He is a senior course director with the Colorado Outward Bound School and the National Outdoor Leadership School. Previously he served in financial management positions with the Boeing Company.

Chrislip has worked nationally and internationally with many communities and organizations and has conducted leadership development programs for stu-dents, managers, and community leaders. He has published articles on politics, civic engagement, and civil society and is the coauthor, with Carl Larson, of *Col-laborative Leadership: How Citizens and Civic Leaders Can Make a Difference* (San Fran-cisco: Jossey-Bass, 1994).

Chrislip received an M.S. from Wichita State University in economics and an M.P.A. from Harvard University's John F. Kennedy School of Government.

# THE CONTRIBUTORS

**James Butcher** is founder of and principal with Entegra Consulting, which focuses on strategic planning, thinking, conversation, and organizational learning. He has worked with the private and public sectors and led many strategic planning efforts, most recently in the high-tech, telecommunications, and steel industries. He has worked with communities on growth management planning and with the President's Council on Sustainable Development on developing long-term sustainable policies for the U.S. energy and transportation sectors. He has assisted environmental nonprofits with strategy development. He is a senior alliance principal with Global Business Network, which specializes in scenario planning, and with Generon Consulting, which specializes in emergent thinking and multistakeholder convening.

**Adam Kahane** is a founding partner of Generon, an international management consulting firm that helps clients sense and actualize emerging opportunities. He is an expert in the design and facilitation of processes that help diverse groups of leaders work together to shape the future. He has worked in this area with corporate leaders in more than fifty countries, as well as with politicians and guerillas, civil servants and community activists, trade unionists and clergy. He was head of Social, Political, Economic and Technological Scenarios at Shell International in London and held research posts at universities and institutes around the world. He received an M.A. from the University of California at Berkeley and the Leadership Institute of Seattle.

**William R. Potapchuk** is president and founder of the Community Building Institute, which works to strengthen the capacity of communities to conduct public business inclusively and collaboratively. The former executive director of the Program for Community Problem Solving, Potapchuk works as a consultant, trainer, facilitator, and mediator. He is widely published. Potapchuk joined the AmericaSpeaks team to work on Neighborhood Action just after the first Citizen Summit.

**Thomas J. Rice** is CEO emeritus of Interaction Associates, an employee-owned consulting and training firm. He is cofounder and chair of the Interaction Institute for Social Change, a nonprofit organization dedicated to building the collaborative skills of community-based organizations and to creating "fair chance" partnerships between corporations and low-income communities. He was a professor of sociology at Georgetown University and a research associate at Harvard University School of Education. He has published over forty articles and has contributed to five books.

**Allan Wallis** is associate professor of public policy at the Graduate School of Public Affairs at the University of Colorado in Denver, where he teaches leadership and ethics and directs the Ph.D. program. He was a member of the evaluation team for Leadership Challenge 2001, along with Carl Larson and Dora Lodwick of the REFT Institute. He received his Ph.D. from the Graduate School of the City University of New York.

**Carol A. Wilson** has worked in education for twenty-nine years, as a teacher, high school principal, assistant superintendent, university instructor, and consultant. She is executive director of the Colorado Partnership for Educational Renewal (CoPER), a collaborative of sixteen school districts, eight universities and colleges, and the Colorado Community Colleges system. CoPER's mission is to promote continuous and simultaneous renewal of schools and programs that prepare educators so that all students will be educated well. Her publications and presentations address leadership, organizational change, collaboration, equity, diversity, policy, and education in a democracy. She received a Ph.D. in curriculum and instruction from the University of Colorado at Boulder.

**Christopher Wilson** is senior research fellow and lecturer at the Centre on Governance at the University of Ottawa, Canada. He is a member of the steering committee for SmartCapital, Ottawa's smart community project, and a program evaluation adviser to TalentWorks, a broad collaborative initiative to coordinate information and programs on regional workforce issues. He is also a strategic adviser with OCRI, a collaborative organization similar to Joint Venture Silicon Valley Network. He holds an M.B.A. from the University of Ottawa.

# THE COLLABORATIVE
# LEADERSHIP FIELDBOOK

INTRODUCTION

# THE POWER OF COLLABORATION

*Behind all the current buzz about collaboration is a discipline. And with all due respect to the ancient arts of governing and diplomacy, the more recent art of collaboration does represent something new—maybe Copernican. If it contained a silicon chip, we'd all be excited.*

JOHN GARDNER

Constructively engaging a diverse group of stakeholders poses great challenges and at the same time adds great value. People with different experiences, knowledge, and perspectives make more creative and better decisions. Communities and regions strengthen their capacity to solve problems and implement solutions when those involved and affected participate in decision making. Leadership comes from many segments of society rather than from a privileged few. People with different competencies to solve problems and innovate make adaptive work possible. Those with different experiences enrich the lives of others with their stories and culture.

Research on community building and diversity consistently emphasizes the need for constructive dialogue as a means of working with the tensions of a diverse society. The National Civic League's Diversity Initiative concluded that "broad-based collaborative process should be a feature of 'governance as usual' not a 'last resort' in time of crisis" (Okubo, 1994, p. 10). The Center for Living Democracy identified the existence of cross-cultural collaboration in community services as one of ten success factors for interracial dialogue (Du Bois and Hutson, 1997). A California Tomorrow publication, *Community Building and Diversity*, said that "opportunities to engage in dialogue within and across identity groups" was one of ten principles for working with diversity (Chang, 1997, p. 7).

Collaboration works because it engages stakeholders as peers using skillful means to facilitate dialogue, mutual learning, shared responsibility, and action.

By providing a powerful transforming experience, it allows stakeholders to engage and act together to address mutual concerns. Citizens converse as equals rather than as representatives of parochial interests. Collaboration confronts and changes basic perceptions about others by recognizing community and conversation as the only means for creating a society of tolerance, justice, responsibility, and caring. When it works, it satisfies fundamental human needs. These needs embrace inclusion (a sense of belonging and community), recognition (respect, care, love), a sense of self-worth, a sense of control over one's life, and the opportunity for living up to one's aspirations (personal fulfillment).

Working together offers the possibility of real progress on public concerns without dividing citizens one from another. Collaborative strategies for addressing civic challenges produce tangible and innovative results while developing the capacity of communities and regions to meet future challenges. A sampling of recent initiatives demonstrates the power of collaboration:

- Citizens in Missoula, Montana, worked together to craft policies for land use and planning that help guide future growth. The city council and county commission adopted these policies through legislative action.
- In Denver, Colorado, the city raised millions of dollars through a bond issue to meet physical infrastructure needs. Without broad support from a wide range of stakeholders, a disastrous battle of special interests would have torn the package apart.
- Sitka, Alaska, faces perennial problems disposing of solid waste because of its mountainous terrain and rainy environment. A group of citizens and civic leaders developed an innovative set of strategies emphasizing recycling and off-island shipping to minimize the use of landfills. Stakeholders continue to work with the assembly (that is, the city council) to implement a comprehensive waste management plan.
- In Maine, environmentalists, developers, and state regulators battled over the proper mix of development and preservation of the state's natural resources throughout the development boom of the 1980s. The Maine Environmental Priorities Project brought stakeholders from each of these groups together to identify and rank the state's most urgent environmental issues, develop recommendations to address them, and help implement new policies at local, regional, and state levels.
- Joint Venture Silicon Valley addressed a wide range of needs, including education, transportation, workforce development, environmental issues, and economic development. The long-running initiative led to the creation of several new organizations and numerous partnerships to meet these needs.

• The Colorado Partnership for Educational Renewal helps school districts and higher education institutions work together to renew public schools and teacher education simultaneously. Results include the establishment of numerous partner schools, improved professional and leadership development programs, and the development of state policies supporting these initiatives.

In each of these examples, stakeholders worked together in new and constructive ways. Civic leaders with new leadership capacities convened citizens and helped facilitate their work. Stakeholders learned new skills for working together and for working with the substance of the issue or concern. Specific tools and consciously designed processes helped them define problems, create visions, and decide what should be done. Credible information supported mutual learning and consensus-based decision making. The influence and credibility gained through collaboration helped stakeholders hold implementing organizations accountable for action and real achievement. By addressing each of these dimensions in a synergistic and skillful way, citizens and civic leaders made collaboration possible and productive. *The Collaborative Leadership Fieldbook* provides the concepts and tools that help communities and regions realize the power of collaboration.

PART ONE

## META

# The Importance of Collaboration

Collaboration is not just another strategy or tactic for addressing public concerns. It is a means for building social capital, sustaining a democratic society, and transforming the civic culture of a community or region.

CHAPTER ONE

# AMERICA'S CIVIC CHALLENGES

For more than a decade, political scientists and commentators have argued about the health of the civic culture or civil society in the United States. To put these disputes to rest, Harvard political scientist Robert Putnam set out to prove in his recent book, *Bowling Alone* (2000), that the quality and kinds of civic engagement in the United States have declined substantially over several decades. An extensive search of trends in church attendance, voting rates, union membership, volunteerism, philanthropy, and other areas leads him to conclude that Americans are more isolated and less capable of engaging constructively on public concerns than at any other time in the past fifty years.

Although his evidence is exhaustive and, for many readers, conclusive, Putnam has critics. Some accept his evidence as far as it goes but think he overlooks the phenomenal growth in the number of nonprofit organizations and associations. New and different kinds of associations may have replaced those in decline, like the bowling leagues he discusses. Others find fault with the reasons he gives for the decline in civic engagement. Some of the criticisms seem mere quibbling—more denial than acceptance. It may simply be that graphs and statistics fail to capture the disillusion, disappointment, and despair that many Americans feel about public engagement in their communities. Listening to the stories of civic engagement—or the lack of it—playing out in American communities like Boulder, Colorado, may provide a better place to start.

School board members in Boulder have been fighting over the need for honors classes in middle schools as part of a larger school reform effort for several years. In 1994, the majority voted to halt discussion of the issue because, as one board member put it, "This has been disruptive to our school communities. You don't turn around every time there's an election and say we changed our mind and we're going the other way" (Taylor, 1994a, p. 1). An opposing board member angrily responded, "I am losing the battle, no doubt, but I intend to win the war!" (Taylor, 1994b, p. 1). In 1995, the woman who was "losing the battle" became the new board president when citizens elected a new majority. Exploiting her new position, she pushed to reverse past decisions about middle school policy. After only two years, citizens, dissatisfied with her heavy-handed attempts to impose her views on the community, voted her out of office. Her defeat removed a divisive force; the damage of a community deeply divided could not be so easily undone. Although few citizens doubt the need for fundamental change in education, opposing views of school reform fragment efforts to achieve sustainable improvement. Everyone is losing.

Other subtle aspects of Boulder's civic culture contribute to its inability to engage constructively on public concerns. Known far and wide as a politically active community, the city is often called "The People's Republic of Boulder" because of its tradition of taking controversial stands on social, environmental, and foreign policy issues. The recent Social Capital Community Benchmark Survey (Saguaro Seminar, 2001), conducted by Harvard University's John F. Kennedy School of Government, confirms this history of civic engagement. Boulder ranks sixth in civic engagement out of forty communities studied. This measure, however, glosses over a more troubling statistic. A large number of community activists and grassroots organizers call Boulder home. As a result, the city ranks third, behind San Francisco and Seattle, in terms of protest politics. Boulder's limited repertoire of tools for civic engagement helps instigate the city's "wars."

Virtually every community has similar stories. The details differ, but the dynamics are the same. One side organizes around a particular position and tries to find allies and gain enough influence to have its way. Meanwhile, others in the community organize in similar ways backing opposing positions. Having mastered the capacity to advocate for particular positions or interests, these groups use their skills to browbeat, oppose, pester, pummel, or otherwise beat their opponents into submission. If one side wins, the victor takes all without much grace. If no one wins, each group can, at the least, stop or delay the action.

Experts have turned this practice into an art form. Partisan groups transform the most trivial or transparently self-serving interest into a cause célèbre, as if no other issue merited consideration. This capacity to narrow issues, stake out exclusive positions, and divide citizens obviously diminishes the community and precludes constructive action. Indeed, Peter Drucker describes the current situation in the United States as "battlefields between groups, each of them fighting for absolute victory and not content with anything but total surrender of the enemy" (1994, p. 80).

This antagonistic approach to public engagement has significant negative consequences. It cannot produce sustainable change because of fickle alliances and shifting majorities. It divides citizens one from another and alienates many from public life. And it sets up future conflict on issues yet to come. No one can argue with the need for progress in addressing complex public issues, but the means to do this have become unproductive and divisive. The way we decide is destroying civility and the fragile bonds of community that bind us together.

## The Civic Challenges

Several disparate factors converge to incite confrontation as the emerging civic norm. Many more people with a stake in public problems demand a voice in the political decision-making process. The problems themselves are complex and systemic and not amenable to expert or top-down solutions. Few people agree about the precise nature of the problems, so few agree on solutions. Lack of shared vision or values prevents concerted action. Distrust and mistrust pervade the relationships between sectors, races, and other disparate groups and interests. Most of these groups do not know how to work with others.

These conditions present unprecedented challenges for America's governing institutions, civic leaders, and citizens and raise a set of critical questions about the future of America's communities and regions:

- With the increasing diversity of citizens in virtually every American community, will we be able to create opportunities for all citizens to participate in the public life of their communities without inviting chaos?
- Given the tradition of adversarial politics and increasingly strident public discourse, will communities be able to develop constructive and effective means for addressing public concerns that engage citizens rather than alienate them?
- As the population of communities becomes more diverse, will we be able to build relationships of respect and tolerance across the dividing lines of race, ethnicity, gender, sexual orientation, and class?
- With the increasing impact of human activity on the natural environment, will human action be congruent with a healthy and sustainable environment?

- As family, school, and community problems magnify, will we be able to meet the basic personal and social needs of citizens necessary for a healthy and fulfilling life?
- As tensions over educational goals and curriculum increase, can we provide education necessary for civic and economic life in a democracy to all citizens?
- With the increasing pace of change in a global and technologically driven economy, will we be able to build and sustain healthy and effective institutions and organizations?
- As the discord between race, ethnicity, gender, sexual orientation, and class intensifies, will we be able to effectively address issues of social justice and equity?

The future health and well-being of America's communities and regions depends on how we answer these questions and how we go about searching for these answers.

## New Standards for Civic Engagement

This foreboding analysis does not mean that Americans are not troubled by the way they make public decisions. Citizens and civic leaders alike seek to improve public decision making in a variety of ways, but with little success. Rather than more haphazard efforts at political reform, America needs new standards for civic engagement to guide political innovation. Adopting standards such as these would once again make politics a source of hope rather than despair:

• *Any response to the emerging political challenges must produce tangible, substantial, and sustainable results.* Civic practices and governing institutions must be capable of constructively addressing the real concerns of a community or region, especially in circumstances involving diverse groups with competing values. Public conflicts commonly juxtapose arguments about differing technical or bureaucratic responses to complex problems when, in reality, different perspectives and experiences, disparate and competing values, and a diversity of interests keep citizens apart. Current civic and governing practices supported by the best of expertise fail to cope with this complexity. Quick fixes and shallow solutions offer only the illusion of real change. Fickle alliances and changing political tides bring only temporary and unstable results.

• *Responses to emerging political challenges must bring people together in ways that heal rather than divide.* Civic practices and governing institutions must bridge the dividing lines of race, ethnicity, class, sexual orientation, interest, and sector in ways that help address the needs of the community or region as a whole. Citizens and civic groups everywhere express exasperation at the lack of appropriate tools for working across these lines. When asked by *USA Today* ("Meeting Race Relations Head On," 1993) what troubled him most about race relations, Cornel West, author of *Race Matters*, said, "We're living in Balkanized spaces mentally as well as physically. There seem to be few spaces where human interaction can actually take place across the races, and that prohibits a coming together which for me is requisite for revitalizing democracy" (p. 11A). This balkanization makes it nearly impossible to focus on the broader concerns of communities and regions. Adversarial politics has left a legacy of anger, distrust, and alienation.

• *Responses to emerging political challenges must engage citizens in new and deeply democratic ways in the process of defining visions and strategies for their communities and regions.* Civic practices and governing institutions must provide avenues for citizens to take an active and substantial role in public life. According to political researcher Richard Harwood, "Citizens say that politics has evolved into a 'System' made up of various institutions and political forces that have seized control of the political process and driven a wedge between citizens and politics" (1991, p. 19). They feel "cut off from political debate: they neither see their concerns reflected in the way current issues are discussed nor believe there are ways to participate in discussions on those issues" (p. 11). Any new response to emerging political challenges must reengage citizens in public life in order to restore confidence not just in governing institutions but in democratic governance itself.

• *Responses to emerging political challenges must enhance the civic culture of the community or region.* Civic practices and governing institutions must build and sustain a civil society. Political scientist Robert Putnam (1993) documented the necessary relationship between what he calls the "civic community" and the performance of governing institutions. In a thoroughly researched comparative study of the twenty governing regions of Italy created in 1970, Putnam discovered that the degree to which trust, reciprocity, and civic engagement pervade the social fabric of the region—not the usual measures of prosperity such as wealth, level of education, or access to natural resources—determines the relative success or failure of each region. His findings were unambiguous: "Civic context matters for the way institutions work. By far the most important factor in explaining good government is the degree to which social and political life in a region approximates the ideal of the civic community" (p. 120). Civic practices, like those characterizing the civic community, must develop the capacity of the community or region to address future issues rather than subvert it.

    Imagine if standards like these became the norms for how we make public decisions. The stilted, archaic language of governance would be replaced by a living language of stories and experience. Citizens would be legitimized and valued for the perspectives and values they bring to public life rather than alienated and discounted. The experiences that shape their values would inform public decisions as much as abstracted, analytical information. Governance would become a learning process where needs are understood and ideas shared in place of unilateral, unequivocal edicts. The outcomes of the public decision-making process would be responsive to both time and place rather than constricted by an obsessive focus on politics and jurisdiction. Citizens would be engaged in a process of dialogue with the primary intent of discovering the best interests of the community or region instead of a contest between a few powerful groups over narrow ends.

## Evaluating Alternative Responses to Civic Challenges

In the American tradition of innovation and adaptation, citizens and public leaders continue to experiment with new ways of responding to emerging political challenges. Some approaches attempt to restore confidence in existing institutions, while others seek revolutionary change in governance systems and civic values. The more reactionary, knee-jerk responses to the failure of traditional practices often lead to unintended and devastating consequences. Many of these responses fall short of meeting new standards for civic engagement. Without reflective analysis, no one knows which of these responses work and which should be cast aside; no one knows which of these responses is the more effective and enhancing of democratic governance.

### Campaign Reform

Recent congressional and presidential elections set new highs for money spent and new lows for mud slinging. Coupled with disconcertingly sluggish election turnouts, these statistics pointedly mark citizens' lack of confidence in representative democracy. David Mathews, the Kettering Foundation president, says citizens find the skyrocketing costs of campaigns particularly abhorrent: "It reinforces the sense that money rules" (1994, p. 20). Citizens want effective ways to cope with the distorting influence of money on election results. They want to be informed about the issues without having every campaign cloaked in accusation, ideology, and innuendo. They rightly seek reform, but fairer elections and better candidates will not necessarily lead to better public decisions.

Campaign reform endeavors to make elections fair, informative, and accessible. It presumes, appropriately, that representative democracy underpins democratic governance. But representative democracy cannot, by itself, respond effectively to emerging political challenges. For one thing, it does not guarantee tangible, substantial, and sustainable results. Too many other factors stand in the way. Some public issues—the escalating cost of social security, for example—are so politically explosive that public officials fear to deal with them. The polarization of debate among political leaders prevents dealing effectively with the complexity of most public problems. The resulting policies may address a narrow range of symptoms but fail to come to grips with underlying causes. Political alliances shift, overturning recent policy decisions. Court challenges as well as initiatives and referenda nullify or subvert decisions.

The voting process and decision making by representatives too often do not bring people together in ways that heal rather than divide. Public decisions determine winners and losers, and the losers, like the school board member in Boulder, press their case through confrontation, further inflaming the community.

Other than campaign activities and the physical action of pulling levers in the voting booth, representative democracy offers few opportunities for citizens to engage in public life. Mechanisms for public participation are notoriously ineffective and alienating. Once elected, public officials maintain only perfunctory contact with constituents and too much contact with lobbyists representing powerful interest groups. Most American citizens know they have little real influence over public officials.

With limited roles for citizens, representative democracy offers little help in improving civic culture. Campaign reform may restore confidence in the voting process and, at some point, in those elected, but it rarely builds relationships among citizens. It does little to build a sense of community or to help citizens work together on shared concerns. Campaign reform cannot by itself overcome the inherent shortcomings of representative democracy.

## Direct Democracy and Ballot Initiatives

States and communities have sharply increased their reliance on the initiative and referendum process as a means of making controversial decisions. Part of the rationale for putting more issues on the ballot reflects a genuine desire by both citizens and elected officials to increase public participation in decision making. But there are more troubling reasons for the increased use. Citizens lack confidence in their elected leaders; elected leaders fear tackling politically dangerous issues. The use of direct democracy does little to enhance America's civic culture.

In November 1994, Californians voted 59 percent to 41 percent on ballot Proposition 187 to deny illegal immigrants access to the state's public health and education services. Equally contentious issues like tax caps on spending, prayer in schools, abortion, gay rights, and so on commonly adorn the public ballot. Voting outcomes on ballot issues like these regularly face court challenges. Opponents organize to overturn decisions in subsequent elections. Most initiatives or referenda fail to address underlying causes of complex problems as they oversimplify solutions to accommodate a yes or no vote. The problems themselves remain vague and undefined. Given these conditions, ballot measures rarely lead to tangible, substantial, and sustainable results.

By presenting simplistic solutions, initiatives and referenda polarize citizens and, when the issue is as controversial as Proposition 187, inflame tensions between them. The distorting role of the media and money in campaigns aggravates this divisiveness. Political scientist Tom Cronin concluded in his study of direct democracy, "In general, the side with the most money . . . [has] the best chance of influencing voter thinking and voter preferences. As a result, the rights of those who cannot afford to be heard are diminished in direct democracy elections" (1989, p. 124).

Direct democracy provides neither the opportunities nor the incentives to engage citizens in addressing complex public problems. It cannot help communities and regions develop the civic networks and norms that improve civic capacity to address future public problems. The fight over parochial interests subsumes the broader public good. Direct democracy's burdensome costs far outweigh the meager benefits of quick action and desultory participation.

## Public Participation

One of the purposes of the public interest reform movement of the 1960s and early 1970s (initiated by Ralph Nader and others) was to open up public access to governmental decision making. By providing avenues for public participation, policymakers would receive input from all affected parties, and decision making would become an expression of the broad public interest. Helped by legislative measures that forced government agencies to provide for maximum feasible public participation and by sunshine laws that required meetings to be open to the public, the reform movement accomplished its immediate goals. For a short time, these mechanisms worked.

Lobbyists, associations, and interest groups quickly figured out how to regain a dominating role in the process. As public hearings proliferated, those interests with the necessary resources attended meetings and developed information that could influence the process. Public interest groups and ordinary citizens with little time or money were unable to keep pace. In some cases, court decisions limited participation of public interest groups to those with standing (interpreted as an identifiable selfish stake). Rather than opening up the process, the reforms, in William Greider's words, "raised the cost of entry and participation. Democratic expression became much more expensive—too expensive for most Americans to afford" (1992, p. 50).

When citizens do participate in public hearings, they quickly become discouraged. Most find the process frustrating and intimidating and come away feeling they had no opportunity to make a difference. Even when public officials listen to citizens, the structure of the hearings provides no opportunity for dialogue and mutual learning. For many people, the hearings are a waste of time where grudging officials perfunctorily fulfill an obligation to solicit public input and subsequently do as they please. Public managers and well-organized groups reach decisions accommodating their own interests while ignoring public comment. Where citizens hoped for engagement, dialogue, and collaboration, hollow procedures developed. Where the broader public interest was to be reflected, those with money and information still dominate.

The ritualized, asymmetric structure of public participation subverts its intended purpose. When citizens do not see evidence that elected leaders or government agencies have considered their comments, they may challenge the process or the decision and impede implementation and action. Public participation routinely prevents real engagement, leading to distrust and alienation. Rather than healing divisions, it commonly exacerbates them. Public participation, at least in its current guise, cannot transform civic culture.

## Reinventing Government

In 1992, David Osborne and Ted Gaebler published their popular and influential book, *Reinventing Government: How the Entrepreneurial Spirit Is Transforming the Public Sector.* Believing deeply in government as a critical component of civil society, they propose ways to restore trust and confidence in the public sector to counter growing public cynicism. They want not more government but better government through a model they call *entrepreneurial government.*

They concentrate on how government operates, not on what it should do. The traditional bureaucratic approach is, in their words, "bankrupt" (Osborne and Gaebler, 1992, p. 12). Instead of relying on market forces with built-in incentives or on a system of government driven by overly bureaucratic rules and regulations, they focus on how the public sector can become more efficient and innovative in the delivery of services.

Despite a growing number of success stories with these approaches, "reinventing government" does little to respond to the emerging civic context. America's civic challenges have less to do with service delivery than with the much more challenging problem of gaining political agreement about what government should do to help cope with complex, emotionally charged public issues.

Regaining the confidence of citizens will take more than efficiency and innovation in government services. By avoiding the questions that divide people, reinventing government cannot bring citizens together. By ignoring the desire of citizens to have a larger role in public policy decision making, it cannot engage them. Defining citizens as customers denies a partnership with government in addressing the needs of the community. Without fundamentally changing the role and relationship of government and citizens, reinventing government cannot strengthen the civic culture of a community. It may contribute to revitalizing America's public institutions, but it cannot transform the civic culture.

## Charismatic, Heroic Leadership

American culture glorifies the "heroic" leader who recognizes danger and galvanizes people into quick action and sure-fire results. This kind of leader knows what to do and has the charisma to convince others. From time to time, this myth of the hero becomes reality: people are rewarded with a leader who measures up to their excessive expectations.

Charismatic, heroic leadership naturally attracts followers. In a political world characterized by gridlock and hostility, people gravitate to leaders like Ross Perot and Ronald Reagan with their facile answers and comforting confidence. But the easy promise of heroic leadership cannot save citizens from themselves when impatience for change and action lead to blind trust in the charlatan.

The practical ability of the heroic leader to act in the face of today's political challenges is deeply suspect. Few political leaders have the credibility to bridge the deep chasms between races, sectors, and ideologies. The complexity of today's public issues precludes any one person (or group) from having *the* answer or from acting unilaterally. The old approach of finding the best and the brightest to develop policy initiatives no longer works in a world where there are no expert solutions. Even when the best and the brightest do come up with appropriate answers, those not consulted in developing them will not support the results precisely because they were not consulted. Consider the failure of the Clinton administration's health care reform initiative: the primarily expert-driven task force excluded representatives of significant interest groups such as the American Medical Association and ordinary citizens. The apparent complexity of the resulting plan and the exclusiveness of the process alienated many who might otherwise have supported it.

A more troubling aspect implicates the attraction to charismatic leaders: appealing to heroic leadership allows followers to escape responsibility for addressing common concerns. The German philosopher Karl Jaspers (1947), writing about the darkest aspects of charismatic leadership expressed in Nazi Germany in World War II, concluded that people—citizens—must ultimately be held accountable, collectively, for the way they are governed and the society they live in.

The charismatic leader who focuses on influencing others to follow his or her vision cannot take this responsibility away.

By definition, heroic leadership cannot enhance the civic community because it denies, fundamentally, the notion of shared responsibility. America needs leaders who can help citizens face common problems, not someone who can tell them what to do.

## The Communitarian Movement

Communitarians begin with the observation that the culture of individualism in America undermines the capacity to focus on the broader good. This overemphasis on individual rights, communitarians believe, precludes the notion of responsibility to the larger community. The founder of the movement, Amitai Etzioni, points out that "Americans are all too eager to spell out what they are entitled to but are all too slow to give something back to others and to the community" (1993, p. 15).

Etzioni and his fellow communitarians seek to correct this imbalance. They advocate "a return to a language of social virtues, interests, and, above all, social responsibilities" grounded in an emphasis on family, self-restraint, and community service (Etzioni, 1993, p. 7). This "shoring up of our moral foundations" would provide a new "spirit of community" that would reduce contentiousness and enhance social cooperation (p. 11). Communitarians want to create a massive social movement that will lead to lasting reform in local, state, and federal government. They want democratic governance to be more representative, more participatory, and more responsive to all members of the community.

Despite its lofty goals, controversy plagues the communitarian movement. Some critics worry about the movement's interest in social policy. They fear the possibility of an assault on individual rights that could lead to narrowly defined, exclusive, repressive, and coercive communities. Others agonize over politicians' co-opting communitarian language for their own purposes. Still others see the movement as empty rhetoric with little capacity to create the change of heart communitarians count on to achieve their goals.

Communitarianism remains a fledgling movement, an idea still in flux. It has yet to prove that it can achieve results of any kind, tangible or otherwise. Although the ideas may be right, strategies for action have not followed. A new language of social virtues would undoubtedly improve the quality of public debate and bring people together in ways that heal rather than divide, but so far, no one has been able to communicate these virtues in ways that others can understand, let alone practice. Communitarians preach the value of civic responsibility and engagement but have not demonstrated the ability to go beyond books, position papers, and legislation drafted mostly by scholars and theorists, not citizens. More exhortatory than engaging, communitarianism has yet to transform the civic culture.

## Implications for Democracy and Civic Engagement

So what can we make of the varying effectiveness of these responses to emerging political challenges? What do these responses tell us about democratic governance when viewed through the lens of new standards for civic engagement? If these responses are not enough, what else do we need?

Representative democracy remains the backbone of democratic governance. Campaign reform may reenergize interest in elections. Neither can cope with today's civic challenges without the support of a strong and vital civil society. Mechanisms of direct democracy like initiatives and referenda are too simplistic and damaging to rely on. The limited venue offered by public participation undermines its goals. Reinventing government and charismatic, heroic leadership promise much but do not deliver enough. Communitarianism appeals to goodwill but has yet to put forward a coherent philosophy and plan for action. None of these approaches can transform America's civic culture.

Collaboration offers a way out of this quagmire. It provides a means for crossing the lines drawn by confrontation by bringing all parties together and creating the safety and space for constructive engagement. The possibility of working together embodies the hope for a new kind of politics—a politics of engagement—with a new role for government as a partner with citizens rather than as the primary source of public initiative. Citizens would be the force behind politics instead of its victims. Civic leaders and public officials would take on new leadership roles by bringing citizens together to address common concerns rather than telling them what to do. The skills of consensus building and collaboration would help build a new civic culture. All of these aspects would lead to a deeper, more constructive, and more inclusive form of democracy.

## A Historical Legacy

Efforts to transform politics in ways that lead to more constructive ways of making public decisions are not new. Gandhi, Martin Luther King, Jr., and the Dalai Lama asserted that nonviolence could be more productive than violence. They might not put it this way, but they saw the use of the strategy of nonviolence as a wager; there was no guarantee it would make life better, but they knew violence could make life worse. They took a chance and matched their courage against the world's cynicism, and they came out ahead. In the face of oppression and impotence, they brought hope and healing.

Similarly, to choose to make public decisions differently, to be guided by another set of standards, is to make a wager. But it is a wager informed by the certain knowledge that the consequences of the current ways we make these decisions cost more than the country can bear.

CHAPTER TWO

# CIVIL SOCIETY, DEMOCRACY, AND COLLABORATION

Few people in the United States recognize democracy as an evolutionary process. American democracy emerged in the eighteenth century as a set of institutions and procedures defined by a constitution, sanctified by the founding fathers, and codified by law. These principles and practices have become hallowed ground not subject to alteration. The formal practices of American democracy remain entrenched despite changing needs and circumstances and a growing sense of frustration.

A discriminating eye can easily discern the shortcomings of current democratic practices. The usual one-sided venue provided for public participation allows citizens to speak to elected leaders with little expectation of a response. The resulting alienation and discontent mean little to many public officials. A multitude of competing interests gridlocks the public policy process. With competing interests driving the public agenda, those with the most influence or resources dominate, leaving the broad middle ground of Americans frustrated and alienated. The lack of confidence in public institutions leads to cynicism and the failure to imagine more constructive possibilities.

Escaping these dilemmas requires an expanded understanding of democracy as an evolutionary process. This broader understanding opens new possibilities for improving the way American democracy works and for developing compensatory mechanisms to mitigate its destructive tendencies.

## Democracy and Civil Society

Democracy as an ideal envisions a political system responsive to the wishes of the people. It presumes that all citizens have equal voice and equal access to the system. A democratic system requires formal institutions, procedures, and rules that offer opportunities for people to express their wishes and elicit a response. It needs a free press, free elections, and the rule of law to maintain a free and open society. But the system needs more than these formal aspects in order to succeed. Without a political culture in which citizens are both willing and able to take advantage of these opportunities, democracy is a meaningless concept. Democracy requires an informed public able to (1) check government authority, (2) advance its diverse interests, and (3) develop grounds for constructive political agreement. This is the role of civil society.

Civil society complements the formal governing institutions of a society or state. The capacity of civil society to meet civic needs depends on the sense of possibility and self-efficacy embodied in the citizenry and the organizational norms and skills for working together. A healthy civil society creates the conditions for democracy and helps it flourish.

Civil society provides citizens with a means for controlling the forces that influence their lives. Historically, these forces include tyranny, oppression, party despotism, and ethnic nationalism. More recently, they extend to such phenomena as the free-market economy, globalization, information technology, biotechnology, population growth, and urban sprawl. Civil society provides the means to oppose, guide, or shape these apparently overwhelming forces. Without an energizing civil society, citizens live in fear, isolation, or frustration.

One function of civil society circumscribes the role of government in such a way that citizens become participants, not subjects. In its simplest guise, citizens organize themselves to counterbalance the strength of the state and prevent it from dominating or fragmenting society. In China, where few avenues exist for organizing, citizens remain at the mercy of the state. The absence of civil society's countervailing force there limits the potential for democracy.

A second function of civil society in a democracy ensures that public life offers the opportunity for all citizens to participate and that the public agenda includes the issues and problems that concern them. Political movements, organizations, and associations advocate for particular interests or groups. Emerging democracies like Hungary, the Czech Republic, and Poland need advocates to expand possibilities for participation. The want of the freedom and capacity to organize for political ends impoverishes democracy, making it narrow, exclusive, and oppressive.

But the freedom and capacity to organize around political causes can, in the extreme, lead to debilitating, and perhaps intractable, conflicts. A third function, overlooked in the current understanding of civil society, mitigates conflicts caused by the vigorous advocacy of special interests in ways that serve the broader public good. A society's ability to confront the conflictual potential inherent in modern life depends on the capacity of its citizens to cooperate for mutual benefit. Mature democracies like the United States and Western European nations must encourage this dimension of civil society in order to sustain the trust of citizens in governing institutions.

All of these functions help citizens in a democratic society exert some measure of control over the forces that influence their lives. All of these functions help civil society meet different needs for democratic development. This flexibility is both necessary and desirable. But what do each of these three functions entail, and when should they come into play? What sort of civic culture supports these different functions? What societal or national examples illustrate this need for flexibility of form and function?

## Resisting Oppression

Democracy needs institutional space in order to develop. In the classical understanding of its function, civil society secures this space. Ernest Gellner describes it as "the idea of institutional and ideological pluralism, which prevents the establishment of monopoly of power and truth, and counterbalances those central institutions which, though necessary, might otherwise acquire such monopoly" (1994, pp. 3–4). This pluralism manifests itself as a network of civic associations independent of the state and capable of energizing resistance to tyranny and oppression. Civil society creates the possibility for democracy and self-government when necessary and maintains it when established.

In some places, civil society developed sufficient strength to force the possibility of democracy into existence by creating a sphere of power independent of the state. In Poland, this oppositional sphere evolved into a "parallel polis" that was able to pressure the state to change. Aleksander Smolar, a senior research fellow at the Centre National de la Recherche Scientifique in Paris, describes it as a "society-first" strategy that relied on a variety of associational forms, including the Solidarity trade union, to counterbalance the power of the communist party-state (1996, p. 26). The motivational power of these associations came from their moral critique of state domination and coercion. A politics of values or morality offered hope for independence and democracy.

A civil society that defines itself in opposition to the state can help create the possibility of democracy, but only in the appropriate historical moment or societal context. "A civil society whose essence was radical opposition to the [communist] state could not survive the disappearance of the state. Civil society, it turned out, had been a historical costume; its usefulness disappeared with the times that dictated its wearing" (Smolar, 1996, pp. 28–29).

## Advocating for Inclusion

The unfortunate first lesson of new democracies established after the collapse of tyrannical regimes is that politics soon reasserts itself in very different terms. Instead of opposing oppression as the impetus for action, issues of social, political, and economic inequality take precedence. Instead of the cohesiveness of opposition that led to the possibility of democracy, the fragmentation of proliferating interests challenges prospects for building democracy. "The moral civil society could endure as a viable ideal only so long as it remained unencumbered by the need to make real choices" (Smolar, 1996, p. 37). Civil society must now call forth a politics of interests or advocacy to push real choices onto the agenda and allow people affected by these choices to participate in their resolution.

Civil society's capacity to get people to the table and issues on the table is crucial for two reasons: first, as an avenue for meeting the parochial needs of different groups in a society and, second, as a way of renegotiating the existing political settlement. Politically motivated, interest-based civil associations challenge governing institutions to meet particular needs. These associations generally push for their ends by influencing actors within the existing political system. Similarly, social and political movements help renegotiate the rules of the game about who participates and how they should participate when trust in existing agreements has broken down. Political scientist Michael Foley and sociologist Bob Edwards point out that these movements play a crucial role "by taking up neglected or repressed demands and pushing the political system to engage forgotten or marginalized sectors and issues" (1996, p. 47). Some of these movements, such as the civil rights movement in the United States in the 1950s and 1960s, operate outside the existing political settlement in order to achieve their ends.

Civil society in this costume creates and guarantees opportunities for participation in a democracy. A society where citizens cannot organize or advocate effectively to meet their needs or exert some control over the forces influencing their lives bankrupts the idea of democracy. But once the possibility of democracy exists, a civil society that creates only a politics of interests or advocacy will inevitably founder as the proliferation of interests degenerates into chaos. Civil society will again have to assume a new guise as the historical moment changes and new needs arise.

## Mitigating the Conflicts

The tradition of politics as a contest among interests saps the strength of mature democracies like the United States. The third function of civil society asserts the need for a politics of engagement about the public good; parochial interests must ultimately defer to communal interests. This involves a continuing search for consensus about the public good rather than simple reliance on liberalism's supposedly neutral procedural ground for resolving competing interests. This search requires asking questions that many societies either never asked or have forgotten how to ask: What is the public good, and what actions or policies are most amenable to democracy and self-government (Sandel, 1996)? The existence of a particular form of social capital provides the possibility for this kind of engagement.

In political science, the qualities of social organization that foster communication and cooperation define the nature of social capital. Robert Putnam distinguishes two forms of social capital: *bonding*, or exclusive, and *bridging*, or inclusive (Putnam, 2000). The presence of bridging social capital distinguishes the third conflict-mitigating function of civil society from its second function advocating for inclusion.

Bonding social capital underpins advocacy of particular causes or interests. Groups bind together through loyalty to each other or to an underlying cause. On the one hand, this binding force helps marginalized groups powerfully assert themselves in order to fulfill legitimate unmet needs. On the other hand, it assists narrow, exclusive, ideologically based groups to repress legitimate interests of diffuse or unorganized populations.

The presence of bridging social capital facilitates the coming together necessary for discovering the broader public interest. It brings people together across society's dividing lines in constructive ways. In Putnam's words, bridging social capital encompasses "the sense of mutual reciprocity, the resolution of dilemmas of collective action, and the broadening of social identities" (Putnam, 1995, p. 76).

The failure to distinguish bonding and bridging social capital muddles the understanding of the role of civic associations in building it. Some civic associations build bonding social capital in the narrow sense and contribute little to a democratic civil society. Others turn bonding social capital into bridging social capital by reaching out to fashion a more equitable and democratic society. In recent years, new forms of associations have taken on a mediating, conflict-mitigating role specifically to build social capital of the bridging sort. More research may be necessary to define what associations capable of developing bridging social capital look like, the extent to which they exist, and the capacities that make them work. To a large extent, the capacities necessary to perform the third function of civil society—mitigating the conflicts—may need to be learned.

Some critics argue that responsibility for this conflict mitigating function lies with democratic institutions not civil society. Foley and Edwards assert, "The key to the success or failure of democratic institutions will lie not in the character of civil society but in their responsiveness as institutions—in their ability to mediate conflict by hearing, channeling, and mediating the multiple citizens' demands that modern societies express through civil and political associations" (1996, p. 49). But can any democratic institution of the state consistently play this central mediating role without the support of a healthy civil society? Agreements reached within the confines of state institutions often lack broad legitimacy. Although constitutions establish and legitimize processes for political action, citizens regularly challenge decisions of elected representatives and public agencies through referendums, court challenges, and attempts to recall elected leaders. In most of these examples, a more inclusive and engaging learning process initiated or encouraged by a healthy civil society could have created the broader legitimacy necessary for acceptance. Michael Ignatieff, director of the Carr Center for Human Rights at the Kennedy School of Government at Harvard University, makes a similar point: "A civil society strategy assumes that formal democracy is not enough. Indeed, democracy will degenerate into authoritarian populism unless the democratic habits of debating what needs to be done and then organizing to get it done take root in civil society's institutions themselves" (1995, pp. 135–136).

## Civil Society and the Evolution of Democracy

For democracy to evolve, civil society must develop apace. As societies move from nondemocratic to developing democracies to deep democracy, the capacities of civil society must shift to match the circumstance. Recent conditions in China, Slovakia, and the United States illustrate the changing demands on civil society if democracy is to become possible or allowed to mature (see Figure 2.1).

In China, the state embodies the Marxist contempt for civil society in its attempt to encompass and control all aspects of civic life. Historically, forces opposing the state have had little power or influence. But revolutionary changes in the economy are providing the impetus for a fledgling civil society. A global and professional economy creates more autonomy for businesses. Regional economic development policies instead of national ones diminish the influence of the state. Growing income disparities between rural and urban areas lead to resentment and an urgency to address the imbalances.

## FIGURE 2.1. CIVIL SOCIETY AND DEMOCRATIC DEVELOPMENT.

| Stages of Democratic Development | **Nondemocratic** | **Developing Democracy** | **Deep Democracy** |
|---|---|---|---|
| The Challenges of Civil Society | • Tyranny<br>• Oppression<br>• Citizens as subjects, not participants | • Proliferating interests<br>• Differing needs and priorities<br>• Varying levels of power and influence | • Polarization<br>• Confrontation<br>• Fragmentation<br>• Gridlock<br>• Alienation |
| The Functions of Civil Society | **Opposing the State**<br>• Oppose tyranny and oppression<br>• Check government authority | **Advocating for Inclusion**<br>• Negotiate rules of the game<br>• Secure rights of all citizens<br>• Advance diverse interests | **Mitigating the Conflict**<br>• Develop grounds for constructive political agreement<br>• Engage citizens<br>• Advance the public interest |
| Social Capital Needs | *Bonding* | *Bonding* | *Bridging* |
| EXAMPLES | **China** | **Slovakia** | **United States** |

These pressures loosen state control and provide opportunities for the growth of a civil society that can counterbalance the state. For example, the number of private associations in China had reached 180,000 in 1993 (WuDunn and Kristoff, 1994). Although the government sponsors many of these, they have achieved some level of autonomy through their sheer number and rapid proliferation. Access to international radio, television, and the Internet offers opportunities for many Chinese to hear other perspectives about their country. The proliferation of religious groups and belief systems brings about a more questioning attitude. An increasing variety of and tolerance for artistic expression facilitate greater imagination about future possibilities. Chinese society is changing so quickly that its aging leaders and decrepit institutions may not be able to forestall the emergence of a dynamic and powerful civil society.

In Eastern Europe, Slovakia struggles with the transition from communism to democracy. Unlike Poland with its trade unions and other associations, Slovakia had no significant history of a morally driven civil society opposed to communism. The split with the Czechs in 1992 forced Slovaks to fend for themselves. A "politics of interests or advocacy" quickly emerged. Nongovernmental organizations (NGOs) proliferated around a wide variety of interests and causes. Concurrently, Vladimir Meciar, the prime minister, began to consolidate political power in his own hands. By appealing to Slovak nationalism and ethnic prejudices against gypsies and Hungarians, Meciar built his political popularity sufficiently to roll back economic privatization and other reforms begun by the Czechs before the "velvet divorce." In 1995 and 1996, Meciar used this power to impose significant restrictions on the press and to pass laws that would constrain or eliminate most of the newly formed NGOs. In the face of these restrictions, an impressive number of influential NGOs coalesced to help defeat Meciar in the 1998 elections. Slovakia's growing and dynamic civil society pushed a repressive democracy into a more deeply democratic state.

As Peter Drucker (1994) noted, politics in the United States has become a battleground between competing interests. Antagonistic and adversarial political practices leave communities polarized and fragmented. Cynicism and apathy characterize a civic culture that offers little hope for working through these divisions. The capacities of civil society that helped create this multiplicity of interests do not serve for working through their differences. The procedural republic of rights and entitlements preempts the development of the social skills and an ethic of responsibility and reciprocity necessary to cooperate for mutual benefit. "Despite the expansion of rights in recent decades," says political scientist Michael Sandel, "Americans find to their frustration that they are losing control of the forces that govern their lives" (1996, p. 72). If Americans cannot build a civil society capable of mitigating the conflicts inherent in a politics of competing interests, they cannot control these forces. Current political practices in the United States impoverish the concept of democracy and weaken the possibility of evolution toward a more deeply democratic society.

In each of these examples—China, Slovakia, and the United States—the concept of civil society shifts as the historical or political setting changes. The capacity to make these adjustments as different needs arise measures the strength of civil society. Democracy cannot evolve without a civil society to match its needs.

## Toward a Deeper Democracy in the United States

"The civic virtue distinctive to our time," says Sandel, "is the capacity to negotiate our way among the sometimes overlapping and sometimes conflicting obligations that claim us, and to live with the tension to which multiple loyalties give rise" (1996, p. 74). Despite the battleground nature of much of American politics, some citizens and local governments negotiate their way through competing interests and obligations in ways that offer hope. They create public processes that complement and work in parallel with the formal institutions of governance to cut across the divisiveness of interest group politics. These initiatives are pragmatic, heuristic responses to real problems in communities energized by frustration with existing divisiveness, not by communitarian optimism.

Collaborative strategies for addressing public concerns have an importance far beyond that of just another pragmatic tactic for achieving results in the public arena. When these initiatives work, they mitigate conflicts between competing interests, engage citizens deeply in addressing the problems that concern them, and build the capacity to negotiate future conflicts in ways that better reflect the common good. Working together creates the networks, norms, and social trust that facilitate communication and cooperation for mutual benefit, building bridging social capital rather than destroying it. The continued evolution of the United States as a democratic society depends on civil society's capacity to foster a new culture of collaborative civic engagement.

CHAPTER THREE

# BUILDING THE CIVIC COMMUNITY

A chain of logic leads from America's civic challenges to the need for more constructive forms of civic engagement. That logic reveals the systemic relationship between the depth and difficulty of America's civic challenges, the inability of current norms of civic engagement to respond to these challenges, the egregious consequences of these norms, and the concurrent decline of social capital. If democracy needs more constructive norms for civic engagement grounded in a healthy civil society in order to thrive, this vicious circle must be reversed.

An equally powerful virtuous circle creates much more beneficial results. The "civic community," as Putnam (1993) defined the elements that support democracy and good governance, includes widespread civic engagement; political equality; norms of solidarity, trust, and tolerance; and associations or social structures of cooperation. These elements combine to generate a steady focus on the broader good and build bridging social capital. In short, the civic community leads to civic action in the broader interests of the community that builds bridging social capital, further enhancing the elements of the civic community, and so on.

Examples of both vicious and virtuous circles of civic engagement exist, as Putnam demonstrated in his research in Italy. But can specific actions transform a vicious circle into a virtuous circle? Is the emergence of the civic community entirely accidental or contingent on historical circumstance and tradition, or can it be consciously created? The deep historical roots of civic community found in Italy made Putnam pessimistic about creating it in places where it does not now exist: "Where norms and networks are lacking, the outlook for collective action appears bleak" (1993, p. 183). Recent experience confirms the opposite, however: certain activities can have an immediate and beneficial effect on civil society, social capital, and the civic community.

## Defining Civic Capacities

Chapter Two defined a third form of civil society necessary for mitigating the conflicts of a politics of competing interests. This politics of engagement encourages a wide range of stakeholders to work through complex, conflict-ridden public concerns in constructive ways. Bridging social capital provides the cornerstone for these efforts. The existence of certain beliefs, knowledge, skills, and structures in a community or region helps make them work.

Communities need a widespread awareness of alternative ways for addressing public issues. This requires understanding a range of possible approaches, knowing how to assess the current situation, and making an appropriate choice. Without these critical capacities, communities respond to public problems in habitual ways. Good results depend on strategies that match the challenges.

Appropriate skills and leadership help make these strategies work. Citizens and civic leaders with good working relationships and skills for interacting across social lines ease the challenges of working together. Process experts help design and facilitate integrative, adaptive, learning engagements that lead to new understandings of problems and innovative, previously inconceivable strategies for addressing them. Civic leaders energize the work by catalyzing, convening, facilitating, and sustaining collaborative engagements. Developing and cultivating these exceptional relationships, group skills, and leadership capacities help transform the civic culture of a community or region.

Putnam identified social structures of cooperation as a crucial component of the civic community. Citizens need public places and spaces where they can come together to build relationships, understand issues, and address public concerns. These forums provide a safe ground for civic engagement and for informing and facilitating the work of the community.

A longer track record of working together provides stories and guidance for future efforts and encourages the belief that challenges can be met in constructive ways. Success stories spawn future successes. A history of collaboration builds relationships of trust and respect.

# Investing in the Civic Community

Communities and regions with enough of these civic capacities and a track record of using them have the potential to turn vicious circles into virtuous ones. The results of this transformation are more profound than people think. Just as good governance depends on the presence of the civic community, economic success depends on similar qualities. In his 1995 book, *Trust*, social scientist Francis Fukuyama, correlated the prosperity of a country or region with the presence of what he called the "social virtues." Fukuyama's social virtues mirror Putnam's civic community.

The broader implications of Putnam's and Fukuyama's findings contrast sharply with the symptomatic focus of traditional strategies for strengthening government and improving local economies. Rather than attending to external factors like campaign finance reform, term limitations, and voter turnout or providing economic incentives to attract businesses, investing in the civic culture offers far greater returns. If good governance and prosperity depend on the presence of the civic community or social virtues, then strategies for enhancing them need to be redirected to investments in the civic culture. Sound investments in the civic culture lead to tangible results, a healthier community, and a deeper democracy.

## Educating for Democracy

A century ago, the American philosopher John Dewey forcefully described the link between education and democracy. Following Dewey's tradition, political scientist Benjamin Barber concluded that "the autonomy and the dignity no less than the rights and freedoms of all Americans depend on the survival of democracy: not just democratic government, but a democratic civil society and a democratic civic culture. There is only one road to democracy: education" (1992, p. 15). Educator John Goodlad reached similar conclusions about the public and civic purposes of education in his recent book *In Praise of Education:* "Education and democracy share a mutual instrumentality: A flourishing democracy nurtures education; education nourishes democratic character" (Goodlad, 1997, p. x). Long-term efforts to enhance civil society must build on the efforts of primary and secondary education systems that teach students the meaning and practice of citizenship in a democracy.

Unfortunately, current efforts to reform public education rarely reflect these public and civic purposes. Standards and accountability dominate the agenda. Preparing students for a productive worklife in a technology-driven economy takes precedence. This business- and economic-oriented impetus shifts the focus away from preparing students for citizenship in a democracy. Some state school districts explicitly reject any reference to civic life or democratic values in the stated purposes of primary and secondary education.

A few exceptional initiatives counter this trend. In 1985, Goodlad created the National Network for Educational Renewal (NNER) with an ambitious mission of simultaneously renewing primary and secondary education and teacher education programs in colleges and universities. Historically, despite their obvious systemic relationship, few activities connected these institutions, and little collaboration took place. Both sides suffered as a result. The lessons of teaching in an increasingly diverse society did not filter back to higher education, so new teachers were ill equipped to succeed in their new jobs. Lessons from research on pedagogy and curriculum in universities rarely found their way into public education. To correct these shortcomings, the NNER helped establish school-university partnerships in twelve states that work to renew the capacity of schools and universities to provide education that builds and supports a healthy civil society.

Unlike many educational reform efforts tied to economic needs, Goodlad's vision goes deeper. Education must prepare students to participate in the human conversation and in a democratic society. Teachers and educators nurture student learning and become stewards of the public education process. For Goodlad, these are the primary purposes of education.

- See Chapter Fourteen, "Equal Partners, Shared Vision: The Colorado Partnership for Educational Renewal," for an example of a collaborative organization striving to achieve Goodlad's vision.

## Developing Civic Leadership in Colleges and Universities

Just as primary and secondary education need to develop the capacities for citizenship in a democracy, colleges and universities must build on this foundation. A quick survey of course offerings in higher education, however, shows little emphasis on civic education. Traditional civics and political science courses provide little more than a basic overview of the political system. These courses define a limited role for citizens: participation in the formal system through voting, initiatives and referenda, and political campaigns. Students gain no knowledge of democratic theory and the role of civil society. Similarly, they learn little about current challenges, the capacity of the formal system to respond to these challenges, and alternative, perhaps more deeply democratic ways to address the challenges.

In response to these shortcomings, the number of leadership development programs in colleges and universities concentrating on civics and citizenship has grown rapidly in recent years. These programs complement the more traditional academic curriculum. Their interdisciplinary nature, however, often makes it difficult to gain legitimacy within the institution and for students to earn academic credit. Nevertheless, a number of these programs have demonstrated the capacity to enhance students' public commitment, political awareness, and civic leadership skills significantly (Zimmerman-Oster and Burkhardt, 2000). They accomplish this through a wide range of program activities and methods, including service-learning (one of Putnam's few prescriptions for addressing the decline of civic engagement), self-assessment and reflection, team building, outdoor experiential activities, community involvement, intercultural training, collaborative group skills, and public policy analysis. The programs reach a broad cross-section of students and vary in size from small, highly selective cohorts to campuswide involvement.

The Student Leadership Institute (SLI) at the University of Colorado in Boulder completed its twenty-eighth year in 2000. From the start, the SLI concentrated on developing students' leadership capacities and commitment to community service. In 1997, responding to the call for more and better leaders, the SLI created a new residential program, Community Trusteeship, that uses cocurricular activities and service-learning to allow participants to learn leadership by practicing it. It develops skills for addressing issues and problems through critical inquiry and collaborative processes. The living and learning center approach to leadership development adds a powerful dimension to this educational experience.

As the number of programs has grown, new networks like the National Leadership Symposium (NLS) emerged to connect these initiatives and share lessons about pedagogy and curriculum. More than forty colleges and universities sent teams to the NLS four-day annual conference in 2000 to learn from each other and from visiting scholars and to develop new programs and activities for developing civic, servant, and character leadership. These programs bring a fresh and much-needed perspective to civic education and leadership development with tremendous potential for building the civic community.

## Building Social Capital in Communities

At the community level, other powerful initiatives improve civic life and empower citizens. These community-building efforts build capacity at the neighborhood level to address local issues such as home renovation and housing, renewing schools, and attracting new businesses. With new skills and better working relationships, citizens can take control of their lives and their communities with less reliance on government.

These place-based programs respond to the needs of people living in a geographically defined area. The experiences build relationships of trust and respect and develop skills for problem solving and working together. The programs increase awareness of issues, improve communication skills, develop an appreciation for good process as well as good results, clarify roles and responsibilities, bring in more diverse leadership, spawn unlikely and unexpected partnerships, and help make the most of local resources.

One such initiative, the Common Enterprise (TCE) in San Antonio, Texas, began in 1995. Its president, Juan Sepulveda, describes its mission as "increasing civic and political participation and leadership and helping make individuals, organizations, and the larger community more effective in the public work they perform" (Sepulveda, 2000, p. 39).

Building relationships among unlikely partners is a central part of TCE: "Unlikely partners shake up the process" (Sepulveda, 2000, p. 40). By mobilizing new partnerships, communities use local resources better. Diverse communities share a common problem: they need more people involved in addressing public problems as the most active leaders burn out and others disengage. TCE brings more people to the table and develops their leadership skills. In order to avoid overcrowded agendas that preclude real work, community members learn to think strategically in order to set priorities. They learn how to identify and build on local community assets, which produces far more results than convincing outsiders to invest in a needy neighborhood. Citizens reflect on their own work—what is working or not working—and incorporate lessons of experience from other places. All of these activities enhance San Antonio's civic community and thus create the possibility of effective citizen involvement and real change.

## Forums for Civic Engagement

Certain kinds of associational life help build civic networks that encourage engagement in public life. Citizens learn civic skills in many places. Participation in parents' and teachers' associations and book clubs, for example, help people learn to organize work, build trust, communicate, and negotiate. At a more formal level, nonprofit organizations and associations help improve civil society. Some of these organizations create bonding social capital. As public advocates, environmental and public health organizations put their concerns on the public agenda. Racial, cultural, and ethnic associations create solidarity within marginalized groups in order to ensure participation in public deliberations. More recently, freshly created mediating organizations convene disparate stakeholders to work together in constructive ways. They build bridging social capital.

A growing number of citizens' leagues in communities and regions serve as social structures for cooperation. These forums provide neutral ground for citizens to understand issues, set priorities, and decide how to meet community and regional challenges. They encourage participation by a wide range of stakeholders and provide resources to inform and support their engagement.

Central Oklahoma 2020, a regional visioning process completed in 1994, supplied the impetus for starting the Citizens League of Central Oklahoma (CLCO). Participants in Central Oklahoma 2020 particularly appreciated the open and respectful conversations that occurred in the visioning process and wanted to continue this kind of engagement. CLCO, a self-governing association of individual, family, and organizational members, provides a forum for discussion, problem solving, and community involvement. It helps ensure that the vision provided by Central Oklahoma 2020 continues to reflect the desires and needs of the region.

CLCO has sparked a number of initiatives responding to particular needs, including, in 1999, a thorough study of ways to improve public schools in the region. This study continues to inform and shape emerging efforts to renew public education. Mediating organizations like CLCO create forums for civic engagement to support the civic community.

## Developing Networks of Responsibility

Public philosopher John Gardner calls for "networks of responsibility" to address public concerns in communities and regions. Civic leadership development programs offer a means for developing these networks.

Historically, community leadership programs built relationships and issue understanding among up-and-comers in the business community. Few focused on developing the civic leadership capacities to address public issues. As the demographics of communities changed and marginalized groups pressed their demands for inclusion and social justice, the old guard of civic leaders lost its hold on the public agenda. Public decisions could no longer be made in the exclusive atmosphere of the rich and powerful. New skills for working across social dividing lines were needed in order to get anything done.

These conditions sparked the emergence of new programs promoting the civic aspects of leadership development for citizens from different segments of society. These programs help participants learn more constructive ways of working together to address issues of shared concern. They teach people how to be catalysts, convenors, and facilitators of collaborative action. They encourage participants to apply these skills to specific issues both within and outside the programs. They build trust across social boundaries, create new civic networks, and teach the organizational skills necessary for a healthy civil society.

The Institute for Civic Leadership (ICL) in Portland, Maine, is an example of this new breed of civic leadership development program. Founded in 1993, the

ICL filled a leadership vacuum exposed when Portland's economy collapsed in the early 1990s after the great boom of the 1980s. When a small group of concerned civic leaders investigated this gap, they found little reason for optimism: a lack of political leadership at the state level, a lack of dialogue between special interest groups and narrow constituencies, and little or no concern about public issues within the private sector. In their words, "the old models of corporate leadership were dead."

In response to these findings, the group convened a broad cross-section of citizens to define leadership needs and design a program to meet these needs. The resulting program would have to bring together a diverse group of people, develop a shared commitment to civic life, and create a new network of concerned citizens from all sectors. It would have to teach participants experientially the skills and capacities for working together to address the challenges of the region. Each year, twenty-five to thirty civic leaders would spend two to five days a month for ten months in order to transform the civic culture of the region.

Since the program began in 1993, more than two hundred citizens have completed the program, building new relationships and learning new civic skills. A number of unlikely partnerships have emerged to address a range of public concerns achieving substantial and measurable results. The region's leadership vacuum disappeared. In its place, a new network of responsibility serves the broader civic needs of the region.

- See Chapter Ten, "Developing 'Networks of Responsibility,'" for information about how to design and initiate civic leadership development program.
- See Chapter Sixteen, "Building Civic Leadership in Portland, Maine," for more on the ICL.

## The Experience of Working Together

Citizens working together increase bridging social capital and enhance civil society. These initiatives build relationships of trust, tolerance, and solidarity, leading to political equality. They promote civic engagement by establishing social structures of cooperation. They reproduce, by experience and example, the elements of the civic community and encourage a deeper form of democracy.

Collaborative initiatives bring together broadly inclusive groups of stakeholders to address issues of shared concern. These groups have no formal power. They gain influence through their inclusiveness, creating a constituency for change that can hold formal institutions accountable for action on their recommendations. They purposefully engage community members with diverse, even opposing, perspectives and positions in order to make better decisions and prevent gridlock. Through a constructive process for learning together, they reach implementable agreements that more accurately reflect the broader public good.

Infighting among developers, timber interests, and environmentalists has plagued Missoula, Montana, for years. Hamstrung and held hostage by competing factions and interest groups, elected leaders had scant control over these battles. Little could be done to manage or shape the forces that were threatening Missoula's greatest assets: the physical beauty of the mountains and the high quality of life that its citizens enjoyed.

This impotence stoked Missoulians' greatest fear—stalemate—and helped move them to action. Spurred in part by its visionary mayor, Daniel Kemmis, the city council and county commission put together the Growth Management Task Force (GMTF) made up of elected leaders, business interests, and neighborhood groups. The GMTF used its broad credibility to convene a larger stakeholder group reflecting the perspectives and experiences of the region to wrestle with the conflicts.

The eight-month process began by creating scenarios highlighting the future challenges the city could face. The scenarios allowed citizens to confront the possible impacts of outside forces and to understand the consequences of their own actions or inaction. One scenario, Status Quo Vadis, and its tale of continued gridlock, inaction, and deterioration galvanized the group to put together a vision of how they would like to see Missoula's future development. This experience led to a series of recommendations defining land use management tools and planning processes consistent with the vision. Finally, the city council and the county commission had the coherent plan and the political backing needed to take concerted action. Because of the credibility of the group doing the work and the thoroughness of the process, elected leaders enacted the recommendations of the stakeholder group with little modification. The process led to real results as it reinforced the civic community.

- For stories and examples of civic collaboration, see Chapter Eleven, "Joint Venture Silicon Valley"; Chapter Twelve, "Transforming Civic Culture: Sitka, Alaska, 1999–2001"; Chapter Thirteen, "Neighborhood Action Initiative: Engaging Citizens in Real Change," in Washington, D.C.; and Chapter Fifteen, "Scenarios: Catalysts for Civic Change," in the Central Carolinas, Missoula, Montana, and Boston.

## From Vicious to Virtuous Circle

All of these activities either create the conditions for a healthy civil society or build civil society itself. They actively promote the attitudinal and organizational capacities for meeting civic needs—the sense of possibility and self-efficacy of the citizenry and the organizational norms and skills for working together in effective ways. With experiences like these, the development of civil society, social capital, and the civic community need not be left to tradition or chance.

The remainder of this book probes the workings of two of these civic investments: collaborative civic engagements and civic leadership development programs.

PART TWO

---

# MACRO

---

## Premises and Principles
## of Successful Collaboration

A s collaborative strategies for addressing complex public issues have become more common, much more is known about what makes them work. New definitions, essential concepts, underlying assumptions, and lessons learned from research and experience inform its practice. These aspects provide an organizing framework for how a community or region gets to the point where collaboration is possible and for putting these ideas into practice.

CHAPTER FOUR

# ESSENTIAL CONCEPTS OF COLLABORATION

Collaboration emerged as a strategy for addressing environmental and natural resource disputes in the 1970s. Since then, its use has extended to a wide range of problems at state, regional, community, and neighborhood levels. These initiatives address a myriad of problems, including economic development, urban sprawl, neighborhood empowerment, education, transportation, health care, and governance.

Working together entails a profound shift in the premises Americans hold for how public issues should be addressed. Instead of advocacy, collaboration demands engagement, dialogue instead of debate, inclusion instead of exclusion, shared power instead of domination and control, and mutual learning instead of rigid adherence to mutually exclusive positions.

## Defining Collaboration

Collaboration, as Carl Larson and I defined it in our 1994 book, *Collaborative Leadership,* goes beyond communication, cooperation, and coordination: "As its Latin roots—*com* and *laborare*—indicate, it means 'to work together.' It is a mutually beneficial relationship between two or more parties to achieve common goals by sharing responsibility, authority and accountability for achieving results. It is more than simply sharing knowledge and information (communication) and more than a relationship that helps each party achieve its own goals (cooperation and coordination). The purpose of collaboration is to create a shared vision and joint strategies to address concerns that go beyond the purview of any particular party" (Chrislip and Larson, 1994, p. 5).

Our definition referred to community or regionally based multistakeholder collaborative initiatives. Sometimes called ad hoc initiatives, these processes respond to specific needs and often dissolve when the work is done. They differ from similar processes in another arena: interorganizational or interagency collaboration. Community and regional initiatives include a broader range of stakeholders, while interagency collaborations usually limit participation to representatives of concerned or affected organizations. For the most part, ad hoc initiatives focus on policymaking through collaboration, whereas interagency collaborations pay attention to implementing decisions already made. Other types of collaborative initiatives support mutual learning but do not seek consensus. This book concentrates on community and regional multistakeholder collaborative initiatives relying on consensus-based decision making.

Collaborative efforts gain credibility and influence by ensuring inclusiveness, managing a constructive learning engagement, providing information necessary for making good decisions, building the coherence of the group, and helping negotiate agreements that lead to action. Many of these efforts operate in parallel with the public sector. In public policymaking, these informal recommending groups rely on their collective credibility to provide a credible and influential link with legislative bodies and implementing agencies. Sometimes communities and regions use collaboration to create new programs and partnerships independent of the public sector to address specific needs. These efforts build shared responsibility for solutions and strategies among implementing organizations.

## Working Assumptions

Several working premises or assumptions inform the practice of collaboration. These assumptions contrast starkly with the usual assumptions about how public decisions are made:

• *Political practices must be congruent and compatible with the commitment to democracy and a healthy civil society.* Since the late 1980s, Americans have debated the status and health of the country's democracy and civil society. When current political practices lead to division, alienation, and distrust, they expend social capital. Collaboration provides an alternative means of civic engagement more compatible with the idea of a democratic society—one that builds social capital rather than destroys it.

- *The quality of public decisions stems directly from the quality of the engagement used to make them.* All public decisions come from some form of public engagement, whether through representatives, public participation, or alternatives like collaboration. There are no high-quality public decisions absent high-quality civic engagement except inadvertently. Effective engagement comes through conscious intent, purpose, and design. More inclusive, constructive, and well-informed engagements lead to better decisions. Working together offers a constructive response to a divisive civic culture, instability in policymaking, alienation from public engagement, and lack of trust in governing institutions.

- *Public decisions must respond to the real needs of the community or region.* Constructively engaging citizens in addressing the concerns that affect them enables public decisions that meet the real needs of a community or region. Policies imposed by outsiders typically fail because of lack of local support or lack of understanding of local concerns. Contemporary research on community and regional development unequivocally concludes that the best public policies come from the people most concerned and affected by those policies. Similarly, people commit to action because of their involvement in making the decisions. Collaboration offers a deeply democratic way of engaging people in a place in defining and addressing their own concerns.

- *People in a place should have some control over the forces that affect their lives.* The apparently overwhelming forces of the free market economy, globalization, information technology, biotechnology, population growth, and urban sprawl threaten the capacity of representative democracy to mitigate their impacts. The fragmentation of political interests prevents the coming together necessary for acknowledging these forces and guiding their impacts. A society lacking the means to shape these forces undermines the essence of democracy. Collaboration provides an alternative that leads to more encompassing and coherent responses to these challenges.

- *Understanding of others and of essential information about public concerns comes before judgment and decision.* In public engagements, Americans tend to shoot first and ask questions later. In contrast, collaborative processes seek to build understanding before agreement. By creating a safe space, stakeholders let go of preconceived notions to allow new solutions and strategies to emerge. Appreciating values, perceptions, and experiences of others builds trust and mutual respect while destroying stereotypes. Perspectives shift by taking the time to clarify and comprehend information. Before rushing to judgment, collaboration creates shared understanding.

- *Constructive ways for bridging cultural boundaries will not be the norm of any one participating culture.* Practitioners learned the hard way that processes peculiar to one culture do not work with other cultures and different traditions. Dominant cultural norms especially do not work with minorities. People do not intuitively know how to bridge cultural boundaries. Most do not have the attitudes or skills for working effectively with people from divergent backgrounds. Engagement across cultural boundaries requires respecting the diverse norms of participating cultures and, at the same time, providing a new and legitimate norm for working together across those boundaries. The practice of collaboration helps create new norms with the potential to reach across these lines.

- *In order for collaboration to work, all participants must engage as peers.* In a collaborative engagement, each participant has equal opportunity to speak, be heard, and shape decisions. No one person or group dominates. People participate as peers with no distinctions made for position, money, power, role, race, sector, and so on. Working together helps meet the needs of all affected parties by engaging them as peers.

- *If you are going to collaborate, collaborate.* Collaborative initiatives planned by a narrow, exclusive group of leaders or policymakers and then imposed on a broader group of stakeholders generally fail. In order to succeed, every phase of collaboration, from conception to implementation, must be accomplished by people who reflect the broader community through a credible and open process. Only by modeling collaboration can collaboration work.

## Basic Concepts

Collaboration as an alternative strategy for addressing public concerns grows out of the increasingly destructive consequences of current political practices. The idea of working together incorporates several closely related concepts fundamental to its practice: the distinction between adaptive and routine challenges, the notion of a holding environment to contain the stresses of collaboration and to do adaptive work, the use of facilitation to guide or orchestrate adaptive work, and the use of consensus-based decision making rather than majority rule.

### Adaptive Work

At the end of the nineteenth century, the Progressive political movement envisioned a new model of governance. Technical and bureaucratic expertise could counter the corrosive and corruptive influence of powerful economic interests on government officials of the time. Because of the Progressives, a certain faith endured that experts and professionals in government could think through public concerns in a rational way and conceive comprehensive solutions that would work. Citizens and elected leaders identified priority issues through a political process and then mobilized the best and the brightest within government ranks to solve them. Public problems were routine in the sense that the expertise to address them either existed or could be developed. For most of the twentieth century, this expert-driven approach to public problems lived up to its early promise. At the turn of the twenty-first century, this approach rarely matches the challenges of public life.

Most contemporary public problems have no clear right answers. Some involve conflicts between differing technical or bureaucratic responses, while for other problems, no precise answer exists. Conflicting values impair the capacity of elected leaders and public agencies to develop acceptable solutions. Ronald Heifetz, codirector of the Center for Public Leadership at Harvard University's John F. Kennedy School of Government, says these kinds of issues cannot be resolved by technical expertise or routine behavior: "To make progress, not only must invention and action change circumstances to align with values, but the values themselves may also have to change" (Heifetz, 1994, p. 35). Solving these problems requires new learning and adaptive work. Answers must be invented or discovered heuristically since they cannot be determined by experts.

## Holding Environment

If competing values and differing positions mark public problems, the work of defining problems and solutions must be done by the people who hold these values and positions. Coping with a diversity of perspectives and values requires a suitable environment to facilitate this work. A collaborative process provides a structure for adaptive work.

Adaptive work requires learning, and learning requires engagement. Heifetz describes the need for a "holding environment" in which to do adaptive work and a means to "orchestrate conflict" inherent in these kinds of issues (Heifetz, 1994, p. 103). Put another way, adaptive work requires a conducive environment and appropriate tools to facilitate learning and discovery among diverse stakeholders. An effective holding environment provides a safe container with a purposefully designed sequence of actions and events—a process—that helps a group work together in ways that lead to agreement.

A collaborative process engages a disparate group of stakeholders with differing positions and, often, a long history of conflict and mutual distrust. A holding environment provides a safe setting—both physically and emotionally—and a fair process for adaptive work. Skilled facilitators may orchestrate conflict and guide the process. Leaders who can establish and maintain the holding environment pace the work to contain and regulate stress within the container (Heifetz,

1994). An effective holding environment helps maintain sufficient pressure on the group to accomplish real work without overwhelming participants.

## Facilitation

Facilitation is a way of managing meetings that allows groups to work together constructively. The verb *to facilitate* means to make easier. A facilitator in a collaborative process helps make the work of stakeholders easier in a meeting or a series of meetings. A facilitator guides the process of how a group works together while remaining neutral about the content of its work. A process defines the way a group works together; content defines the substance of the issue itself.

For good reason, this is not a book about facilitation. Other excellent books cover this topic. Twenty-five years ago, the groundbreaking work of David Straus and Michael Doyle in *How to Make Meetings Work* (1976) helped define the roles, tasks, and tools of the facilitator's discipline. Others, like Sam Kaner's *Facilitator's Guide to Participatory Decision-Making* (1996) and Roger Schwarz's *The Skilled Facilitator* (1994), built on these concepts but always within the parameters of the earlier work. Collaboration and collaborative leadership extend the original ideas that Doyle and Straus put forward. Collaboration builds on three of the foundational concepts of facilitation.

First, *comprehensive agreements evolve from a series of smaller, less consequential agreements.* The complexity of public problems and the diversity of stakeholder groups make larger agreements impossible or incomprehensible without parsing them into smaller steps. Starting with basic agreements about what concerns should be addressed and the willingness to work together, collaboration then builds more complex agreements about solutions, strategies, and actions.

A second basic concept of facilitation recognizes that *meetings or collaborative processes break down unless participants engage in the same activities at the same time.* The open-narrow-close framework organizes the work of a group in a consistent, predictable way. "All meetings are a series of discussions where participants are opening, narrowing, and closing on different topics and building agreements as they go" (Interaction Associates, 1991, sec. 4, p. 6). A group gathers and clarifies information in an opening phase, before organizing and evaluating information in a narrowing phase, and reaching agreements in a closing phase. This framework informs the overall design of a collaborative process, the stages within the process, particular meetings in each stage, and subparts of these meetings. The framework helps groups stay focused on the task at hand while moving forward in a coherent fashion.

A third basic concept of facilitation recognizes that *the work done ahead of time to create an environment for working together is as important as what is done in the engagement itself.* Preventions anticipate and help prevent problems in meetings or collaborative engagements. For example, gaining initial agreement on the process for working together helps prevent future problems. Similarly, seeking agreement on desired outcomes and an agenda for a particular meeting at the start provides a means for maintaining or regaining focus later in the meeting. Experience demonstrates that planning a meeting or a series of meetings requires at least as much time as the meetings themselves. Collaborative processes cannot work unless the meetings themselves work.

## Consensus-Based Decision Making

For more than two centuries, majority rule has helped Americans make public decisions. It may now have outlived its usefulness. The tradition of majority rule and politics as a contest among interests has become increasingly destructive in the United States. When one side wins the zero-sum political game, the consequences are devastating. When no one wins, gridlock or stalemate results. Rather than leading to progress and action, the tradition of majority rule divides the country, erodes civil society, and undermines trust in the democratic ideal.

Instead of majority rule, a collaborative process seeks consensus on critical agreements. Through a constructive process, "groups *can* forge agreements that satisfy everyone's primary interests and concerns" (Susskind, 1999a, p. xvii) and avoid the worst consequences of majority rule. Consensus-based decision making recognizes that adaptive work generally leads to deeper, more creative agreements with broader support for action. Innovative solutions and strategies emerge from a learning engagement, not from a win-lose battle of positions. Consensus becomes possible through well-planned and well-executed collaborative processes. Through an inclusive, engaging, and constructive process—a good-faith effort to meet the interests of all stakeholders—overwhelming agreement can be reached.

# Realizing the Promise of Collaboration

Realizing the promise of collaboration can be likened to building a wheel: assembling a number of disparate parts creates a powerful tool. New working assumptions lead to new ways of making public decisions, and new concepts and tools help fashion new processes. Consider what a community or region creates when collaboration works: a credible and influential stakeholder group with the cohesion that comes from constructive engagement, a carefully considered rationale for its recommendations, and strong leaders within the group that help facilitate its work. Stakeholders reflect the makeup of the broader community so they cannot be mistaken for another special interest group or coalition. A fair and constructive process engages stakeholders as peers, so no one dominates the results. The creative use of good information helps avoid bias. This powerful constituency for change leads to real results because of its capacity to hold implementing organizations accountable for action. Like a well-built wheel, a carefully crafted collaborative process is a powerful tool.

CHAPTER FIVE

# A FRAMEWORK FOR COLLABORATION

For people with little or no experience, the concept of collaboration remains distant in theory and in practice. The apparent complexity and difficulty of most collaborative endeavors obscure the premise and principles that make it work. Gifted facilitators use their skills and knowledge with grace and artfulness concealing long years of training and experience. The seemingly esoteric practice of collaboration hides the evidence that it can be learned. Despite this opacity, lessons of experience from practitioners make the practice of collaboration intelligible. Research findings (see Appendix A) provide a framework for thinking about and organizing collaborative initiatives. An emerging state of the art informs the practice of collaboration from conception to implementation.

## Getting to Collaboration

Getting to collaboration is never as easy as it sounds. Potential participants must have an incentive to invest the time and energy in a collaborative effort. For many, the practical possibility of a better outcome than could be achieved by other means offers the most compelling reason. For others, the community-oriented aspirations of good leaders spark engagement. Collaborative leaders tap into these differing motivations to overcome the obstacles to collaboration.

### The Incentive to Collaborate

Many examples of collaboration began as reactive responses to difficult and challenging situations: a few people seek a less destructive and more effective means for addressing public concerns. Gridlock and stalemate provide compelling reasons for working together. The impetus to collaborate comes more often from futility or crisis rather than from proactive, visionary leadership.

Absent a crisis, other contextual factors help spark collaboration. Sometimes civic leaders create a sense of urgency when none exists by forcefully publicizing pressing needs. Previous success stories help catalyze collaboration. Citizens know that it works. A widespread awareness of collaborative alternatives and the leadership capacity to encourage them facilitates working together.

### Convening Leadership

Once an incentive exists to pursue collaboration, leadership moves it into practice. Leaders with a vision of a different way of solving problems mobilize others to participate. Taking advantage of opportunities and finding allies throughout the community or region, convening leaders use their credibility to convince others that a new approach to public concerns is needed.

## The Collaborative Premise

The collaborative premise identified in *Collaborative Leadership* remains at the heart of successful collaboration:

> If you bring the appropriate people together in constructive ways with good information, they will create authentic visions and strategies for addressing the shared concerns of the organization or community [Chrislip and Larson, 1994, p. 14].

It defines three key elements and exposes the underlying beliefs that make it work. Each element works synergistically with the other elements to affirm its conclusion.

"If you bring the appropriate people together" might be misread as excluding certain parties, but, in fact, it means just the opposite. "Appropriate people" includes both usual and unusual voices—those traditionally engaged and those who have been excluded or otherwise disengaged. It joins advocates on all sides of the issues with those directly affected by the issues. It includes citizens with the resources to address or influence these concerns. The appropriate people credibly reflect the larger community; they are as diverse as the community itself and have the perspectives and experiences to address the presenting issues and the collective credibility to move their recommendations to action.

The addition of a second element—"in constructive ways"—recognizes that bringing the appropriate people together in traditional ways will not work. The conflict inherent in a group of diverse stakeholders requires a carefully designed and well-executed process—a holding environment—to facilitate the group's work. A constructive process takes the time to build trust, skills for working together, and an understanding of issues necessary for effective engagement. A skillfully orchestrated process focuses on a particular issue or concern yet has no predetermined outcomes. Advocacy follows inquiry and collective learning. The process seeks consensus. A series of smaller agreements lead to deeper, more meaningful, more comprehensive agreements. A constructive process builds a constituency for the whole that reflects the knowledge and wisdom of the larger community.

A third element, "with good information," ensures that the work of the stakeholders is well informed. Some group facilitators assume that the wisdom and knowledge necessary to address a shared concern reside in the group itself. This may be true for issues particular to the group, but complex public problems require additional knowledge. Stakeholders must take the time to understand their own perceptions and experiences about public concerns, as well as to learn what others know and how other communities have dealt with similar problems. Collaborative engagements use expert information and advice to inform the process but not to drive it.

The synergistic combination of these three elements leads to the collaborative premise's powerful conclusion: "They [the appropriate people] will create authentic visions and strategies for addressing the shared concerns of the organization or community." When collaboration works, authentic visions and strategies result because of who does the work, how they do it, and the information they use.

One must trust collaboration to work and let go of preconceived notions about what the solutions or strategies should be. Appropriate, more responsive, and more innovative solutions than anyone imagines emerge through engagement. Good results come from the right people in a good process, not from manipulation and control. Stakeholders must learn to share power and understand that it does not have to be a zero-sum game. A few credible people in the community or region must lead in different ways to catalyze, convene, and sustain collaboration.

## Four Critical Requirements

Collaborative processes work when they are well conceived and well executed. Stakeholders become a constituency for change that leads to real action and results. Process expertise helps stakeholders work together constructively. Content experts support and inform the work of the group. Strong facilitative leadership energizes and sustains the process.

### A Constituency for Change

Successful collaborative efforts build a constituency for change with the credibility and influence to achieve real and lasting results. If a stakeholder group does not have enough credibility and influence to achieve real results, the group is either incomplete or engages the wrong people. To continue without addressing these shortfalls wastes time and precious political capital. Ostensibly collaborative initiatives like blue-ribbon panels and governor's or mayor's task forces rarely build a constituency for change. These narrow and exclusive efforts often provide little more than political eyewash. A true constituency for change has the collective credibility and influence to hold implementing organizations, elected leaders, and public agencies accountable for acting on their recommendations.

A constituency for change reflects the perspectives, experiences, and concerns of the broader community. Including unusual voices from the unengaged middle along with more vocal and better-organized interests with well-defined positions changes the usual polarizing dynamic. Bringing new and different perspectives to bear dilutes the influence of the extremes. The broader needs of the community, rather than parochial interests, drive the process.

The careful reader will note the use of the word *reflect* rather than *represent* in this description. The idea that certain people represent others undermines collaboration. Representation implies the capacity to speak for all members of a group with similar views, yet many claims to represent these positions or interests simply cannot be verified. It often leads to a numbers game, where the group with a thousand members expects to have twice as many representatives as the group with five hundred. Representatives without decision-making power stall initiatives as they check for approval with their constituencies or superiors. The multiple roles played by stakeholders and the variety of perspectives and experiences they bring to the table invalidate the notion of representing a particular and narrow point of view. In a collaborative process seeking consensus, each person has, in essence, veto power, negating the need for proportional representation. Stakeholders speak from their own perspectives and experiences and only for themselves. The shift from *represent* to *reflect* changes the dynamic of the process. It clarifies the role of the stakeholder and encourages authentic participation.

## Process Expertise

The formation of a constituency for change creates the potential for successful collaboration. Engaging stakeholders in constructive ways with good information transforms this potential into reality. Some stakeholder groups rely on their own skills to facilitate a constructive process. This works best when some or all group members have training in facilitation and group process skills. Other groups bring in neutral third parties skilled in the design and facilitation of collaborative efforts. The more diverse the stakeholder group is and the more complex and conflict ridden the issue, the more imperative it is to have a skilled facilitator to guide the work of the group.

Process experts help the stakeholder group build agreement and a constituency for change. A good facilitator helps the group learn together by creating a safe space or container for constructive engagement and ensuring that participants have equal voice. A strong facilitator teaches skills for collaboration and consensus building while managing the inherent conflict in ways that do not tear the group apart.

The process expert gains the trust of the group by encouraging the process while remaining neutral about the content of the presenting issues. Neutrality about content, however, does not mean ignorance. Content knowledge helps process experts recognize strategic moments in the engagement where skillful facilitation can lead to deeper understanding and agreement.

## Content Experts

Stakeholders need access to reliable information in order to make good decisions, not someone to tell them what to do. Traditionally, public entities retain experts to study an issue, develop and evaluate alternative ways to address it, and make recommendations for specific actions. In a collaborative effort, content experts support the learning of the group by providing background information and education needed to understand the issue, describing pertinent lessons of experience, and surfacing critical considerations for decision making. If content experts cannot make this shift, stakeholders and facilitators must sort out the biases or predilections of the specialist. The group evaluates the usefulness of the information and decides how to use it. This information becomes part of a learning process, not a fixed idea or position. Stakeholders remain in control of information gathering, analysis, and interpretation.

### Strong, Facilitative Leadership

Strong, facilitative leaders come from the community or region and share a vital concern for the issues at stake. Some are present at the start, while others emerge as the process evolves. Sometimes they hold strong positions about the issues but trust the collaborative process to reach appropriate conclusions. They provide the motivation and leadership to help people work together. No one from outside the community or region can play this role.

Collaboration cannot work without a few strong facilitative leaders in the stakeholder group. These collaborative leaders promote and safeguard the process by keeping stakeholders at the table through periods of frustration and skepticism, acknowledging small successes along the way, helping stakeholders negotiate difficult points, and enforcing group norms and ground rules (Chrislip and Larson, 1994). They articulate the incentives for collaboration and serve as catalysts for moving to more inclusive ways of working together. They use their credibility to bring other leaders together to accomplish the initiating and convening work necessary to start a collaborative process. They ensure inclusion of usual and unusual voices reflecting the broader community, help design a constructive process, and define the educational and informational needs of the initiative. These leaders provide a key link to formal decision-making bodies and implementing organizations using their credibility to move recommendations to action.

## Four Phases of a Collaborative Process

A collaborative process builds a series of progressively deeper and more comprehensive agreements among stakeholders. The evolution of these agreements follows a general pattern and shapes the phases of a collaborative process:

1. Agreement that shared concerns exist that should be addressed
2. Agreement to work together to address the concerns
3. Agreement on how to work together
4. Agreement on a shared understanding of the relevant information
5. Agreement on the definition of the problem or the vision
6. Agreement on the solutions to the problem or the strategies to achieve the vision
7. Agreement on the action steps or implementation plans for implementing the solutions or strategies

Each phase of a collaborative process helps stakeholders reach particular agreements. Figure 5.1 outlines these phases and defines the tasks that need to be ac-

## FIGURE 5.1. A GUIDE TO THE PRACTICES
## OF SUCCESSFUL COLLABORATION.

| *Getting Started* | → | *Setting Up for Success* | → | *Working Together* | → | *Moving to Action* |
|---|---|---|---|---|---|---|

**Analyzing the Context for Collaboration**
1. Understanding the political dynamics
2. Understanding how citizens think about public issues

**Deciding on a Collaborative Strategy**
1. Determining the feasibility of collaboration
2. Defining the purpose, scope, and focus

**Identifying and Convening Stakeholders**
1. Understanding the principle and practice of inclusion
2. Finding the credibility to convene
3. Identifying stakeholders
4. Inviting, recruiting, and convening stakeholders

**Designing a Constructive Process**
1. Defining the decision-making method
2. Establishing ground rules
3. Designing a constructive process

**Defining Information Needs**
1. Defining information and education needs

**Defining Critical Roles**
1. Selecting process experts
2. Selecting content experts
3. Identifying strong, facilitative leaders

**Managing the Process**
1. Establishing a steering committee
2. Staffing the effort
3. Documenting the process

**Finding the Resources**
1. Developing the budget
2. Funding a collaborative process

**Building Capacity**
1. Building relationships and skills

**Ways of Engaging**
1. Engaging through dialogue
2. Working with written information

**Informing the Stakeholders**
1. Understanding the content
2. Understanding the context
   • Analyzing strengths, weaknesses, opportunities, and threats
   • Developing scenarios

**Deciding What Needs to Be Done**
1. Collaborative problem solving
2. Visioning
3. Strategic planning

**Reaching Out**
1. Building a broader constituency
2. Engaging with decision makers and implementing organizations

**Managing Action**
1. Developing action plans
2. Organizing and managing implementation

complished in order to build successive agreements. The *getting started* and *setting up for success* phases cover the tasks necessary for initiating the process. These two phases build agreement to work together on particular concerns and on how to work together. In the *working together* phase, stakeholders build a shared understanding of the issues, define problems or create a vision, and develop solutions or strategies to address the issues. The *moving to action* phase connects stakeholders and their work with the broader community, decision makers, and implementing organizations.

## Getting Started

Collaborative initiatives usually begin with a few people lending their time and credibility to catalyze and convene the effort. Doing some early homework helps define the purpose and scope of the process. Understanding the context for collaboration helps civic leaders choose and design an appropriate intervention. Because communities and regions differ, no one model for working together applies to all situations. Using the premise and framework for collaboration, each place must develop a process that fits its particular needs.

The contextual conditions—the political dynamics of a community or region surrounding a particular concern—provide the starting point for any process. These conditions include the level of conflict in the community or region about an issue, the readiness or capacity to address the issue, the history of previous efforts to deal with the concern, or the status of other community efforts that may complement or compete with the proposed initiative. Understanding these conditions helps determine the feasibility of collaboration, define the scope and purpose of the initiative, provide an initial understanding of the range of stakeholders that need to be involved, and identify the challenges a collaborative process will face.

To be compelling, a collaborative process needs a well-defined purpose and scope. The focus of collaboration can be broad or narrow or anywhere in between. It must identify, for example, an issue or, at least, an area of concern to provide direction yet refrain from defining it or specifying what should be done. The possibility of collaboration depends on an open agenda. An appropriate focus helps provide compelling reasons for stakeholders to come together.

If a stakeholder group credibly reflects the broader community or region, collaborative leaders must also reflect this diversity. They inspire, compel, cajole, persuade, or otherwise convince others to work together. No one person or group has the credibility to do this. Since governments, businesses, special interest groups, and other organizations cannot convene stakeholders by themselves because of parochial agendas, collaborative leaders build partnerships among disparate leaders to form initiating groups with the credibility to bring stakeholders together. These initiating groups help educate the community about the process, plan the effort, and invite or recruit stakeholders. Without collective credibility early on, most collaborative efforts fail.

- See Chapter 6, "Getting Started," for specific tools for this phase.

## Setting Up for Success

With enough understanding of the context, a well-defined purpose and scope, and the collective credibility to convene a larger stakeholder group, initiating work shifts from getting started to setting up for success. The work accomplished in setting up for success helps gain agreement on how to work together. The initiating group must be willing to invest a substantial amount of time in designing the collaborative effort. This work often takes several work sessions spread over a few weeks to complete. The thoroughness and quality of this work makes or breaks the subsequent working together phase.

The work performed in the setting up for success phase includes several tasks. An initiating group must choose what method to use to address the issue or concern from a spectrum of possible approaches, including collaborative problem solving, visioning, and strategic planning. The group must identify stakeholders, design a constructive process for engaging them, determine information needs, and provide process expertise to support the work. The group's responsibilities include estimating and finding the resources necessary to support the effort. The quality of this work helps convenors communicate the importance of the initiative and provides more compelling reasons for stakeholders to participate.

- See Chapter Seven, "Setting Up for Success," for specific tools for this phase.

## Working Together

In the working together phase, stakeholders engage with the content of the issues or concerns. They build a shared understanding of information relevant to the issues, fashion agreement on problem definitions or create a vision, decide what needs to be done, and agree on next steps that lead to implementation and action.

Collaboration is a process for doing adaptive work, not a debate or power struggle. A learning engagement loosens the hold that initial positions have on stakeholders by first legitimizing these positions and then encouraging new possibilities to emerge. This shift begins when stakeholders start to trust each other and have a better understanding of what collaboration means and how it works. Developing a shared understanding of relevant information helps stakeholders learn how to engage with the issues and each other in more constructive ways. A process of inquiry leads to understanding and clarification, not advocacy or argument. Stronger relationships, new skills for working together, and better understanding of the issues provide the foundation for the more difficult subsequent work.

"If you don't agree on the problem, you won't agree on the solution." So goes the old facilitator's adage. More time spent defining problems or visions leads to less time spent defining solutions and strategies. In a crisis, collaboration usually begins by defining problems. Immediate needs preempt the possibility of more proactive action. Diagnosing the disease determines the prescription. When time permits, a visionary approach may lead to strategies that go far beyond the symptomatic responses that often come out of a problem-oriented process. By analyzing the context for collaboration, an initiating group can choose an appropriate approach.

With a clear definition of a problem or a compelling vision, the work of deciding what needs to be done begins. Past experiences have prepared stakeholders for creative work. They know each other, know how to work together, know what they need to know in order to make good decisions, and know how to identify alternative solutions and strategies, evaluate them, and decide what to do. Sometimes solutions or strategies emerge with a clarity no one could foresee. At other times, hard choices and difficult trade-offs make for challenging work. In either circumstance, recommendations coming out of a collaborative process will be well informed, carefully considered, and broadly supported. More traditional means for making public decisions would be hard put to make these claims.

- See Chapter Eight, "Working Together," for specific tools for this phase.

## Moving to Action

Putting these qualities to work ensures success. The link between citizen-driven efforts and legislative bodies and implementing organizations moves recommendations to real results and action. This can take different forms. Sometimes recommendations from a collaborative process provide the conceptual framework for coherent public policy that considers the true complexity of the issues. Elected leaders understand in a deeper way what needs to be done and have a more comprehensive and visionary basis for action. Elected leaders use the credibility of the stakeholder group and its work to provide the backing they needed to take politically risky actions. At other times, the stakeholder group uses its collective influence to negotiate with elected leaders or other implementing organizations in order to move its recommendations to action. The group understands that by its makeup and the processes it uses, it has sufficient credibility to work with other powerful organizations to create new partnerships that achieve real results. Rather than just another interest group, the stakeholder group becomes a constituency for the whole that can speak credibly for the larger community or region.

- See Chapter Nine, "Moving to Action," for specific tools for this phase.

## From Theory to Practice

Collaboration is not simply an act of will. It is a carefully conceived and well-executed process that emerges and evolves in response to particular needs. No two collaborative processes will ever be the same because each is tailored to a unique time, place, and situation. An emerging body of knowledge about what makes collaboration work informs its practice. The collaborative premise and the principles that derive from it shape the process and lead to action. Understanding and applying these lessons of experience helps collaborative initiatives achieve real results.

As in all other collective human endeavors, the quality and kind of leadership brought to bear ultimately determine whether collaboration works. Unless people who care deeply for their community or region recognize the possibility of better ways to address public concerns and use their leadership capacities in new and different ways, collaboration cannot work.

# PART THREE

# MICRO

## Practices of Successful Collaboration

Chapters Six through Nine define the tasks in each of the four phases of collaboration: getting started, setting up for success, working together, and moving to action. Each of these tasks needs attention in a collaborative process. The tools described can help perform the tasks and can be combined in different ways to meet particular needs. Civic leaders or facilitators and process experts can use the tools on an informal basis or as part of a formal, comprehensively designed process. Chapter Ten describes how to design and initiate a civic leadership development program.

CHAPTER SIX

# GETTING STARTED

Initiating a collaborative process requires civic leaders to shift attention from the content of an issue to its political dynamics or process challenges. Analyzing the context for collaboration helps identify the challenges the process will face. By exposing these challenges, a community or region can make better decisions about how public concerns should be addressed. Figure 6.1 highlights the "Getting Started" phase of the collaborative process.

## Analyzing the Context for Collaboration

Two approaches help civic leaders gain a better understanding of the context for collaboration. The first poses general questions about the political dynamics of the community or region. The second uses open-ended questions to identify how citizens think about particular issues and how they might be approached. These questions help identify the emerging public agenda in the community or region. Both approaches can be used on an informal basis or as part of a formal and disciplined effort. The information can be gathered through interviews, focus groups, or interactive community processes. Including people from different parts of the community or region enriches the insights from these questions.

## FIGURE 6.1.  A GUIDE TO THE PRACTICES
## OF SUCCESSFUL COLLABORATION.

| Chapter Six | Chapter Seven | Chapter Eight | Chapter Nine |
|---|---|---|---|
| *Getting Started* | *Setting Up for Success* | *Working Together* | *Moving to Action* |

**Analyzing the Context for Collaboration**
1. Understanding the political dynamics
2. Understanding how citizens think about public issues

**Deciding on a Collaborative Strategy**
1. Determining the feasibility of collaboration
2. Defining the purpose, scope, and focus

**Identifying and Convening Stakeholders**
1. Understanding the principle and practice of inclusion
2. Finding the credibility to convene
3. Identifying stakeholders
4. Inviting, recruiting, and convening stakeholders

**Designing a Constructive Process**
1. Defining the decision-making method
2. Establishing ground rules
3. Designing a constructive process

**Defining Information Needs**
1. Defining information and education needs

**Defining Critical Roles**
1. Selecting process experts
2. Selecting content experts
3. Identifying strong, facilitative leaders

**Managing the Process**
1. Establishing a steering committee
2. Staffing the effort
3. Documenting the process

**Finding the Resources**
1. Developing the budget
2. Funding a collaborative process

**Building Capacity**
1. Building relationships and skills

**Ways of Engaging**
1. Engaging through dialogue
2. Working with written information

**Informing the Stakeholders**
1. Understanding the content
2. Understanding the context
   • Analyzing strengths, weaknesses, opportunities, and threats
   • Developing scenarios

**Deciding What Needs to Be Done**
1. Collaborative problem solving
2. Visioning
3. Strategic planning

**Reaching Out**
1. Building a broader constituency
2. Engaging with decision makers and implementing organizations

**Managing Action**
1. Developing action plans
2. Organizing and managing implementation

## Understanding the Political Dynamics

The information from this analysis helps determine the feasibility of collaboration; define the purpose, scope, and focus of the initiative; understand the dimensions of the stakeholder group; and identify parameters of a constructive process. When the analysis is completed, highlight the particularly challenging aspects exposed by the analysis. These aspects will have to be considered and addressed in the design of the process.

---

# Understanding the Political Dynamics

- *The dynamics of the community relevant to an issue.* Four questions help define the challenges that must be addressed: (1) What makes leadership difficult on this issue? (2) What is the level of conflict among stakeholders? (3) What is the perceived need to address the issue in the community or region? (4) What is the capacity to address the issue in the community or region? Use a graduated scale such as low, medium, and high to identify relative levels or numbers where appropriate rather than seeking precise information. Stick to the questions, and avoid jumping ahead to prescribe what should be done.
- *Background information about the possible scope and focus of a collaborative process.* Are there currently or have there been other initiatives in the community or region to address this issue? What are or were the results? Who were the primary players in these initiatives? What interest groups are most concerned about the issue? How many stakeholders might be engaged in a collaborative process? Are there other stakeholders or leaders who would support a collaborative initiative to address this issue or support new efforts on existing initiatives? Where is the appropriate locus of work (neighborhood, community, region, state, national)?
- *The level of stakeholder agreement.* Three questions help assess the initial level of stakeholder agreement: (1) Have stakeholders agreed there are concerns that should be addressed? (2) Have stakeholders agreed to work together to address the concerns? (3) Have stakeholders agreed on how to work together to address the concerns? The initial planning for a collaborative process begins with the first negative answer.

---

## Understanding How Citizens Think About Public Concerns

Comprehending how citizens think about public issues provides invaluable information for initiating a collaborative process. Open-ended questions stimulate thinking and conversation in creative and engaging ways. These questions help identify priorities, expose the political dynamics of the community, and develop an agenda for addressing the community's concerns. Using the questions in individual interviews or with homogeneous focus groups offers opportunities for people to speak openly about their concerns. A more inclusive and interactive community process can spark shared understanding and insight if participants feel comfortable speaking frankly.

Open-ended questions elicit comments about both content and process. Several questions ask the same thing in different ways. Participants may respond better to one way of asking a question than another. Sometimes a slightly different question elicits a very different response.

If using individual interviews, fifteen to twenty-five interviews should suffice. After that, new information from additional interviews declines dramatically. When using focus groups, include a variety of participants from different sectors or parts of the community or region. Sometimes political considerations determine the number of interviews or focus groups. Certain people or groups may need to participate in order to trust the process and what it produces. Participants—like stakeholders in a collaborative process—need to reflect the diversity of the community or region.

---

## Understanding How Citizens Think About Public Concerns

1. *Set up interviews or focus groups.* In order to elicit a candid assessment of the situation, the facilitator must build an open and trusting relationship with the individual or group. Participants need to know how the information will be used and that a safe environment for conversation exists.
2. *Conduct the interviews or focus groups.* Once the interview or process begins, the facilitator listens actively and keeps the conversation going without directing it or allowing someone to dominate. In general, the facilitator does not comment on individual or group responses but may probe further with directly related follow-up questions.
3. *Develop the interview or focus group protocol.* Questions can be asked in a general way focusing on the community or region as a whole or with reference to a particular issue—for example "When you think about the future of the community or region, what concerns you the most?", and "When you think about the future of public education in your community, what concerns you the most?"(See van der Heijden, 1996, for information about individual interview questions.)

"When you think about the future of the community or region, what concerns you the most?"

"Imagine that I am oracle and can foretell the future. What three questions about the future of the community or region would you like to have the answers to?"

"You have mentioned several issues and concerns about the future of the community or region. What would be a good scenario in terms of how things might turn out? What would be a bad scenario?"

"What critical decisions will have to be made in the near future? What are the forks in the road?"

"What in the culture of the community or region either helps or hinders addressing these issues and concerns?"

"From your perspective, what are the three most important factors affecting the future of the community or region?"

"In relation to the issues and concerns you have mentioned, what have you learned from the past? What has surprised you?"

4. *Record the information.* Virtually every comment or perspective provided by participants needs to be noted, so extensive note taking is necessary. This must be done quickly and thoroughly to keep from disrupting the pace of the interview or conversation.

5. *Sort and present the information.* Thorough note taking generates hundreds of information points that need sorting in a systematic fashion. Some facilitators look for patterns in the answers to each question, though this may limit what can be learned since some questions ask for the same information in different ways. A more organic method of sorting leads to deeper insights. Transcribe each information point onto a small sticky note (there may be hundreds of them). After completing the transcription, match each sticky note with others with similar or related points. Let categories of responses emerge rather than trying to identify them up front. It make take some time to get comfortable with the way the points sort themselves out. Once a comfort level is reached, name the groupings, and look for relationships among them. Once the sorting is complete, look for ways to communicate the information in a straightforward, easily accessible way.

6. *Check for accuracy.* When possible, check the information for accuracy with the participants. Begin by describing the interview process and how the information was recorded, sorted, and organized. Present the information, and check with the group as to whether it accurately reflects what they said. Make adjustments based on the group's feedback without violating the integrity of the perspectives provided by the participants. The process should offer a means for raising and legitimizing hard issues not covering them up.

---

The richness of perspectives that come from these questions is clear: an understanding of different positions on issues, an emerging set of priorities for addressing them, mental models of how people think about them, an understanding of the level of conflict in the community or region, a sense of the barriers and challenges to addressing the issues, the interrelationships of different issues or stakeholders, an understanding of how people see themselves as leaders or change agents, and others.

This information helps determine the existing level of concern about a particular issue. It may spark interest in looking for collaborative ways to address an issue. It helps define the purpose, scope, and focus of a collaborative initiative. It can help civic leaders choose an appropriate intervention, design a constructive process, and identify stakeholders. Short presentations based on this information can provide a useful starting point for any collaborative process. A compelling summary helps others understand the need for a new and different approach.

- Chapter Twelve, "Transforming Civic Culture: Sitka, Alaska, 1999–2001," provides an example of how information from a series of interviews helped develop strategies for enhancing Sitka's civic culture.

# Deciding on a Collaborative Strategy

Choosing an appropriate way to address public concerns is a central task of civic leadership. Conscious choices from a range of possibilities can be made. Analyzing the context for collaboration and understanding how citizens think about public issues provides the basis for making these choices. With this deeper understanding, citizens and civic leaders can determine the feasibility of collaboration and define the purpose, scope, and focus of a collaborative process.

## Determining the Feasibility of Collaboration

Some people think of collaboration as the strategy of last resort for addressing public issues. As one practitioner put it, "If you think you can get a better result another way, do it." The history of collaboration lends weight to this argument. As noted in a previous chapter, many collaborative initiatives start when other means break down. There are no other ways to achieve better results. Progress depends, finally, on working together. The current context of complexity and diversity in the public arena implies the need to look at collaboration as a primary choice rather than as a last resort. Civic leaders intent on addressing public issues should consciously and deliberately consider it first.

Collaboration is one of many strategies for addressing public concerns. These strategies fall in three categories: strategies that work in opposition to the system (the formal system of democratic governance through elected representatives), strategies that work within the system, and strategies that work in parallel to the system. Figure 6.2 provides an overview of this spectrum of strategies. Civic leaders choose from this range of alternative strategies depending on the situation.

Several considerations inform the choice of an appropriate strategy. Which alternative offers the greatest likelihood of satisfying the primary interests and concerns of stakeholders? Which strategies produce positive outcomes for a wide variety of interests? Which strategies produce positive outcomes for some interests and negative ones for others? Which strategies produce negative or no results for all interests? Realistically, how long will it take to get results with alternative strategies? (Some people argue that collaboration takes too much time, yet other common strategies often end in gridlock or in legal battles that never achieve satisfactory results.)

Civic leaders need to understand the potential consequences of a particular strategy. Are the parties involved willing to live with the consequences? Will the use of a particular strategy divide and polarize the community or bring it together? Does it alienate citizens from public life or engage them in constructive ways? Will it spend or destroy social capital rather than build the capacity of the community or region to address future issues?

Contextual conditions may encourage or preclude the use of certain strategies. Does the history of the community or region rule out or encourage certain strategies? Does the culture of the community or region lend itself to different strategies? Does the level of conflict on the issue suggest that certain strategies may be better than others? Does the complexity of the issue require adaptive work? Are there a number of stakeholders with relatively equal power with the capacity to block action?

Few places make conscious choices about appropriate strategies. Most citizens and civic leaders lack awareness of alternative strategies for addressing public issues. Collaborative leaders take the time to evaluate alternative strategies, understand their consequences, and match the strategy to the situation.

## FIGURE 6.2.  A SPECTRUM OF STRATEGIES FOR ADDRESSING PUBLIC ISSUES.

| **Against the System** | **Within the System** | **Parallel to the System** |
|---|---|---|
| ← | | → |
| • Civil disobedience | • Executive action | • Collaboration |
| • Economic action (for example, strike, boycott) | • Legislative initiative | • Mediation |
| | • Voter initiative | • Negotiation |
| • Physical violence | • Judicial action | |

## Defining the Purpose, Scope, and Focus

In the early stages of a collaborative process, presenting issues often lack definition. Citizens may recognize an area of concern but know little about the precise nature of their concern. This vague unease may not be enough to compel people to engage. Without defining the purpose, scope, and focus of a collaborative initiative further, citizens have little impetus for working together.

Defining a focus does not mean defining the problem, creating a vision, or developing solutions or strategies. Stakeholders do this work. In this initial phase, convening leaders must develop a focus that brings people together yet leaves an open agenda for collaborative engagement. Too broad a focus may leave citizens unmoved; too narrow a focus may lead to limited symptomatic responses.

The process of understanding how citizens think about public issues helps define the focus. This information often leads to a natural framing of the issues and concerns reflecting the perspectives and priorities of the people engaged. Understanding the "political" dynamics provides more insight. Identifying other stakeholders or leaders who might support a collaborative process builds understanding of their interests or positions. Defining the locus of work helps define the geographical scope. Understanding what other initiatives do or have done defines the niche to be filled by a new initiative. Creating a matrix of related activities comparing dimensions like substantive focus, time lines, range of stakeholders, geographical scope, similarities or differences in approach, and the likelihood of achieving real results exposes gaps and prevents competition with or duplication of other efforts.

# Initiating a Collaborative Process

Most collaborative initiatives grow out of informal conversations among a few concerned civic leaders. Analyzing the context for collaboration helps determine the feasibility and focus of a potential process. This deeper understanding makes the case for collaboration more compelling. Collaborative leaders use this understanding and their credibility to convince others that something can and must be done. The informal work of getting started leads to the more disciplined work of setting up for success.

CHAPTER SEVEN

# SETTING UP FOR SUCCESS

Setting up for success moves collaboration from concept to practice. This planning work ensures a well-conceived process. Investing time and effort in this preparatory work prevents far more problems than could ever be dealt with by subsequent interventions. Whether civic leaders do this work informally or in a structured process, each task needs attention. Figure 7.1 highlights the "Setting Up for Success" phase of the collaborative process.

In each phase, a collaborative process expands the circle of people engaged. Those who participated in the initial feasibility work bring in others to strengthen the credibility of the effort. These convening groups reflect the diversity of the larger community. When citizens see some reflection of themselves in the convening group, they trust the process and, hence, participate. The need for credibility determines the size of these groups. A convening group includes enough people from different parts of the community or region to have the collective credibility to convince stakeholders to work together.

The work of the convening group, whether formal or informal, includes several tasks. The group identifies and recruits stakeholders, designs a constructive process, defines critical roles, and determines the information needs of the stakeholders. A convening group helps establish a management structure and finds the resources to support a collaborative process. This planning work may take up to a few months to complete. Figure 7.2 provides an example of how this work might unfold.

# FIGURE 7.1. A GUIDE TO THE PRACTICES OF SUCCESSFUL COLLABORATION.

| Chapter Six | Chapter Seven | Chapter Eight | Chapter Nine |
|---|---|---|---|
| *Getting Started* | ***Setting Up for Success*** | *Working Together* | *Moving to Action* |

**Analyzing the Context for Collaboration**
1. Understanding the political dynamics
2. Understanding how citizens think about public issues

**Deciding on a Collaborative Strategy**
1. Determining the feasibility of collaboration
2. Defining the purpose, scope, and focus

**Identifying and Convening Stakeholders**
1. Understanding the principle and practice of inclusion
2. Finding the credibility to convene
3. Identifying stakeholders
4. Inviting, recruiting, and convening stakeholders

**Designing a Constructive Process**
1. Defining the decision-making method
2. Establishing ground rules
3. Designing a constructive process

**Defining Information Needs**
1. Defining information and education needs

**Defining Critical Roles**
1. Selecting process experts
2. Selecting content experts
3. Identifying strong, facilitative leaders

**Managing the Process**
1. Establishing a steering committee
2. Staffing the effort
3. Documenting the process

**Finding the Resources**
1. Developing the budget
2. Funding a collaborative process

**Building Capacity**
1. Building relationships and skills

**Ways of Engaging**
1. Engaging through dialogue
2. Working with written information

**Informing the Stakeholders**
1. Understanding the content
2. Understanding the context
   - Analyzing strengths, weaknesses, opportunities, and threats
   - Developing scenarios

**Deciding What Needs to Be Done**
1. Collaborative problem solving
2. Visioning
3. Strategic planning

**Reaching Out**
1. Building a broader constituency
2. Engaging with decision makers and implementing organizations

**Managing Action**
1. Developing action plans
2. Organizing and managing implementation

# FIGURE 7.2. INITIATING TIME LINE.

| Phases / Tracks | Initiating Phase | | | | | |
|---|---|---|---|---|---|---|
| Convening Group | • Review and refine purpose and focus of project<br>• Review lessons of experience about successful collaboration<br>• Define role of convening group | • Begin stakeholder identification<br>• Begin design of collaborative process | • Continue design of collaborative process<br>• Continue stakeholder identification<br>• Define information and education needs of stakeholder group<br>• Define critical roles | • Complete stakeholder identification<br>• Complete design of collaborative process<br>• Identify resource and logistical needs<br>• Develop budget | • Complete resource planning<br>• Review budget<br>• Create strategies for securing resources<br>• Complete logistical planning<br>• Recruit stakeholders | • Convene first stakeholder meeting |

**It usually takes five to eight meetings (two to four hours each) for a convening group to complete the tasks.**

# Identifying and Convening Stakeholders

Practitioners use the word *stakeholder* to describe a participant in a collaborative process: those responsible for problems or issues, those affected by them, those with perspectives or knowledge needed to develop good solutions or strategies, those with power and resources to block or implement solutions and strategies, and anyone else who wants to be engaged.

Collaboration implies the inclusion of all citizens concerned with a public issue. A stakeholder group reflects the diversity of the community or region and includes people with different, perhaps conflicting, interests. Stakeholders do the real work of collaboration in defining problems and visions, solutions and strategies. When collaboration works, stakeholders become a constituency for change who are able to hold decision makers and implementing organizations accountable for action. The makeup of this group makes or breaks a collaborative process.

## Understanding the Principle and Practice of Inclusion

Communities and regions strive for inclusiveness for both pragmatic and moral reasons. Pragmatically, if some groups or individuals can block the work of others, no action can occur without the willingness to negotiate a broader agreement. If one coalition of interests overpowers another, changes may not last if the opposing side regains power. Action and change cannot be sustained over long periods if they leave the community divided. Ultimately, citizens are responsible for the problems of the community and the solutions that address them. The quality of solutions depends on the quality of engagement. Sometimes elected officials and public agencies do not have the power to address public issues without engaging citizens. Coping with public challenges and achieving long-lasting results can be achieved only by bringing diverse perspectives together, not keeping them apart. Pragmatically, inclusion is necessary in order to solve problems.

Morally and ethically, collaboration implies a deeper, more intimate, and inclusive kind of democracy. It brings together citizens as peers, ignoring their social, economic, or political standing. Working together bridges diversity and difference. It also legitimizes the right and responsibility of each citizen to have a voice in public deliberations and to participate in the decisions that affect everyone. Inclusiveness does not mean that a collaborative process involves every citizen. It does mean that the stakeholder group accurately reflects the makeup of the larger community.

Mapping two contrasting dimensions of a stakeholder group helps define the meaning of inclusion. The first dimension measures a person's stake or interest in the issue as defined by how much or how little it affects or concerns him or her.

The second dimension delineates a person's relative influence in the community or region. Since influence tends to be perceived as synonymous with a person's position in a hierarchy, the influence axis uses position in a business, nonprofit, or governmental organization as a measure of relative influence. The higher the position and the more prominent the organization is, the more relative influence a person has. Figure 7.3 uses these two dimensions as axes. Identifying people in each quadrant helps define the dimensions of a stakeholder group that reflects the broader community.

In the earliest stages of a collaborative process, civic leaders begin to speculate about who needs to be involved. They easily identify the usual voices—those with influential positions in prominent organizations with high stakes (the upper right quadrant in Figure 7.3). Unfortunately, the visibility of usual voices often obscures the need to include others. A collaborative process, if it is to succeed, also includes unusual voices—those in the upper left quadrant. Citizens with high stakes but low influence in the traditional sense engage as peers with the usual voices. A stakeholder group that reflects the broader community includes both usual and unusual voices (the circled area in Figure 7.3 covering the two upper quadrants). Expanding the stakeholder group changes the dynamic of the usual voices by bringing in new perspectives and experiences. A collaborative initiative is neither a grassroots effort nor an insider job.

Successful collaborative initiatives tap people in the lower right quadrant to serve as strong, facilitative leaders. These influential people lend credibility to the effort without the burden of particular interests or positions. Retired government

**FIGURE 7.3. STAKEHOLDER MAP.**

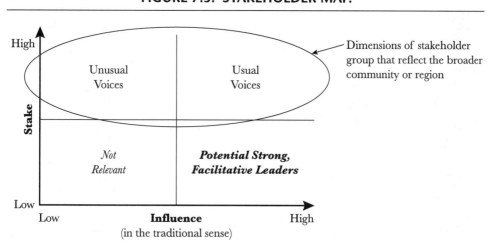

and business leaders, church leaders, higher education executives, and others with broad credibility can help motivate others to work together. Jimmy Carter, for example, uses his considerable influence as former president to bring people together in challenging situations.

Expanding the dimensions of the stakeholder group beyond the traditional terms of money, power, and position creates the potential for a constituency for change. A thorough and credible stakeholder identification process greatly enhances the prospects for success and puts the principle of inclusion into practice in a meaningful way.

## Finding the Credibility to Convene

If a stakeholder group includes usual and unusual voices, then the convening group must have the collective credibility to attract both. Most convening groups find it easy to identify usual voices and much more challenging to discover other unknown or unrecognized voices. The four questions and matrix in Figure 7.4 help

### FIGURE 7.4. EXPANDING THE STAKEHOLDER MAP.

**Arenas**

| Players | Neighborhood | Local | Regional | State | National |
|---|---|---|---|---|---|
| Individuals | | | | | |
| Nonprofit Organizations | | | | | |
| Educational and Philanthropic Organizations | | | | | |
| Public Sector | | | | | |
| Private Sector | | | | | |

**Questions:**
• What players in what arenas are engaged in addressing this issue?
• What new players in what arenas must be engaged in order to make this a truly collaborative endeavor?
• What actions can be taken to engage new players in a collaborative endeavor?
• Who, collectively, would have the credibility to convene the expanded stakeholder group?

specify the dimensions of the stakeholder group. Understanding these dimensions helps determine the need for recruiting new people to a convening group to enhance its credibility. New convenors or others with deeper knowledge of different parts of the community may need to be recruited.

## Identifying Stakeholders

Assembling a credible stakeholder group is a central task of convening leaders. Four criteria guide the process. First, a credible stakeholder group reflects the diversity of the broader community or region. Second, it includes people with the perspectives and experiences necessary to address the presenting concern or issue. Third, the group must have the potential to hold formal decision-making bodies and implementing organizations accountable for action on its recommendations. Fourth, it includes several strong, facilitative leaders from different sectors or parts of the community or region to energize its work.

---

# Identifying Stakeholders

1. *List the perspectives and experiences necessary to address the presenting concern or issue.* Do not start by listing the names of powerful individuals or organizations—the usual voices—that need to be represented. Instead, begin by identifying the perspectives and experiences necessary to address the presenting issue. This approach helps break the trap of focusing too much on the usual voices and opens the way for the inclusion of unusual voices. Listing perspectives and experiences highlights arenas needing new voices.

2. *Create a matrix of perspectives and experiences and prospective stakeholders.* A matrix helps organize the work. List perspectives and experiences on one axis, and provide a space for names of potential stakeholders on the other axis. The matrix makes it easy to see that most people bring multiple perspectives and experiences to the effort. Rather than identifying one person for each of the perspectives and experiences, a person with multiple perspectives reduces the number of people necessary for success.

3. *List potential stakeholders.* Begin to list names of potential stakeholders, and put an X on the matrix to identify the perspectives and experiences each person brings. As the list develops, expand the search for potential stakeholders by checking for gaps in coverage of perspectives and experiences. Look for areas that are heavily covered by the list of names, and reduce the number of potential stakeholders in these areas. Continue this process until all perspectives and experiences are covered by names of potential stakeholders. Add usual voices

such as members of influential groups or organizations that must be present if not already identified.

4. *Check the stakeholder list against the criteria already defined, and refine as necessary.* The criteria help determine the appropriate number of stakeholders. Pragmatically, it may take twenty people or two hundred to meet the criteria. The fear of large numbers should not limit the size of the stakeholder group.

5. *Check for balance in other dimensions.* Check other dimensions, such as race, ethnicity, gender, age, geography, and sexual orientation, and revise the list as necessary.

6. *Finalize the list, but leave it open for revision.* Check the list against the criteria once more and refine as necessary.

## Inviting, Recruiting, and Convening Stakeholders

A credible stakeholder group includes multiple and possibly conflicting perspectives and interests. It includes those necessary to implement solutions, those who can block action, and those who control power and resources. Diverse stakeholders have different levels of motivation or willingness to work together. Bringing them together takes more than an invitation.

Elected officials and public agencies traditionally work with anyone who shows up at public hearings and town meetings. Generally, well-organized and well-financed interests dominate these engagements. Other citizens may have no reliable way to know about the meetings or opt out because of the hostile environment. Many ostensibly collaborative engagements do no better.

Stakeholders in a collaborative process must be invited and recruited to prevent the shortcomings of most public meetings. Members of the convening group solicit participation sometimes on a one-on-one basis. The credibility of the convening group and their good work on stakeholder identification and process design sells citizens on the viability of collaboration. As the invitation and recruitment of stakeholders occur, the possibility of participation remains open to others who may want or need to be engaged. Any hint of exclusiveness about who participates dooms the effort to failure. Collaborative initiatives cannot work without a credible stakeholder group that includes usual and unusual voices along with strong, facilitative leaders to support the work.

## Designing a Constructive Process

A diverse, conflict-ridden, skeptical, and mistrusting stakeholder group cannot reach agreement without a constructive process. Stakeholders need some knowledge of how decisions will be made, the ground rules for working together, and the nature of the engagement in order to commit to it. Any collaborative initiative, formal or informal, can benefit from a carefully planned process.

## Defining the Decision-Making Method

Collaborative initiatives seek consensus—unanimity—about what to do or, at the least, overwhelming agreement. Defining consensus or overwhelming agreement, specifying how it will be measured or tested, and identifying how decisions will be made if consensus cannot be reached prevent potential misunderstandings later in the process.

Many practitioners argue that "groups [should] seek consensus but not require it to reach closure on the group's recommendations or decisions" (McKearnan and Fairman, 1999, pp. 327–328). The goal of unanimity may allow one or a few stakeholders to hold the group hostage to their demands. After due diligence efforts to reach consensus, stakeholders should settle for overwhelming agreement. Others believe that consensus should be the only goal and that groups should continue working through issues until unanimity is reached. This requires skillful facilitation and strong, facilitative leaders in the stakeholder group to prevent a few people from exerting too much influence in the decision process.

One measure of consensus uses a gradient of agreement scale, with the scale ranging from full agreement to veto. Sam Kaner provides an example of this in his book, *Facilitator's Guide to Participatory Decision-Making* (1996). He suggests an eight-point scale (p. 212):

- Endorsement
- Endorsement with a minor point of contention
- Agreement with reservations
- Abstain
- Stand aside
- Formal disagreement but willing to go along with the majority
- Formal disagreement with request to be absolved of responsibility for implementation
- Block or veto

The facilitator polls participants from time to time using this scale to check the level of agreement. When a high level of support for a decision exists with few reservations or objections, consensus can be acknowledged. Low levels of support indicate the need for further efforts to build consensus or fall back to an alternate method for making decisions.

David Straus and others recommend a fallback decision-making rule if consensus cannot be reached (Straus, 1999b). Sometimes stakeholders designate a formal decision-making body or other group to make the decision. Other fallback decision-making rules use some form of voting. Such a rule defines what a majority means: 51 percent or a two-thirds majority or some other variation. Sometimes the decision to vote may itself require a vote. A vote to vote rule usually sets a high threshold, for example, an 80 percent majority might be required in order to prevent premature or overuse of voting. Traditional means for making public decisions often provide a de facto fallback along with their attendant negative consequences when attempts to reach consensus fail. The threat of deferring to the fallback decision-making option often motivates stakeholders to keep working toward consensus.

## Establishing Ground Rules

Establishing ground rules for working together sets the tone of the engagement. Ground rules prevent future trouble. By gaining agreement early in a collaborative process, they establish norms and expectations for behavior. An effective set of ground rules is congruent with the working premises of collaboration.

The best ground rules come from the stakeholders themselves to meet the particular needs and challenges of the group. Examples of possible ground rules help stakeholders get started, and then the group adds to or modifies them as they see fit. Once the rules are established, stakeholders need to agree to abide by them. Ground rules therefore become a binding contract that commits the group to constructive ways of engaging and serves as a basis for intervention when violated or ignored. Stakeholders should revisit ground rules regularly and refine them when necessary.

Mark Gerzon's work with congressional bipartisan retreats provides a good example of possible ground rules. Gerzon and others designed the retreats to help rebuild a culture of civility in the U.S. Congress. When more than two hundred representatives met for the three-day retreat in 1999, six ground rules set the tone of the engagement:

- Respect—for people and process
- Fairness—equal time for speakers
- Listening—listen to understand
- Openness—to other points of view and to outcome
- Privacy—confidentiality
- Commitment—be present

Groups that consistently observe ground rules like these have a more constructive dynamic than do groups with no rules or with indifference toward the rules.

## Designing a Constructive Process

Collaboration is not a free-for-all. The work of stakeholders must be conducted in an orderly fashion, building deeper and more meaningful agreements in each succeeding stage. Designing a constructive process defines the working together phase in sufficient detail for potential stakeholders to understand what they are getting into. In particular, this design work includes the following steps: selecting an appropriate approach to the issue or concern; defining the work flow of the process, the number and types of meetings that will take place, and a time line; identifying the tracks of activity; and creating a graphic map for the process. Members of the convening group or another designated working group perform this task. On complex public issues, the assistance of a skilled process expert may be helpful.

David Straus of Interaction Associates, a consulting group focused on collaboration in organizations and communities, helped develop the process design discipline. What follows builds from Straus's work (1999a).

***Selecting an Appropriate Approach.*** Common approaches to public concerns include collaborative problem solving, visioning, and strategic planning. Many collaborative processes use aspects of all three. Selecting an appropriate approach shapes the remainder of the process design work.

Collaborative problem solving approaches the issue as a problem. Stakeholders define the problem in some depth and then define the solution. This approach works well in highly conflictual situations where particular problems must be solved before other issues or concerns can be addressed. It also works well on issues that are narrow in scope.

Visioning is more creative and proactive. Stakeholders create a vision of a desired future state and then develop strategies for achieving it. Visioning works when a community or region needs new ways of looking at public concerns and possibilities for addressing them. An effective vision provides a compelling picture of the future that inspires action to achieve it.

A strategic planning process defines strategic goals or objectives and the specific actions necessary to achieve them. It places particular emphasis on current realities, a desired future state, and the strategies for connecting the two. Strategic planning works best on very complex or interdependent issues. Visioning often plays an important role in strategic planning.

- See Chapter Eight, "Working Together" for more on the use of these three approaches.

The situation and the nature of the issue or concern help determine which approach, or combination of approaches, to use. Among the aspects to consider are these:

- The level of conflict surrounding the issue or concern
- The time frame for dealing with the issue
- The barriers to action (for example, what makes leadership difficult)
- The need for or opportunity to create something new or to revitalize existing arrangements
- The complexity of the issue

Selecting one or a combination of these approaches shapes how the work will progress and specifies the tasks that need to be accomplished.

*Defining the Work Flow.* A collaborative process builds a series of agreements, each one deeper and more encompassing than the last. These agreements help define the phases of the process (see Chapter Five). In the working together phase, stakeholders build the capacity to collaborate, build shared understanding of content and context, define problems or create visions, decide what needs to be done, and plan for action.

The initial work sets the tone for the remainder of the process. Stakeholders begin building trust and working relationships among themselves and learning new skills for working together. They learn about the process, how it works, and who participates, and they set ground rules and refine the process as necessary. This work confirms their agreement to work together.

Subsequently, stakeholders build a shared understanding of the information and knowledge about the concern. They help determine what information needs refining and complement the preliminary work of the convening group in the setting up for success phase. This builds trust in the sources and credibility of the information. Stakeholders begin to understand the information without debating it, clarify information and check for shared understanding, and learn new ways for engaging with information and with each other. Taking the time to do the educating work allows new perspectives to emerge. New perspectives create possibilities for learning together, shifting positions, and accomplishing adaptive work.

With a shared understanding of the issue or concern, stakeholders move to defining problems or creating a vision. Once this work is complete, the group must decide what to do. Alternative possibilities are identified and evaluated and decisions made. A clear rationale for the recommendations helps stakeholders make their case to the broader community.

Finally, stakeholders define the steps that lead to action. They must determine how to take the recommendations to the community, formal decision-making bodies, and implementing organizations in a way that will gain agreement and support. This may include a plan for managing the implementation work and a definition of roles and responsibilities. Deciding how the recommendations themselves will be implemented occurs in the moving to action phase.

Each of these aspects may take a meeting or a series of meetings to accomplish. Stakeholders do some of the work in plenary sessions while delegating other work to subcommittees or task forces within the group. The convening group lays out a proposed schedule for meetings and an initial organization of subcommittees and task forces.

*Identifying Tracks of Activity.* A number of concurrent activities occur in a collaborative process and define the different levels of involvement required of stakeholders and others: process management, stakeholder work, subcommittee or task force work, outreach to the community or region, and outreach to formal decision-making bodies and implementing organizations

The process management track covers the activities of a steering committee or other group responsible for planning specific meetings and activities. This group manages the process and has no decision-making responsibilities related to the content of the issue or concern. The stakeholder track and the subcommittee or task force track cover the work of these groups through the activities identified earlier. The work of the stakeholder group does not go on in isolation. The outreach tracks help stakeholders inform others and gain a broader level of support for their work.

*Creating a Process Map.* A graphic process map provides a visual picture of the prospective work and thus helps potential stakeholders know what they are committing to. Defining the work flow and identifying the tracks of activity provide all the information needed. The work flow and tracks identify the horizontal and vertical dimensions of the map, respectively. Symbols define meetings and other engagements (see Figure 7.5). Figure 7.6 is an example of a process map from an initiative in central Oklahoma addressing the quality of teaching in public education.

# Defining Information Needs

Once the process design has been established, the convening group makes an initial assessment of the information and education the stakeholder group will need in order to make good decisions. Differing perspectives on the quality or credibility

## FIGURE 7.5. PROCESS MAP SYMBOLS.

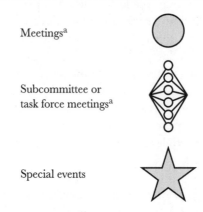

Meetings[a]

Subcommittee or
task force meetings[a]

Special events

[a]The size of the circle indicates the relative number of participants.

of available information make this a critical task. A stakeholder's willingness to participate depends in part on confidence in content information and the way it is used.

### Defining Information and Education Needs

The process begins by listing the kinds of information that stakeholders need in order to make good decisions along with possible sources. Outside expert advice may help. Surfacing the biases in the information and its sources can help the convening group decide how to deal with them. Understanding these biases assists in identifying and selecting content experts. Stakeholders will review and refine this initial assessment in the early stages of a collaborative process. If information needs are vague or uncertain, the convening group can define a process for helping stakeholders identify and gather the information they need.

## Defining Critical Roles

In a collaborative process, stakeholders do the work, process experts facilitate the work, content experts inform the work, and strong, facilitative leaders sustain the work. The stakeholder identification process defines a group of citizens who could become a constituency for change. Specific people need to be identified and selected to fill other critical roles.

## Selecting Process Experts

Process experts facilitate the work of the stakeholders. They inform and educate the group about effective collaborative processes while remaining neutral about the content of the group's work. They may help the convening group design the process and its component work sessions. Process experts help build the group's identity, help them work through issues and concerns arising from the group's experience, and provide the connecting links through the various elements of the initiative. The process experts should have substantial prior experience working with similar groups as a trainer, consultant, and facilitator of organizational and community collaboration. Their skills and capacities should include

- A working knowledge of successful collaboration in communities and regions
- The capacity to manage and facilitate extended multistakeholder, collaborative engagements that lead to meaningful agreements and effective implementation
- The ability to work in partnership with the convening group to help design, set up, and facilitate a collaborative process
- Substantial knowledge and experience of group dynamics and the ability to facilitate the stakeholder group's work around its issues and concerns
- The capacity to use a wide variety of tools and techniques to help address specific problems and needs arising out of the work of the stakeholders
- Knowledge and experience in using experiential group and team-building tools and techniques that engage the whole person
- The ability to empathize with the varying experiences of the stakeholders
- The ability to coach and counsel individual stakeholders as necessary
- The capacity to command the respect of the stakeholders over an extended period of time in a variety of challenging situations
- The ability to provide a positive role model that reflects the goals, objectives, and methodological beliefs of the initiative (including credibility as a content neutral facilitator)
- Knowledge of the content or substance of the issue in order to recognize and use strategic moments or turning points in the collaborative process

## Selecting Content Experts

Content experts inform the stakeholder group. Ideally, they should provide information to help stakeholders make good decisions. More often, they try to tell the stakeholders what to do.

Sometimes people in the stakeholder group have content expertise. If participants trust those with special expertise, this can be helpful. But people who use

## FIGURE 7.6.  PROCESS MAP EXAMPLE.

| Phase / Track | Orientation | Understanding the Challenges | | |
|---|---|---|---|---|
| *Steering Group* | ○ | ○ | ○ | ○ |
| *Stakeholder Group* | ⬤ | ⬤ | ⬤ | ⬤ |
| *Task Groups* | | | | |
| *Meeting Outcomes* | • Review purpose of initiative<br>• Build relationships<br>• Understand collaborative process<br>• Agree on guidelines for working together<br>• Understand concerns about quality of teaching | • Understand current performance of schools and how measured<br>• Understand how education system operates<br>• Understand Central Oklahoma rankings<br>• Identify what is working and not working<br>• Understand how other initiatives identify challenges<br>• Identify what makes change difficult<br>• Explore and understand various perspectives on the purpose of education | | |
| *Outreach to Region* | | | ☆ | |
| *Outreach to Implementing Organizations* | | ⬤ | | ⬤ |

**Improving the Quality of Teaching**

| Defining the Vision | Defining the Strategies | From Strategy to Action |
|---|---|---|
| • Define vision<br> - Purpose of education<br> - Quality of education<br> - Quality of teaching<br> - Supporting quality of teaching<br>• Define key performance areas for improving the quality of teaching<br> - Identify gaps between current reality and vision<br> - Identify priorities for improving the quality of teaching | • Understand the lessons of experience for improving the quality of teaching<br> - Current research<br> - What is working in the region (to build on)<br> - What is working in other areas<br>• Define alternative strategies for improving the quality of teaching<br>• Agree on strategies for improving the quality of teaching | • Define action steps and links with implementing organizations<br>• Develop strategies for working with implementing organizations<br>• Create oversight and evaluation plan |

**in the Central Oklahoma Region**

their knowledge to influence the agenda create problems. Content expertise from outside sources may provide more credibility.

Outside sources include recognized experts such as academics, consultants, or other professionals in particular fields. Stakeholders engage with these experts individually or in panels made up of experts with different perspectives on the issue or concern. Sometimes specific consulting or academic groups can meet all information needs if they have the confidence of the group.

The selection process ensures the credibility of content experts. Either the convening group or a subcommittee of the stakeholder group—whoever is responsible for selection—develops the process. Stakeholders must trust the group doing the selection work. A useful selection process could include developing a set of criteria for selecting content experts, describing the kind of information stakeholders need (including what form it should take), listing possible sources, evaluating possible sources against the criteria, and selecting the content experts.

### Identifying Strong, Facilitative Leaders

Strong, facilitative leaders in the stakeholder group provide the glue that holds a collaborative effort together. They help create and support an inclusive and constructive process, convince others that collaboration is necessary, help do the initiating work, convene the stakeholders, keep them focused and engaged, and link stakeholders with formal decision-making bodies and implementing organizations. Their capacity to accomplish these tasks depends on their credibility. With a diverse stakeholder group, several participants must take on this role to provide the collective credibility to keep the initiative moving.

Identifying strong, facilitative leaders means finding people with recognized influence in the stakeholder group who will use their credibility to support the collaborative process. By keeping an open mind about the outcomes of the process, they encourage the work of the stakeholders. Some people who have the potential to serve in this capacity are retired government and business leaders, church leaders, and higher education executives. Others with credibility limited to certain sectors or interests may be necessary for specific segments of the stakeholder group. In addition to those identified during the preparatory work, new collaborative leaders emerge during the process itself. A steering committee recognizes, encourages, and supports these emerging leaders.

## Managing the Process

A collaborative process is a complex enterprise involving people, information, and resources over a significant period of time. It requires a great deal of logistical work and support. Defining a management structure, identifying roles, and assigning responsibilities help organize the work.

## Establishing a Steering Committee

Most extended collaborative processes need a steering committee to manage the process. The steering committee has no authority for working with the content of the issue or decision making; rather, it helps plan and organize the work of the stakeholders—for example:

- Developing agendas for specific meetings
- Determining information needs of stakeholders and coordinating the work of content experts
- Overseeing the recording and communication of information and agreements within the stakeholder group
- Tracking group dynamic issues within the stakeholder group and determining how to deal with them
- Maintaining regular communication with stakeholders about meeting schedules and places
- Identifying and addressing the logistics needs of the process
- Evaluating the progress of the initiative and finding ways to improve it
- Planning and initiating outreach activities to the community, formal decision-making bodies, and implementing organizations
- Working with the media to communicate the work and progress of the stakeholders
- Advising staff and process experts on the conduct of the initiative
- Tracking financial aspects of the process

Most steering committees meet prior to each meeting of the full stakeholder group to accomplish this planning work.

Members of the steering committee come from the stakeholder group itself. Sometimes convening group members carry over into new roles with the steering committee. As with the convening group, committee members must have the trust of the stakeholders. In order to build trust, stakeholders may choose some or all of the committee members. Ultimately, the steering committee is responsible to the stakeholders.

## Staffing the Effort

Managing the process through the work of the steering committee relies on volunteer work. Supporting this work requires committed staff. Many initiatives have an executive or project director to oversee management functions and at least one other administrative person to carry them out. Staff members support the work of the stakeholders.

The executive or project director needs a high level of credibility with the stakeholder group. The director must work constructively with stakeholders as well as funders, media, and the broader community. Supporting staff members need skills in writing memorandums, scheduling meetings, taking care of logistics needs, transcribing meeting notes, contacting stakeholders by telephone, and so on. Staff members have the following roles:

- Communicating with stakeholders
- Meeting logistics
- Financial management
- Resource development
- Coordinating steering committee, stakeholder, and other working group meeting schedules
- Organizing outreach to media, the public, and formal organizations
- Working with process and content experts
- Documenting the process

## Documenting the Process

Maintaining a visible record of stakeholders work supports group learning and adaptive work. Past work informs subsequent work. By keeping work visible, the group can continually verify its accuracy and make any needed corrections. Recording information and agreements in the moment in the words of the stakeholders in a visible fashion supplies this need.

Many groups use a designated recorder in partnership with the facilitator to keep track of the group's work. The recorder writes, under the direction of the facilitator, important points tracking the group's work and agreements reached on large flipchart or newsprint sheets. The recorder uses participants' words as much as possible without interpretation or paraphrasing. The group and the facilitator check the recorder's work for clarity and accuracy. This group memory must reflect the meaning the group intends. A visible group memory legitimizes the work of the stakeholders and helps prevent the revisiting of prior work. Because ideas are visible, participants know they have been heard and that their contributions will be considered.

Recording the proceedings of the stakeholder group in this fashion creates an ongoing record. Support staff transcribe or copy the work of the recorder with minimal editing to preserve the spirit and accuracy of the group's work. Direct copying ensures that stakeholders see their own work, reducing the potential for misinterpretation. The staff maintains the group memory in a readily accessible format and provides copies for stakeholders as soon as possible after a meeting.

# Finding the Resources

A complex undertaking like a collaborative initiative needs financial resources or in-kind contributions to support it. The convening group takes responsibility for defining resource needs and finding financial support. Securing funding or other support prior to convening the stakeholder group ensures the continuity and success of the initiative.

## Developing a Budget

With stakeholders identified, a constructive process designed, and information needs determined, a budget can be developed that covers expenses in the following categories:

- Administrative expenses, including salaries and office expenses for staff
- Meeting expenses (for example, meeting rooms, meals or refreshments, materials, equipment, and transportation)
- Process expertise, including fees and expenses
- Content expertise, including fees and expenses

## Funding a Collaborative Process

The credibility of a collaborative initiative depends in part on the credibility of its funding sources. Multiple funding sources help mitigate the perception that organizations making larger contributions have an inordinate voice in the outcome of the process.

A community or region can call on several funding sources, including corporations, government organizations, individual contributors, and foundations. Contributions can be financial or in-kind. In-kind contributions often support administrative and office needs. Universities and government organizations may be willing to provide content expertise. Local foundations and community service organizations can help identify potential funding sources. Sometimes federal and state government agencies fund programs that support collaboration. When funds are secured, the convening group or steering group should develop a means for allocating them in a clear and transparent way.

## Setting Up for Success

Collaborative initiatives do not fail because the concept is flawed. They fail because of poor planning and poor execution. Foresight and good preparation prevent failure from poor planning. Good preparation brings credibility to the effort and helps motivate stakeholders to participate. A well-conceived process and a credible stakeholder group provide the foundation for future success. The disciplined work of setting up for success facilitates working together.

CHAPTER EIGHT

# WORKING TOGETHER

Collaboration engages stakeholders in new and constructive ways. Stakeholders need relationships of trust and respect and new skills for working together. They need information that supports mutual learning and consensus-based decision making. They need specific tools and consciously designed processes to help them define problems, create visions, and decide what should be done. Addressing each of these dimensions in a synergistic way makes collaboration possible and productive. Figure 8.1 highlights the "Working Together" phase of the collaborative process.

## Building Capacity

Few collaborative initiatives have the luxury of building relationships and skills prior to the engagement itself. Most stakeholders are unwilling to commit additional time to do this. They simply want to get down to work and get it over with. Successful efforts therefore build relationships and skills as part of an ongoing process. In a collaborative initiative, this work begins at the outset and continues throughout the process. Stakeholders learn to appreciate the perspectives of others while learning new skills for working together.

## FIGURE 8.1.  A GUIDE TO THE PRACTICES OF SUCCESSFUL COLLABORATION.

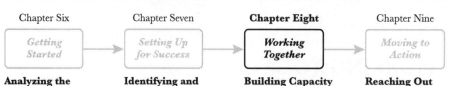

| Chapter Six | Chapter Seven | **Chapter Eight** | Chapter Nine |
|---|---|---|---|
| *Getting Started* | *Setting Up for Success* | ***Working Together*** | *Moving to Action* |

**Analyzing the Context for Collaboration**
1. Understanding the political dynamics
2. Understanding how citizens think about public issues

**Deciding on a Collaborative Strategy**
1. Determining the feasibility of collaboration
2. Defining the purpose, scope, and focus

**Identifying and Convening Stakeholders**
1. Understanding the principle and practice of inclusion
2. Finding the credibility to convene
3. Identifying stakeholders
4. Inviting, recruiting, and convening stakeholders

**Designing a Constructive Process**
1. Defining the decision-making method
2. Establishing ground rules
3. Designing a constructive process

**Defining Information Needs**
1. Defining information and education needs

**Defining Critical Roles**
1. Selecting process experts
2. Selecting content experts
3. Identifying strong, facilitative leaders

**Managing the Process**
1. Establishing a steering committee
2. Staffing the effort
3. Documenting the process

**Finding the Resources**
1. Developing the budget
2. Funding a collaborative process

**Building Capacity**
1. Building relationships and skills

**Ways of Engaging**
1. Engaging through dialogue
2. Working with written information

**Informing the Stakeholders**
1. Understanding the content
2. Understanding the context
   • Analyzing strengths, weaknesses, opportunities, and threats
   • Developing scenarios

**Deciding What Needs to Be Done**
1. Collaborative problem solving
2. Visioning
3. Strategic planning

**Reaching Out**
1. Building a broader constituency
2. Engaging with decision makers and implementing organizations

**Managing Action**
1. Developing action plans
2. Organizing and managing implementation

## Building Relationships and Skills

Deeper relationships emerge as people begin to see others as fellow human beings rather than as strangers or opponents. The experiences and stories of participants become as valuable to the process as expert information about the content. Understanding the experiences of others fosters insight, learning, change, and agreement. Collaborative leaders legitimize the race, gender, culture, class, sector, or sexual orientation identities of stakeholders in order to ensure their engagement. Process experts design experiences that transform how stakeholders see each other. These experiences help people build trust, learn to respect and care for each other, listen to each other, and work together as peers.

Good facilitators teach new skills while facilitating the work of the group. At the beginning of each new task, the facilitator provides an outline of the process and defines and models the skills necessary to accomplish the work. Over time, the group develops a new awareness of process and the tools that make it work, and they begin to incorporate this awareness into their behaviors and actions. They learn preventions to preclude trouble and interventions to regain focus when trouble occurs. They learn to use dialogue and Socratic inquiry to build understanding of others' perspectives rather than debate different points of view. Over time, the stakeholder group's collaborative skills become the norm rather than the exception.

---

## Beginning the Process of Relationship and Skill Building

1. *Introduce participants to each other.* Stakeholders can introduce themselves or another stakeholder. When stakeholders introduce themselves, ask them to define their role in the community rather than identifying themselves with a particular organization or position in a hierarchy. To build understanding of other perspectives, have them describe the concerns that motivated them to participate rather than their position on the issue. When stakeholders introduce others, ask them to interview others whom they do not know or do not know well and create a headline that captures something interesting about the person.

2. *Use small groups to build relationships and skills.* Working in small groups such as dyads or triads made up of people with different or unfamiliar perspectives speeds the relationship-building process and helps participants learn new skills. Groups should include people with different perspectives and experiences. Change the makeup of small groups regularly. Allow people enough time for introductions, and provide a well-defined process to guide their work. Describing and demonstrating relevant skills and designating facilitators for the small groups help ensure productive interaction and full participation. Early successes in small groups set a powerful and positive tone for subsequent work.

---

- See facilitators' guides like *How to Make Meetings Work* (Doyle and Straus, 1976) and *Facilitator's Guide to Participatory Decision-Making* (Kaner, 1996) for ideas for relationship and skill building for the process expert.

# Ways of Engaging

Collaboration develops deeper agreements through shared understanding and mutual learning. The engagement requires critical faculties for listening, inquiring, and advocating. Two approaches for changing the norms of engagement can help: engaging others in dialogue as a means of creating shared meaning and understanding and working with written information to develop understanding of content and the critical assumptions that support different perspectives.

## Engaging Through Dialogue

The process of dialogue changes the norms of public engagement. Rather than producing controversy through debate and argument, productive dialogue creates shared meaning and mutual learning. It builds the stakeholder group's capacity to do adaptive work through active listening and constructive inquiry and advocacy. The process legitimizes and clarifies the diverse perspectives of stakeholders. When dialogue works, learning occurs, new possibilities emerge, and relationships and skills—social capital—improve. Figure 8.2 contrasts the working premises of dialogue with those of debate.

Dialogue, like collaboration, has opening, narrowing, and closing phases. The opening phase provides a sense of safety, allowing people to suspend judgment so that new insights emerge. Participants learn from each other through inquiry—exposing reasoning and underlying assumptions supporting differing perspectives and concerns. New insights appear in the narrowing phase as participants advocate new possibilities in ways that educate and inform. New understanding and agreement develop in the closing phase. At its best, dialogue is an organic process, with each phase unfolding naturally from previous ones.

Stakeholder facility for dialogue depends on the capacity for active listening and constructive advocacy and inquiry. Groups learn these skills through structured group exercises. With regular use, these skills quickly become the norm, allowing dialogue to take place with a less structured process.

In addition to these basic skills, several other factors nurture and support a group's capacity for dialogue. A facilitator can help the group honor its guidelines for working together, raise awareness of group dynamics not apparent to those participating, and help the group work through difficult emotions, misunder-

## FIGURE 8.2. DEBATE AND DIALOGUE.

| Debate | Dialogue |
|---|---|
| • Assuming that there is a right answer and that you have it | • Assuming many people have part of the answer |
| • Combative: participants attempt to prove the other side wrong | • Collaborative: participants work together toward common understanding |
| • About winning | • About exploring common ground |
| • Listening to find flaws and make counterarguments | • Listening to understand, create shared meaning, and find agreement |
| • Defending our own assumptions as truth | • Revealing assumptions for evaluation |
| • Seeing two sides of an issue | • Seeing all sides of an issue |
| • Defending one's own views against those of others | • Admitting that others' thinking can improve one's own |
| • Searching for flaws and weaknesses in others' positions | • Searching for strengths and value in others' positions |
| • Discouraging further conversation by creating winners and losers | • Keeping the topic open even after discussion ends |
| • Seeking a conclusion or vote that ratifies your position | • Discovering new options, not seeking closure |

*Source:* Created by Mark Gerzon for the Bipartisan Congressional Retreat. Adapted from work by the Public Conversations Project, National Study Circles Resources, Educators for Social Responsibility.

standings, and conflict when they arise. Sufficient time—two hours or more when possible—allows the process to work. More than one session may be necessary in order to reach closure on a particular topic or issue. Because dialogue creates shared meaning and understanding, participants speak more to the topic than to each other. A circle of chairs where everyone can see each other works best.

## Learning the Skills of Dialogue

1. *Choose a topic or issue.* A dialogue generally focuses on a particular topic or issue.
2. *Surface personal perspectives on the topic.* Allow stakeholders to reflect on and outline their own perspective about the topic or issue. Have them identify the reasons or rationale for their perspective. Have each person verbally describe his or her perspective and the rationale behind it. This process provides practice in making thought processes visible to others. Other participants listen carefully without interrupting.
3. *Build shared understanding.* Allow listeners to ask clarifying questions that check for understanding. They are not to comment on or rebut what others say. This

provides practice in inquiring to understand others' perspective without attacking them.

4. *Refine personal perspectives.* As stakeholders begin to understand the perspectives of others, ask them to refine their personal perspective based on what they have learned from others.

5. *Focus on new insights and perspectives.* Repeat the process as necessary in dyads, triads, small groups, or the large group. When using dyads or triads, do several rounds, changing partners with each round. Observe how individual and group thinking evolves. New insights and perspectives emerge as learning takes place, and an organic consensus tends to develop as thinking converges.

- See Peter Senge's *The Fifth Discipline Fieldbook* (1994) for further information about the use of dialogue and for very useful protocols for advocacy and inquiry.
- See *The Study Circle Handbook* (Study Circles, 1993), for further information about the use of dialogue for exploring public concerns.

## Working with Written Information

Participants in most public engagements take information apart and debate it rather than try to understand it. Instead of using information to educate, they use it to buttress positions. The medium—the manner of presentation—often becomes more important than the message. Collaboration seeks to change these norms. Working with written information in a manner similar to dialogue fosters the skills of reading, listening, and analytical thinking.

Stakeholders begin by understanding the issues and ideas in a written document regardless of who the author is, the author's biases, or the manner of writing. This Socratic method relies on questioning to probe the meaning of a text. Socrates had a specific lesson in mind that he sought to elicit through leading questions; Socratic inquiry, however, has no particular destination in mind (see Figure 8.3). A process of inquiry using open-ended questions leads to shared understanding of the text. Using this method helps participants

- Gain knowledge and perspective through deeper understanding of written information
- Understand how others think about ideas, values, and information
- Gain new insights and learning from other participants
- Create shared meaning from the text
- Build relationships of trust and respect
- Develop skills for listening, inquiry, and advocacy

## FIGURE 8.3. SOCRATIC INQUIRY.

| **Socratic Inquiry Is** | **Socratic Inquiry Is Not** |
|---|---|
| • Understanding issues, ideas, and values in the text | • Debate |
| • About the text | • Finding the "right" answer |
| • Acquiring new insights and perspectives from the text and from other participants | • About your opinion or position |
| • Making meaning from the text through exploration | • Acquiring organized knowledge |

The technique of Socratic inquiry has been used with all types of audiences, especially in educational settings from kindergarten to higher education. St. John's College in Santa Fe, New Mexico, uses the technique as its central teaching method. Some programs use Socratic inquiry with inner-city and low-income groups to develop skills and knowledge for full participation in civic and political life. This wide application demonstrates that anyone, regardless of age or ability, can access text, contribute worthwhile ideas to a conversation, derive meaning from the insights of others, have their ideas valued by others who might be different from themselves, and create shared understanding and meaning by engaging with others.

As in dialogue, a circle of chairs for participants is essential. Each person should have a copy of the text in order to refer to it. People who have not read the text sit outside the circle and serve as process observers and offer comments after the session. Seminars work well with groups up to thirty people or so. For larger numbers of participants, break the group down into smaller, more manageable groups, conduct a separate inquiry with each, and then integrate learnings later. Most seminars take forty-five minutes to an hour and a half to run their course. The facilitator starts the conversation, keeps it focused on the text and the issues raised by the text, keeps it moving, and ends it at an appropriate or strategic time.

## Learning the Skills of Socratic Inquiry

1. *Select and distribute a relevant text.* The best texts for Socratic inquiry are rich in issues, ideas, and values. Since ambiguity about issues, ideas, and values characterizes most public concerns, texts that uncover ambiguities serve better than those that are narrow or one-sided.

2. *Read the text.* Ask participants to read the text several times before the seminar and to note important points or questions raised by the text. Some seminar leaders

encourage participants to read the text like a love letter, examining every word, phrase, sentence, or paragraph for different meanings or interpretations.

3. *Begin the conversation.* When the group is gathered, ask an opening question to begin the conversation. Opening questions should be open-ended, lead participants deeper into the text, and reflect something about which the facilitator has genuine curiosity. If this fails to start the conversation, drop the question and try another.

4. *Keep the conversation moving.* Once the conversation is moving, intervene only to keep it focused on the text and moving but not to promote your own agenda. Ask participants to indicate and read specific paragraphs and pages within the text that support their points. Encourage them to say more if necessary. Ask what others think or how a point one person raises relates to that of another. Remember that the first objective is to understand what the author says, not to disagree with or critique the author.

5. *End the conversation.* Stop the conversation as energy decreases and before conclusions are drawn. Socratic inquiry is not a decision-making process; rather, it creates shared meaning and understanding that informs future decisions.

6. *Reflect on the experience.* Debrief the experience by quickly eliciting a word or two from each participant about his or her experience in the process. If the seminar is part of an education phase of a collaborative process, capture content points to remember from the text itself.

---

- See Michael Strong's *The Habit of Thought: From Socratic Seminars to Socratic Practice* (1997) and *How to Conduct Effective Socratic Seminars* (1999), a videotape, for further information about Socratic inquiry.

## Informing the Stakeholders

Stakeholders need two types of knowledge in a collaborative process: content information about the concerns or issues and information about the current and future context in which action will take place. Gathering and analyzing content information uses the skills of dialogue and Socratic inquiry to create a shared understanding of the issues. Analyzing strengths, weaknesses, opportunities, and threats and developing scenarios describing alternative futures helps groups understand the context for action.

### Understanding the Content

Gathering and analyzing information about content helps stakeholders make good decisions in a collaborative process. In the early stages, participants build a common base of understanding about the presenting issue. In later stages, they learn about and evaluate alternative courses of action.

A history of conflict about facts and differing interpretations of implications makes finding credible sources of information challenging. Unfortunately, dueling experts and adversarial science commonly do more harm than good in informing stakeholders. More intent on telling stakeholders what to do and impressing them with what they know, content experts too often divide, confuse, and obfuscate rather than enlighten.

Stakeholders have more confidence when they determine their own information needs as well as how they will gather it, analyze it, and use it. This shared understanding becomes a central reference point for the remainder of the process. Gathering and analyzing information in credible and constructive ways serves several purposes. Because most public issues require adaptive work, new insights and perspectives arise from a deeper understanding of the content. Relationships and skills develop through interaction with written information, content experts, and other stakeholders. With more understanding of and confidence in relevant information, stakeholders make better decisions.

## Defining Information Needs

1. *Determine areas of concern.* Ask stakeholders, "When you think about the future of [the issue], what concerns you the most?" Give them time for personal reflection, and then have them share their ideas with others in dyads or triads. Have them use dialogue for clarifying other participants' views without argument. Use two or three rounds to build understanding. Ask all stakeholder to refine their concerns at the end of each round, building on what they hear from others. Once the rounds are complete, ask each person to narrow his or her list to the two or three most important concerns. In the large group, ask each person to share one of those concerns. Write each one on a sticky note and stick it on the wall. Continue until all concerns are out (the number will not be too large because many ideas will be duplicated). Ask the stakeholders to group similar concerns. Once they are satisfied with the groupings, have them name the groups. This becomes the initial list of shared concerns.
2. *Identify the information needed to address the concerns.* Ask the stakeholders to consider the question, "What do we need to know in order to make good decisions?" Use a brainstorming process to develop an initial list. Combine and group ideas as necessary. Have the list checked by an outside source to be sure that nothing significant has been overlooked.
3. *Determine the best sequence for working with the information.*
4. *Determine the process for gathering information.* There are several options: task groups within the larger stakeholder group, individual experts, panels of experts, surveys, or outside assessments by academic or consulting groups. Develop criteria to help determine which approach to use. Stakeholders must agree on how

to gather the information and how to select resources as a key step in building confidence in the information.

5. *Agree on roles and responsibilities for gathering information.* Sometimes task groups within the stakeholder group can be assigned to gather information. Task groups should be given specific instructions about their role and tasks by the larger stakeholder group and should have diverse membership so that narrow interests or perspectives do not bias the findings.

6. *Decide how to use the information.* Stakeholders must decide how the information will be presented, organized, analyzed, and considered.

7. *Record the information for future use.* Record the learnings or things to remember as preparation for moving to the next stage. Check that all necessary information has been gathered and considered. Prepare for problem-defining or visioning activities by asking stakeholders to list what is known and not known about the issue. This helps frame activities in subsequent stages.

---

- See John R. Ehrmann and Barbara L. Stinson, "Joint Fact-Finding and the Use of Technical Experts" (1999), for further information.

## Understanding the Context

Public problems and opportunities do not happen in a vacuum; they take place within a particular context—a bigger picture or a wider regional, national, or even global perspective—and a varied history of efforts to address them. Understanding this larger context grounds the work of stakeholders and helps them make more responsive decisions. New visions and strategies should connect current reality with a desired future state. Stakeholders must respond to both current and future needs. Unfortunately, most interventions on public issues, collaborative or otherwise, pay little heed to understanding the context for action. Decisions are disconnected from both current reality and the vagaries of an uncertain future.

Two powerful tools can help stakeholders understand the current and future context. First, analyzing strengths, weaknesses, opportunities, and threats (SWOT analysis) surfaces the contextual challenges in the near term. Second, developing scenarios exposes the deep uncertainties inherent in any future context and highlights alternate possibilities for how the future might unfold.

*Analyzing Strengths, Weaknesses, Opportunities, and Threats (SWOT).* Businesses have used SWOT analysis as a tool for strategic planning for decades. Now communities and regions use it in the public arena. Strengths and weaknesses describe features of the community or region that help or hinder its capacity to deal with the presenting issues. Opportunities and threats define features of the current and future contextual environment that can affect the community or region in positive or negative ways. Understanding the implications of these features helps inform other aspects of collaborative work, such as developing scenarios, collaborative problem solving, visioning, and strategic planning.

---

## Analyzing Strengths, Weaknesses, Opportunities, and Threats

1. *Identify strengths, weaknesses, opportunities, and threats.* Ask participants to make a list of each of these aspects from their own perspective. Use the tools of dialogue in dyads, triads, or other small groups to build shared understanding and develop a broader perspective. Have participants refine and prioritize their lists. Transfer the top three or four points from each list to large sticky notes. Group them by category: strengths, weaknesses, opportunities, and threats. Further grouping within categories helps emphasize particularly significant features.
2. *Analyze the information.* Strengths describe assets or features of the community or region that support future action. Weaknesses define challenges or barriers that must be compensated for in order to make progress. Opportunities identify features of the contextual environment that can be used to advantage. Potential threats may undermine efforts to move ahead. After identifying these features, ask the group to consider their implications for future action.

---

*Developing Scenarios.* The few trenchant questions in a SWOT analysis help stakeholders understand the current and near-term features of the contextual environment. Understanding a future fraught with uncertainty is more challenging. The key variables or driving forces affecting the future of a community or region—population growth, changing business environments, shifting tax bases, growing social problems, economic globalization, developments in new technology, increasing interdependence with other communities and regions, and others—are generally unpredictable or out of its control. Beyond a few years out, forecasting becomes inaccurate or impossible. Most groups find it easier to assume that the future will be very much like today rather than consciously considering its unpredictability. This limited understanding of the future context can lead to unresponsive and ungrounded decisions with potentially harmful consequences.

When forecasting is unreliable, other tools must be used to consider the inherent unpredictability of the future. Anticipating the future in a rapidly changing environment calls for more than systematic analysis; it demands creativity, insight, and intuition. Developing scenarios or stories about possible futures combine these elements into a foundation for improving community and regional visions and strategies. Understanding the contextual environment helps shape proposed strategies and actions.

Distinguishing three types of uncertainties helps define the purpose and focus of scenarios. First, statistical forecasting techniques can predict some factors affecting the future when sufficient history and data exist. For example, insurance companies use actuarial data about accidents and mortality to identify the probability of future events in order to set premiums.

Second, some factors affecting the future cannot be accurately predicted, though different plausible assertions can be made about what may happen to these "structural" uncertainties. The ongoing debate between the bulls and the bears reflects the inherent structural uncertainty of the stock market. Both sides rely on the same information about the performance of the economy. They discern common patterns while drawing different conclusions. Each side tells a very different yet plausible story about how the future might unfold—one optimistic, one pessimistic. Neither predicts the future with any level of confidence. When structural uncertainties pervade, a scenarios process identifies a range of plausible assertions or assumptions about them and creates stories about what the future might be like. The majority of the most important factors affecting the future of a community or region fall in the category of structural uncertainties.

Third, some uncertainties are virtually unknowable. What are referred to as "acts of God" might include such things as terrorist attacks, catastrophic floods or other weather-related events, collisions with meteors, and surprise acts of war. A community or region can prepare for these events by putting in place structures, protocols, and organizations to deal with potential emergencies. Neither forecasting nor scenarios can help cope with these unpredictable events.

A scenarios process begins by identifying the structural uncertainties—the driving forces—affecting the future of the community or region. Internally consistent stories based on different assumptions about these forces describe possible future contexts. Each story describes a larger world in which a community or region may have to live. A community or region will have little control over this external environment.

Unlike traditional forecasting or research approaches, scenarios present alternative images instead of extrapolating current trends. They embrace qualitative perspectives and the potential for sharp discontinuities that more quantitative models exclude. Creating scenarios requires decision makers and stakeholders to question their broadest assumptions about the way the world works so they can foresee decisions that might be missed or denied. Within a community or region, scenarios provide a common vocabulary and an effective basis for communicating complex, and sometimes paradoxical, conditions and options. By providing a deep understanding of the future context, scenarios allow communities and regions to create realistic, responsive, and grounded visions and strategies.

The use of scenarios as a way of enhancing visioning and strategic planning efforts has expanded in recent years from the corporate world to government and, now, to communities, regions, and countries. Royal Dutch Shell developed the methodology to help make better decisions about volatile oil prices. The Global Business Network, a California consulting group, refined the process in the private sector through its work with large corporations. In the public arena, scenarios have been used to guide South Africa's transition from apartheid to a multiracial democracy, cope with the challenges of economic and population growth in Missoula, Montana, and Charlotte, North Carolina, and restructure the nonprofit sector in the Boston metropolitan region.

Scenarios serve several purposes. They can help a community or region identify an emerging public agenda and build agreement on concerns that need to be addressed. The stories offer a starting point or artifact to react to and build on. They inform the visioning process by helping stakeholders identify qualities or aspects of the future they would like to create or avoid. Stakeholders test strategies by evaluating which options work best in different future environments.

Within communities and regions, the scenarios process helps build trust and skills for collaboration among disparate stakeholders. The process provides a safe environment to explore difficult issues and improve communication. Citizens, not experts, create scenarios. Different and varied perspectives among stakeholders challenge current assumptions about the future. The stakeholder group or a smaller task group can develop the scenarios.

The tools of facilitation, dialogue, and Socratic inquiry support the work of developing scenarios. Some of the subtle aspects of developing scenarios such as identification of driving forces and the development of scenario themes require skillful and experienced facilitators to get good results. Process experts new to scenarios should work with more experienced people when possible.

## Developing Scenarios

1. *Set up the scenarios development process.* Identify the scenario development group participants, and design the scenario development process.
2. *Conduct individual interviews.* Interviews with a cross-section of the stakeholder group help focus the scenario work. They identify pertinent strategic questions and ensure the relevance of the scenario work. These interviews generally follow the format and protocol described in Chapter Six.
3. *Educate the stakeholders or the scenario working group.* Stakeholders need to understand the purpose of scenarios and how they will be developed and used. Background information from individual interviews or other studies provides a shared understanding that ensures the relevance of scenarios to presenting concerns. New perspectives from experts and "remarkable people," that is, unconventional

thinkers with particular insight, inform the work and challenge stakeholders to consider hidden or unspoken dimensions of possible futures (Schwarz, 1994).

4. *Identify the driving forces.* The scenario working group identifies the driving forces: the most important and uncertain factors affecting the future of the community or region. Use dyads, triads, or other small groups to brainstorm possible driving forces. Use sticky notes to rank driving forces first by importance and then by degree of uncertainty. The five to ten most important and uncertain factors become the driving forces for the scenarios.

5. *Develop scenario themes or story plots.* Participants create scenario themes or story plots by making different plausible assumptions about the driving forces. Out of a range of possibilities, the group chooses two to four themes or plots. Good themes or plots are relevant, plausible, provocative, and divergent.

6. *Create the scenarios.* The scenarios working group expands the themes or plots into stories about how the future might unfold. Each story has an internally consistent logic that considers what happens to each of the driving forces, catalytic events that might occur, how the story progresses over time, possible newspaper headlines, early indicators, and a symbolic name that vividly captures the essence of the story and quickly distinguishes it from the others.

7. *Prepare the scenarios for use.* Scenarios are tools for developing visions and strategies, not an end product. The scenarios working group develops a means of presenting the scenarios for use by stakeholders and others. This might include written stories, multimedia presentations, or improvisational theater.

---

- See Chapter Fifteen, "Scenarios: Catalysts for Civic Change," for examples of the use of scenarios in the public arena.
- See Peter Schwartz's book, *The Art of the Long View* (1991), for a good introduction to scenarios. Kees van der Heijden's book, *Scenarios: The Art of Strategic Conversation* (1996), although directed more to the private sector, provides the most help on the subtleties of scenario development and describes specific processes for various steps. *Learning from the Future* (1998), edited by Liam Fahey and Robert M. Randall, offers valuable ideas about scenario themes, story plots and the use of scenarios for developing testing visions and strategies.

## Deciding What Needs to Be Done

New relationships, skills, and understanding prepare stakeholders for the real work of collaboration: deciding what needs to be done. Inquiry and learning shift to building agreements. The open-narrow-close framework provides guidance. Up to this point, the process has been one of opening. Now the work turns to narrowing as stakeholders define problems or create visions and identify alternative solutions or strategies. Finally, closing occurs, with clear and firm agreements about what should be done. This work must be carefully designed, skillfully facilitated, and powerfully led. Most collaborative initiatives use some combination of collaborative problem solving, visioning, and strategic planning to help stakeholders decide what needs to be done.

- See Chapter Seven, "Setting Up for Success," for more information on choosing an approach or combination of approaches.

## Collaborative Problem Solving

Collaborative problem solving relies on a particular set of tools and strategies to help stakeholders define problems and solutions. More specifically, it defines a way of organizing the work of deciding what needs to be done. Public concerns require adaptive work and a heuristic and iterative process for getting results. Though this may sound chaotic, an underlying logic helps make it work. First, a group cannot agree on solutions unless it agrees on the underlying problem or problems. Collaborative problem solving defines problems before defining solutions. Second, each step in collaborative problem solving has its opening or generative phase, its narrowing or evaluating phase, and its closing or reaching agreement phase. Third, a series of specific steps guide the process. For collaborative problem solving to work, groups must engage on the same task at the same time.

---

## Six Steps for Collaborative Problem Solving

Michael Doyle and David Straus (1976) outlined six steps, each designed to answer a specific question, for organizing the work of collaborative problem solving.

---

### Defining Problems

1. *How do stakeholders perceive the problem?* The problem definition phase begins with the perception of the problem. This first step surfaces and legitimizes different perceptions of the problem and helps define its dimensions.
2. *What is the real problem?* This step specifically defines the problem.
3. *Why is it a problem?* The group analyzes the problem, building an understanding of its causes and consequences. This deeper understanding provides the basis for developing solutions.

## Defining Solutions

4. *What are possible solutions to the problem?* The solution phase begins by generating alternative ideas for solving the problem. Creativity rather than practicality shapes this dynamic stage of the process.
5. *How should these alternatives be evaluated?* Alternatives must be evaluated in order to narrow the range of possible solutions. This analytic stage considers the desirability and practicality of alternative solutions.
6. *What is the solution?* What will the group's decision be? This step requires agreement on both how the final decision will be made—the process—and what the decision will be—the content.

- See Michael Doyle's and David Straus's *How to Make Meetings Work* (1976) and Sam Kaner's *Facilitator's Guide to Participatory Decision-Making* (1996) for further information on the concepts and tools used in collaborative problem solving.

## Visioning

Over the past three decades, the concept of vision has dominated thinking about setting direction. Heroic, charismatic leaders show the way by providing an inspiring vision. The leader persuades followers to align themselves in support of the leader's vision and motivates them to achieve it. Some circumstances—a crisis, for example—may require this style of leadership. The complexity of public concerns and the diversity of people affected by them demand a different style.

In the public arena, citizens are more likely to respond to a vision they helped create than to the vision of a single leader. A shared vision leads to mutual understanding and commitment. This does not mean, as some think, a diminished need for leadership. Rather than a solitary, visionary leader painting a picture of what needs to be done (the content), a few credible leaders provide inspiration and a means (the process) for creating a shared vision. Collaborative leaders help stakeholders set direction and inspire them to move in that direction.

Several recurring themes characterize the notion of a vision. A vision describes a desirable future to be realized over a period of time. An effective vision invigorates and inspires people to achieve it. A compelling vision aligns people in pursuit of it. A vision answers the questions of what will be done, why it should be done, and how it will be done. It is not abstract. When in place, a vision provides a context and rationale for decision making and criteria—values—to guide action. Achieving a vision requires creativity, risk taking, and experimentation. A shared vision creates expectations when people can feel what it would mean to achieve it. A palpable tension pulls energy toward the vision. Specific strategies link current circumstances to a desirable future state, grounding the vision in the realities of the current and future context.

When old ways of thinking and acting fail to match changing circumstances, a shared vision can provide a revolutionary reconception of future possibilities. By providing a broader context for action, a shared vision allows people to break out of historic mind-sets. It shifts emphasis from the present to the future by redirecting energy toward positive, desirable outcomes rather than avoidance of negative, undesirable consequences.

---

# Creating a Shared Vision

The best visioning processes integrate personal vision into shared vision by finding common ground. The process is organic and emergent rather than logical and rational. It taps both the heart and the mind of participants. As in other collaborative processes, a visioning process moves from a generative phase—opening—to an evaluative phase—narrowing—to an alignment or agreement phase—closing. A successful process generates alignment with the vision.

1. *Define shared vision and its importance.* Participants understand the definition of a vision, its importance, and the process for creating a shared vision.
2. *Identify personal visions.* Have participants take a few minutes to define their personal vision. Ask them to create a compelling image of a desirable future relevant to presenting issues and concerns that is personally meaningful and fulfilling and serves the needs of society. Have them describe it in terms of what it would look like and feel like, and how they would experience it. Ask them to define the values that inform and support their vision. Have them identify any personal concerns or aspirations. Ask them to see their vision in the present as if it had been achieved and to capture particular images of success. When they are finished, ask them to circle key themes and images.
3. *Expand and refine personal visions.* Ask participants to share their personal visions in dyads or triads. Have listeners look for aspects in common and for ideas that support or enhance their own vision. Listeners can ask clarifying questions but should not critique another's vision. Have participants do two or three rounds of sharing their personal vision and incorporating ideas from others at the end of each round. On completion, have each participant identify three to five key themes or images that are especially important to them.
4. *Record elements of personal visions.* Record essential elements of personal visions on sticky notes. Be sure other participants understand the meaning of each element. Put the sticky notes on a wall where all are visible.
5. *Create a shared vision.* Have the group put common themes or images together with other similar themes or images. Ask group members to describe the rationale

for why particular themes and images go together. Have participants move the sticky notes until all are satisfied with groupings. Ask the group to name the groupings. This label identifies the characteristics, dimensions, and values implicit in the vision. Contradictions within groupings or between groupings should be reconciled if necessary at this point. Check for missing elements that would help make the vision clear and complete. Have participants draft a vision statement incorporating these various aspects and check for alignment.

- See Peter Senge's *The Fifth Discipline* (New York: Currency Doubleday, 1990) and *The Fifth Discipline Fieldbook* (New York: Currency Doubleday, 1994), along with Carl Moore, Gianni Longo, and Patsy Palmer, "Visioning" (1999), for further information on and other approaches to visioning.

## Strategic Planning

Strategic planning incorporates both collaborative problem solving and visioning into a more comprehensive approach. It establishes a disciplined process for responding to a dynamically changing context. The process provides a means for creating a plan while concurrently building support for it. It defines strategic goals and objectives, as well as specific actions necessary to achieve them. The plan itself becomes a means of communication and a structure for management and control. The use of scenarios complements the work of strategic planning under conditions of great uncertainty. A strategic plan provides a rationale for future actions, sets priorities, and describes how work will be done.

Once a discipline reserved for experts, the practice of strategic planning has evolved into a collective endeavor. In the past, policy analysts would study an issue and use their intelligence and education to develop optimal strategies or policies. The increasing complexity of public issues and diversity of political perspectives, coupled with growing distrust of government, undermined confidence in the work of the "best and the brightest." In an age of uncertainty, optimal strategies no longer exist. Sound strategy requires a skillful strategy process capable of accomplishing adaptive work, not a cadre of experts. Sound strategies mobilize the assets of a community or region and lead to synergistic combinations of programs and services that produce results and enhance the health and sustainability of the area. Figure 8.4 contrasts traditional and evolving approaches to strategic planning.

A skillful strategy process builds sound strategy by improving the match between the evolving needs of a community or region and the capacity to respond to these needs. It informs and facilitates a strategic conversation among stakeholders that leads to alignment and commitment. It uses a wide range of techniques and tools to help stakeholders define the concerns or issues that need to be addressed,

### FIGURE 8.4. APPROACHES TO STRATEGIC PLANNING.

| Traditional Strategic Planning | Evolving Strategic Planning |
|---|---|
| • Expert driven | • Stakeholder driven |
| • Looking for "correct" answer or "optimal" strategy | • Looking for most skillful strategy process |
| • Objective, rational, and analytic | • Open, flexible, and adaptive |
| • Predictive | • No one right answer—"best" answer is what stakeholders determine it to be |

identify the challenges or barriers to action, analyze the contextual environment, describe current reality, envision a desirable future, and develop strategies for achieving this future. Figure 8.5 describes this framework.

## Facilitating a Skillful Strategy Process

1. *Define the strategic questions to be addressed.* A skillful strategy process responds to particular needs. Identifying these needs and defining the questions that need to be answered about these concerns determines the focus of strategic planning. Open-ended questions like those described in "Understanding How Citizens Think About Public Issues" in Chapter Six can help inform this work.

2. *Describe the current and future context.* Understanding the context helps ground strategy development. This includes understanding the challenges and barriers to dealing with presenting issues, identifying the relevant structural uncertainties affecting the future of the community or region, and analyzing the current and possible future contexts in which the community or region will have to exist. The tools and techniques described in "Analyzing the Context for Collaboration" in Chapter Six, along with SWOT analysis and scenarios, can help inform this work.

3. *Describe current reality: where we are.* Skillful strategies help communities and regions move from where they are to where they want to be. A description of current reality includes an assessment of the current capacity of the community or region to meet critical needs and an analysis of its capacity for change. SWOT analysis can be particularly helpful in describing current reality.

4. *Envision the desired future: where we want to be.* A vision of a desired future defines the target for strategy development. A skillful strategy process ensures that the vision is robust, that is, it will be viable in a range of plausible future environments. The visioning technique defined in this chapter can be used to develop the vision. SWOT analysis and scenarios can be used to test the viability of the vision.

5. *Define strategies: how we get there.* Strategies define what a community or region should do in order to achieve the desired future state. Strategy development

may include understanding what is known about how this can be accomplished and defining the assets of the community or region relevant to the vision. Sound strategies describe a synergistic combination of policies, programs, and services that can achieve this future. They define the capacities the community or region needs in order to implement these strategies, as well as the actions necessary to build these capacities. SWOT analysis and scenarios can be used to test the viability of proposed strategies.

- See Kees van der Heijden's *Scenarios: The Art of Strategic Conversation* (1996) for further information on evolving approaches to strategic planning.
- See John Kretzmann and John McKnight's *Building Communities from the Inside Out: A Path Toward Finding and Mobilizing a Community's Assets* (1993) for further information on identifying and mobilizing community assets.

## From Recommendations to Action

While a collaborative process builds agreement among participating stakeholders, its larger purpose is to build agreement in the community or region. The makeup of the stakeholder group and the quality of its work provide the credibility to move recommendations to action. By working together in skillful ways, communities and regions build the capacity for moving to action.

### FIGURE 8.5.  STRATEGIC PLANNING FRAMEWORK.

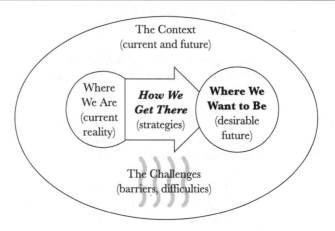

CHAPTER NINE

# MOVING TO ACTION

Citizens must ultimately judge civic leadership strategies by the results they produce. In leadership theorist James MacGregor Burns's words, "Power and leadership are measured by the degree of production of intended effects" (Burns, 1978, p. 22). Successful civic leaders choose strategies most likely to lead to results. If old ways fail, they invent new means for achieving results. Collaboration itself emerged as a leadership strategy in the public arena when more traditional strategies could no longer produce intended results.

Similarly, the success of a collaborative effort depends on the capacity of stakeholders to convert their agreements into meaningful results in the community. Stakeholders must cope with a number of challenges in order to move recommendations to action. Their conclusions will inevitably be misunderstood or misinterpreted. Agreements reached through trust, constructive engagement, and mutual learning may not translate into hierarchical organizations managed by command and control. Parochial politics may undermine collaborative action.

The process of collaboration itself creates the assets for overcoming these challenges. Well-conceived and well-executed initiatives create a constituency for change with carefully considered recommendations and well-informed rationale. Reaching out to the community builds a broader constituency, thus extending and strengthening this work. This expanded influence helps hold formal decision-making bodies, public agencies, and implementing organizations accountable for moving to action. Figure 9.1 highlights the "Moving to Action" phase of the collaborative process.

# FIGURE 9.1.  A GUIDE TO THE PRACTICES
# OF SUCCESSFUL COLLABORATION.

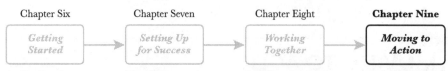

| Chapter Six | Chapter Seven | Chapter Eight | Chapter Nine |
|---|---|---|---|
| *Getting Started* | *Setting Up for Success* | *Working Together* | *Moving to Action* |

**Analyzing the Context for Collaboration**
1. Understanding the political dynamics
2. Understanding how citizens think about public issues

**Deciding on a Collaborative Strategy**
1. Determining the feasibility of collaboration
2. Defining the purpose, scope, and focus

**Identifying and Convening Stakeholders**
1. Understanding the principle and practice of inclusion
2. Finding the credibility to convene
3. Identifying stakeholders
4. Inviting, recruiting, and convening stakeholders

**Designing a Constructive Process**
1. Defining the decision-making method
2. Establishing ground rules
3. Designing a constructive process

**Defining Information Needs**
1. Defining information and education needs

**Defining Critical Roles**
1. Selecting process experts
2. Selecting content experts
3. Identifying strong, facilitative leaders

**Managing the Process**
1. Establishing a steering committee
2. Staffing the effort
3. Documenting the process

**Finding the Resources**
1. Developing the budget
2. Funding a collaborative process

**Building Capacity**
1. Building relationships and skills

**Ways of Engaging**
1. Engaging through dialogue
2. Working with written information

**Informing the Stakeholders**
1. Understanding the content
2. Understanding the context
   • Analyzing strengths, weaknesses, opportunities, and threats
   • Developing scenarios

**Deciding What Needs to Be Done**
1. Collaborative problem solving
2. Visioning
3. Strategic planning

**Reaching Out**
1. Building a broader constituency
2. Engaging with decision makers and implementing organizations

**Managing Action**
1. Developing action plans
2. Organizing and managing implementation

The recommendations of stakeholders must be legitimized and accepted by the community, decision makers, and implementing groups before the actual work of implementation begins. Once this occurs, stakeholders and implementing groups can develop action plans that clearly define roles and responsibilities and establish appropriate structures to manage the work.

# Reaching Out

Consciously planned efforts to build a broader constituency and engage with decision makers and implementing organizations help stakeholders move recommendations to action. Stakeholders help mitigate divisions in the community or region by educating and engaging others while expanding their own influence. Informing decision makers and implementing organizations about the progress of collaborative work prevents future surprises. The success of future negotiations with these bodies depends on the efforts to keep them informed.

## Building a Broader Constituency

The broader community needs to understand the work of the stakeholder group, its thinking process, and the rationale for its conclusions. Reaching out to the community or region begins early and recurs regularly. It uses a variety of media to inform, educate, and work with others in order to gain their support. Consistent with the idea of collaboration, engagements with the broader community use similar processes for working together. Stakeholders reach out to diverse interests to communicate the importance of collaboration. Public forums do more than share information or gauge public support. Citizens have real opportunities to help shape stakeholder recommendations.

The various stages of a collaborative effort provide logical points for reaching out. At the start, letting others know about the process, its purpose, who participates, and how the effort fits with other public decision-making processes helps alleviate suspicion. This clarifies the role citizens can play and informs them about future opportunities to participate. Early efforts to reach out provide an opportunity to expand the stakeholder group if others want to participate. As a collaborative effort progresses, stakeholders can provide citizens with summaries of work in progress and a rationale for their work and engage others in improving it.

The steering committee and the stakeholders manage outreach to the community as a specific track of a collaborative process. They carefully design each effort to achieve specific objectives. Several considerations guide this design work:

- What are the desired results or outcomes?
- What do people need to know at the current stage of the effort?
- How will this information be communicated?
- Who will communicate this information?
- What processes will be used to engage others in useful ways?

As in stakeholder meetings, skillful facilitation helps make these events effective. If public meetings do not work, citizens will not support the effort. Process experts can facilitate the engagement, but stakeholders must provide leadership and speak for their work. Citizens get a firsthand account of the experience of collaboration and learn about the results from the people who did the work.

Public forums offer one way of reaching out. Other media complement face-to-face meetings and reach a broader audience. Stakeholders have used radio call-in shows, live television presentations, extended newspaper coverage, special inserts in newspapers, and messages included in utility bills to communicate their work.

---

## Facilitating a Public Forum

One example of a public forum looks like this:

1. *Review the history and purpose of the collaborative effort.* Citizens need to know the purpose of the initiative, why a collaborative strategy is needed, and how the effort fits with other public decision-making processes.
2. *Review the concept of collaboration.* Citizens need to understand the premise and principles of successful collaboration.
3. *Review and clarify roles and responsibilities.* A clear description of the roles and responsibilities of stakeholders, decision makers, and implementing organizations helps citizens understand how they can engage in the effort.
4. *Identify participating stakeholders.* Citizens need to see the stakeholder group as a microcosm of the community, not as a narrow interest group. The credibility of the stakeholder group enhances the credibility of the effort.
5. *Review the status of the stakeholder process.* Let participants know what work has been accomplished and what remains to be done.
6. *Present an overview of work accomplished and clarify for understanding.* This may include educational information, problem definitions, visions, solutions, or strategies. Describe the considerations supporting this work and the rationale for any conclusions.
7. *Engage citizens.* Ask participants to assess the work in progress. Have them identify strong points, and elicit ideas from them for improving or enhancing the work.
8. *Review next steps.* Identify future opportunities for engagement.

---

## Engaging with Decision Makers and Implementing Organizations

By building a broader constituency, stakeholders demonstrate broad-based support for their work. This augments the capacity of the stakeholder group to influence decision makers and implementing organizations to act on its recommendations.

When recommendations require legislative action, stakeholders work closely with elected officials and public agencies. The nature of this engagement ranges from acquiescence to working partnerships to challenging negotiations. In any circumstance, stakeholders need to recognize that their collective influence can be formidable and compelling even without formal authority. Power does not reside solely in the hands of decision makers. Although the active support of elected leaders enhances the possibilities of collaboration, stakeholders do not need the permission of elected leaders to do their work.

Effective links between citizen-driven efforts and elected leaders help ensure the success of these initiatives and can take different forms. Sometimes elected leaders participate directly as stakeholders. At other times, they help identify and select the stakeholders. Some examples of collaboration move forward without the support of elected leaders. Citizens provide leadership when elected leaders either cannot or will not take the initiative.

Collaborative processes can provide the conceptual framework for coherent public policy. This helps elected leaders understand what needs to be done in a deeper way and provides a comprehensive basis for action. Sometimes elected leaders use the credibility of collaborative stakeholder groups to provide the cover they need to take politically risky actions. At other times, stakeholders use their collective influence to hold elected leaders and formal organizations accountable for action on their recommendations. Stakeholders become, in John Gardner's words, "a constituency for the whole" (Gardner, 1990, p. 109) that can speak credibly for the larger community, not just another interest group.

In many cases, civic action does not depend on legislative approval. Instead, working together leads to new partnerships between existing organizations or the creation of new entities to move recommendations to action. As with relationships with elected leaders, the links between stakeholders and potential implementing organizations take different forms. Where possible, members of these organizations participate as stakeholders in the collaborative process. They provide a communication link to their organizations but are not solely responsible for gaining its support. The stakeholder group as a collective body provides the most important link with implementing organizations.

Just as in reaching out to the community or region, communicating with decision makers and implementing organizations begins early and recurs regularly. Information about the status of the effort, including what the stakeholder group is thinking and why, where it is in the process, what kinds of information it is considering, and who is participating, helps prevent future surprises and enhances the credibility of the initiative. Feedback from these groups helps stakeholders understand potential legislative or organizational constraints, allowing them to formulate better recommendations. The steering committee manages these efforts using stakeholders to convey the value and credibility of the work to other influential parties.

# Managing Action

Successful collaboration produces tangible results that leads to real progress on public issues while changing the way communities do business. Careful and conscious effort turns recommendations into agreements and agreements into action plans, structures, and organizing frameworks to facilitate the transition from vision to action. Most agreements reached through collaboration require coordination of cross-boundary activities, sharing of management responsibilities, finding and mobilizing resources, and mutual accountability. Sometimes complex agreements lead to subsequent smaller-scale collaborative initiatives to refine action plans. Stakeholders need to define action steps, clarify roles and responsibilities, and put structures in place to oversee and evaluate implementation.

## Developing Action Plans

Action plans specify what work needs to be done, who will do it, and when it will be done. A stakeholder group will often designate a special task group to do this planning work. The stakeholder group oversees the work in order to maintain the integrity of their work and ensure that all parties understand its intent. The task group may need to include new people from implementing organizations that were not part of the stakeholder group.

An effective action plan consists of several elements. First, specific action steps relate directly to achieving the desired results. The steps themselves are clear and unambiguous, and each party understands their intent and meaning. Second, action steps define the roles and responsibilities of each participant or organization. Everyone knows what each party is expected to do. Sometimes a type of "job description" formalizes these arrangements. Third, a schedule or time line describes the sequence of events. Fourth, resource needs are specified and budgets or other control mechanisms established. Securing resources becomes part of the action plan. Fifth, accountability standards facilitate managing and evaluating the work of implementation. Finally, action plans need to be communicated to the stakeholder group and to all parties responsible for implementation for review and approval.

### Organizing and Managing Implementation

With action plans defined, many collaborative initiatives establish a separate structure to manage and provide oversight for implementation. Sometimes a new coordinating group or interagency committee performs this function. Some of the original stakeholders provide continuity and guidance working closely with members of implementing organizations. In other circumstances, stakeholders designate a lead agency or organization to coordinate activities or establish a new entity to do the work.

This managing structure helps turn action plans into real work. Its tasks include helping implementing organizations change internal systems to meet new demands, building new partnerships among existing organizations, establishing new organizations to meet new or unmet needs, or organizing further collaborative efforts to define what remains to be done. Analyzing existing arrangements and mapping the relationships between its parts help specify these needs.

## Realizing the Promise of Collaboration

Collaboration helps communities and regions negotiate real differences in values and priorities. Moving to action converts these agreements into real change. Civic leaders choose to collaborate because it produces tangible results and teaches a more productive way of addressing public concerns. By working together, citizens develop a different kind of civic culture that builds social capital and enhances the civic community.

CHAPTER TEN

# DEVELOPING NETWORKS
# OF RESPONSIBILITY

The growth of citizen-driven collaborative initiatives to address public issues is a harbinger of a revitalized civil society in the United States. It reflects a movement to more entrepreneurial and inclusive approaches to public problems and an increasing activism of citizens in public life sparked, in part, by the failures of public institutions. Collaborative leaders nurture and support these initiatives by building social capital and complementing the formal institutions of government. As John Gardner (1981) suggests, "We must develop networks of leaders who accept some measure of responsibility for the society's shared concerns. Call them networks of responsibility, leaders of disparate or conflicting interests who undertake to act together in behalf of the shared concerns of the community or nation."

Emerging political challenges demand new civic practices and different leadership skills. Citizens need to learn more constructive ways for creating change in their communities and regions. Elected, appointed, and professional public officials need new leadership capacities to work with citizens as partners in governance. Community-building skills help a diverse society work across boundaries. Community organizers need to understand how to work in partnership with other stakeholders in the community. Instead of polarizing issues and dividing the community, the media must learn how to help citizens work together.

In America, little capacity to meet these critical needs exists today. Few civic leadership development programs add substantially to social capital. Too many community leadership development programs focus on networking and issues understanding rather than the civic leadership capacities and skills necessary to address public challenges. Frustrated graduates may understand the issues better but know little about how to cope with them. Few resources for training and technical assistance exist to support the growth and development of these programs; there are not enough qualified process experts and leadership educators to meet the growing need.

If collaboration is as an essential strategy for meeting civic challenges, leadership development programs must teach civic leaders the skills for working together. The civic community invests in the development of the capacity to collaborate building social capital and deepening democracy. A growing body of knowledge about civic leadership development informs these investments and helps make them productive. A reconception of existing leadership development programs and the creation of new ones can help build or provide the following aspects of a revitalized civic culture:

- A sense of membership or belonging in a community
- A moral concern for the community and the larger society
- Leadership that can catalyze, convene, facilitate, and sustain collaborative engagements among diverse citizens and groups
- Credible forums where citizens can come together to deliberate in engaging and constructive ways
- New relationships and social skills for interaction across social divisions
- Integrative, adaptive, learning engagements that lead to new understandings of problems and revolutionary, previously inconceivable strategies for addressing them
- Process expertise to design and facilitate these engagements
- Information that is accessible and understandable to citizens
- Constituencies for the whole that can hold the formal implementing institutions in the community accountable for decisions

## Civic Leadership Development: Working Premises

Civic leadership development programs have the potential to transform the civic culture of America's communities by transforming citizens and civic leaders who participate. A demanding curriculum helps participants learn new concepts and skills, as well as new beliefs, attitudes, and behaviors congruent with collaboration and a revitalized civic culture. Powerful experiences in the program itself encourage this transformation and help participants embody new leadership capacities.

## Developing Leadership Capacity

Leadership research demonstrates that the capacity for leadership is widely, not narrowly, distributed. Leadership experience as well as structured leadership development programs can develop these capacities. Leaders are both born and made. Powerful experiences, not didactic teaching, help develop new leadership capacities. Leadership development depends on action learning and reflection in applying new concepts and skills directly to immediate concerns. These experiences help participants master new leadership skills and build the confidence to use them. Effective leadership development programs offer opportunities for participants to learn through experience.

New roles and new expectations of leaders demand self-knowledge gained only through self-discovery and reflection. Effective leadership comes primarily from the leader's thoughts, words, and actions rather than from skills and knowledge. The congruence of inner beliefs and outer behaviors provides more credibility than position in a hierarchy. Exploring and understanding personal mission and purpose helps tap the inner dimensions of leadership. Powerful civic leadership development programs offer opportunities for self-exploration and development.

## Developing a Curriculum

The best leadership development programs respond directly to the needs of a particular place. Although most communities and regions face comparable challenges with similar political dynamics, a curriculum tailored to local needs and culture serves better than a universal one. Using citizens to help design programs helps ensure that they respond to local needs. Citizens with a diversity of perspectives and experiences can identify civic challenges and define the leadership capacities needed to meet them. A consciously designed and well-integrated curriculum helps develop these capacities.

## Working with Diversity

As America's communities become ever more racially and ethnically diverse, different perceptions of leadership and power challenge the capacity of citizens to work together. Efforts to build a better understanding of others in order to "just get along" do not go deep enough. Building relationships of trust and respect across these boundaries requires powerful, transforming experiences that profoundly alter limiting perceptions of others. Leadership development programs with a diverse group of participants help develop leadership capacities to address the challenges of a diverse society.

### Sustaining the Investment

Transforming the civic culture of a community requires a continuous, sustained investment. Program alumni provide the energy to do this. Once participants have completed the initial program, a myriad of opportunities exists for further learning and development. A growing cadre of citizens with the skills and knowledge to catalyze collaborative engagements helps build the civic community. Regular opportunities for them to come together allow them to help assess the challenges facing a community or region, agree on priorities, and develop ways to address them. Alumni help maintain interest in and resources for supporting civic leadership development.

# Designing and Initiating a Civic Leadership Development Program

The best civic leadership programs are designed by citizens through a collaborative process that informs them about experiences in other places, civic leadership, and leadership development. The design group uses this information to define the leadership capacities needed to meet local challenges and design a curriculum to develop these capacities. The members of the group have the credibility and influence to gain the support necessary to implement the program. This process ensures that the leadership program responds to the needs of the community or region and creates support for it.

## Designing a Civic Leadership Development Program

1. *Identifying current and future challenges.* What are the current and future challenges facing the community or region? What makes leadership difficult on these challenges? What are the possible future contexts in which the community or region will have to exist?
2. *Understanding lessons of experience.* What are the lessons of experience from successful communities and regions in terms of meeting civic challenges? What are the lessons of experience about transforming civic culture in communities or regions?
3. *Understanding leadership as a field of knowledge.* What are the key tasks of leadership, and what is the range of leadership approaches for accomplishing these tasks? What are the emerging leadership approaches that facilitate change in communities or regions?
4. *Defining leadership capacities.* What are the leadership capacities the community or region needs in order to meet current and emerging challenges? What existing

capacities rooted in the civic culture will serve the community or region well? What new capacities must be developed? How are these needs similar or different in different sectors or parts of the community or region?

5. *Designing the curriculum.* What are the lessons of experience about civic leadership development? What is known about successful civic leadership development initiatives in terms of form, content, curriculum, and pedagogy? Who should participate in the program in order to develop the necessary leadership capacities? What are the desired outcomes for participants in the program? What perspectives, experiences, and knowledge must participants be exposed to in order to develop new leadership capacities? What are the form, content, curriculum, and pedagogy of a leadership development initiative that will develop the leadership capacities needed by the community or region?

6. *Implementing the program.* How can this initiative be integrated with other leadership programs and initiatives in the community or region? How many people will participate, and how will they be selected? How will faculty be selected? What is the appropriate length and schedule for the program? How much will the program cost, and how will it be funded? How will the program be governed and administered, and who will do these tasks? What are the form and structure of the initiative that best fits with the culture community or region? What are the most effective ways of evaluating the impact of this initiative? How should the initiative continue to evolve based on learning from the evaluation and assessment? How will continuing support for the initiative be generated in the community or region?

## Program Outcomes

Effective civic leadership development programs offer opportunities for citizens to learn new leadership capacities. An inclusive, well-informed, collaborative process for designing the program specifies the particular outcomes a program should produce. Common outcomes in outstanding programs include that participants will

- Develop working relationships of trust and respect as diverse citizens and civic leaders who can act together on behalf of the shared concerns of their communities or regions
- Understand the current and future challenges for leadership in their communities or regions
- Understand the need for adaptive, integrative, and systemic responses to these challenges
- Understand the need for new, inclusive, and collaborative approaches to leadership that can build bridges between disparate groups and address ethical issues of social justice and equity

- Learn how to initiate and sustain collaborative processes to address complex community issues that create the power to act on behalf of the whole community or region
- Identify and define the work necessary to address a significant issue in their community or region, building on new perspectives, skills, and relationships
- Understand the critical aspects of a healthy civic culture and how it can be enhanced
- Learn the leadership skills, capacities, and behaviors that transform the civic culture of their communities and regions
- Transform their understanding of themselves and their roles as civic leaders in their communities and regions
- Learn how to educate others about collaborative approaches to public concerns in the community or region

## Program Description

New roles of collaborative leadership require personal transformation. Transformative change, that is, moments leading to higher levels of understanding and motivation, comes through new insights resulting from powerful learning experiences. Participants habituate themselves to newly acquired skills through reflection and practice. Mutual exploration of personal differences and similarities builds strong, mutually supportive relationships.

An effective program is an intensive, integrated, highly interactive learning experience. Most programs progress through several stages over an extended period of time. The initial stage orients participants to the program and its goals and begins building relationships. Participants identify individual and group expectations for the program. This helps faculty understand the needs of the group and helps participants shape the program to meet their needs.

The next stage helps participants understand the need for change. In order to appreciate the need for new leadership capacities, participants need to have a deep, experiential—even visceral—understanding of the leadership challenges inherent in complex public issues. Participants identify specific public concerns and issues and analyze the challenges they pose for civic leadership. They develop an understanding that these challenges require adaptive, integrative, systemic, and collaborative responses.

In subsequent stages, intensive shared experiences develop individual and group capacities for working together and build a strong group identity. Extended retreats deepen engagement. Many programs use outdoor experiences as a powerful adjunct to other activities. Participants discover a heightened ability to facilitate new responses to old problems. They learn new concepts and skills for collaborative leadership and apply them to specific challenges in the community or region grounding new approaches in practice. Participants design collaborative processes for addressing the issues and challenges, identify stakeholders who must be involved, and define the information and education resources they need. They convene stakeholders and catalyze collaborative processes on selected issues and challenges.

At some point, the program focus shifts from group development and learning new skills to personal development. Participants enter the program with their own perceptions and experiences of what it means to be a leader. Understanding past experience provides a starting point for future development as a leader. Participants identify resources necessary to support future development.

In the closing stage of the program, group members evaluate their experiences in the program and celebrate successes. They identify future development needs and recommend changes in the curriculum. Through personal reflection and group interaction, participants integrate the lessons of the program into daily lives and leadership roles.

## Program Length and Schedule

Good civic leadership development programs are of sufficient length to create noticeable and long-lasting change in participants; twelve to fifteen days over a period of a year or so works best. Groups need at least three to four days to begin the relationship-building process and eight to ten days to learn and practice new skills. Incremental learning begins to decline after fifteen days or so. Programs with several sessions spread over an extended period of time tend to be more powerful than one intensive session over several days. Regular engagement enhances relationship building and new skills through repetition. One- or two-day sessions occur every few weeks. The strategic use of multiday retreats such as Outward Bound dramatically accelerates team building and personal transformation.

## Selecting Faculty

Faculty members in civic leadership development programs need a deep understanding of community building and leadership development. They must possess the group facilitation and experiential teaching skills to produce the specified outcomes for each session and for connecting program elements. They must engage participants in ways that touch minds, hearts, spirits, and bodies. Their behavior must be congruent with the goals, objectives, and pedagogical beliefs of the initiative.

Civic leadership development programs require several different but complementary faculty roles. One faculty member facilitates group development and integrates different parts of the curriculum to provide continuity. Expert faculty teach specific aspects of the program. Coaches or mentors facilitate self-development.

The integrating facilitator helps build group identity, helps participants work through the issues and concerns arising from their experience, and provides the connecting links between program elements. Prior experience working with similar groups as a trainer, consultant, facilitator, or teacher in organizational development, community building, or leadership development supports this work. Capacities, skills, and knowledge should include the following:

- Substantial knowledge and experience of group dynamics and the ability to facilitate the group's work around its issues and concerns
- A working knowledge of organizational development, community building, and leadership development
- Knowledge and experience in using experiential group and team-building tools and techniques that engage mind, heart, spirit, and body
- The ability to work in partnership with the management team and other faculty members to help design, set up, and facilitate program action blocks
- The ability to provide a larger contextual framework and connecting links for the program action blocks
- The ability to empathize with the varied experiences of group members
- The ability to coach and counsel individual group members;
- The capacity to command the respect of the group over an extended period of time and in a variety of challenging situations
- The ability to provide a positive role model that reflects the goals and aspirations of the program

Expert faculty teach and facilitate program action blocks that build specific skills and knowledge. They work with the management team and the integrating facilitator to develop a detailed curriculum, a syllabus, and related materials for each block. Expert faculty need prior experience working with similar groups as a trainer, consultant, facilitator, or teacher in the particular content area of the action block. Capacities, skills, and knowledge should include the following:

- A working knowledge of group dynamics and the ability to facilitate the group's work around its issues and concerns as necessary with the help of the integrating facilitator

- A working knowledge of the fields of organizational development, community building, and leadership development
- A deep understanding of the content to be addressed in the assigned action block, including alternative views and the lessons of experience necessary to help participants use the information
- Knowledge and experience in using experiential teaching approaches related to the particular content of the action block that engage mind, heart, spirit, and body
- The ability to work in partnership with the management team and the integrating facilitator to design, set up, and lead program action blocks
- The ability to empathize with the varied experiences of group members
- The capacity to command the respect of the group
- The ability to provide a positive role model that reflects the goals and aspirations of the program

## Selecting and Recruiting Participants

Participants in civic leadership development programs reflect the diversity of the community and the wide variety of perspectives and experiences inherent in that diversity. These boundary-crossing initiatives engage citizens who have the potential to work together on shared concerns. Participants include both emerging and established leaders who come together as peers. Established leaders know as little about collaborative leadership as anyone else. A group size of twenty to thirty-five facilitates building new relationships and group learning.

Civic leadership programs demand a significant commitment of time and energy. A credible design or initiating group helps attract participants. Having a few high-level visible leaders in the first group makes recruiting easier in subsequent years. After the first year, alumni can speak for the value of the experience and the importance of the time commitment.

## Evaluation

Program evaluation helps faculty and sponsoring organizations understand what works and where adjustments are needed. Understanding impacts on participants and the community or region underscores the value of the program. An effective evaluation plan gathers data on three levels: individual, programmatic, and community or region. On the individual level, evaluation measures leadership characteristics of participants. Possible measures include normed assessment devices or tests such as the Leadership Practices Inventory, the Life Orientation Inventory (an optimism scale), and the Dominators, Influencers, Steadiness, and Conscientiousness personality inventory.

Program evaluation includes assessment of individual instructors, as well as of each training module or program component. Participants evaluate each training module and complete a more comprehensive assessment in the middle and at the end of the year. Participant and faculty feedback provides information about progress toward meeting program objectives. Surveys of citizens, scholars, and media representatives help assess the deeper impacts of the program on the community or region.

## Building the Civic Community

Collaborative leaders operate from a very different premise than traditional leaders do. Instead of pitting groups or coalitions against each other, they look to citizens for power and serve in very different leadership roles. They trust fellow citizens to work together in inclusive, constructive, and well-informed processes. They convene, catalyze, and facilitate the work of others. They inspire people to act, help them solve problems as peers, build broad-based involvement, and sustain hope and participation.

They have new and different leadership capacities. They know how to analyze and understand the challenge of leadership and how to develop change strategies that will overcome resistance and inertia. They know how to bring citizens together and help them build trust and the skills for collaboration. They help design constructive processes to solve problems collaboratively and create shared visions. These capacities have to be learned.

Revitalizing civil society and replenishing social capital demands citizens and civic leaders with the capacity for collaborative action. New networks enhance cooperation through mutual trust and reciprocity. Building the civic community depends on a process of civic learning grounded in both theory and practice. Well-conceived civic leadership development programs provide a powerful means for transforming the civic culture of a community or region.

- See Chapter Sixteen, "Building Civic Leadership in Portland, Maine," and Chapter Seventeen, "Building Leadership Capacity in a Socially Emerging Community," for two examples of civic leadership development programs illustrating these concepts.

PART FOUR

# STORIES AND EXAMPLES OF SUCCESSFUL COLLABORATION AND CIVIC LEADERSHIP DEVELOPMENT

A range of stories and examples reflecting different geographical regions, rural and urban perspectives, and a variety of social, environmental, education, and economic issues provide insight into the practice of collaboration.

In the following case studies, a number of participants have shared their insights through interviews with the authors. We thank them for their help in bringing the stories to life.

CHAPTER ELEVEN

# JOINT VENTURE SILICON VALLEY

## Christopher Wilson

*Joint Venture Silicon Valley (JVSV) is one of the most comprehensive and long-running collaborative endeavors in the United States. Among its interesting features is the initial hesitance of local governments to join the effort. When it became clear that business and nonprofit stakeholders would persevere, the public sector eventually joined the initiative. The combination of credible convening leadership from government, business, and nonprofits allowed JVSV to become a powerful catalyst for collaborative action.*

*The entrepreneurial spirit that pervaded JVSV sparked numerous far-reaching initiatives to address a myriad of concerns in Silicon Valley, such as education, transportation, business and workforce development, the environment, affordable housing, regulatory reform, and smart growth. JVSV created a variety of innovative programs and partnerships in response to these issues. Some were spun off into separate entities; others achieved their goals and concluded their work. None of these efforts would have succeeded without a concentrated focus on moving to action. A carefully conceived and powerfully led management structure facilitated the transition from talk to action.*

*In the long run, JVSV's efforts helped transform the civic culture of the Silicon Valley region, extending an inherent aptitude for networking and collaboration from business to government to community to the region itself. JVSV also reflects the challenges in maintaining the credibility of a convening organization as a neutral broker. The organization's current struggle to redefine its role and reestablish itself as a powerful actor in the region offers several lessons for similar endeavors.*

In the spring of 1992, the future of Silicon Valley did not look rosy. The regional economy seemed to be stalling, and maybe even beginning a slide into decline. Major businesses were leaving, and compared to previous years, the numbers of new businesses being created had dropped by half. Regional unemployment had doubled. The *San Jose Mercury News* ran headlines like "Valley Sliding: Area Outlook Bleak" and "Survey Reveals Growing Dismay." "There's no silicon left

I thank Doug Henton, Rebecca Morgan, Ruben Barrales, John Kennett, Susan Snyder, and Bob Pearlman for sharing their stories and insights into Joint Venture's history and evolution.

in Silicon Valley," proclaimed Brenna Bolger, of San Jose's Chamber of Commerce (Elder, 1992, p. 7C). The world's biggest economic success story appeared to be floundering.

It was under this cloud of pessimism that a new collaborative organization, Joint Venture Silicon Valley, was created as a product of the community learning to pull together. This is the story of its formation and early years and its struggle to renew itself amid the boom-bust cycles in Silicon Valley.

In the early 1990s, California's Silicon Valley had a population of roughly 2 million. Its geography extended from south of San Francisco to San Jose.

The ending of the cold war had produced significant reductions in U.S. defense spending and caused a major contraction among Silicon Valley defense manufacturers. Lockheed, the largest of the region's defense-related employers, had shed some 50,000 of its 150,000 employees. At the same time, the region's semiconductor industry was still badly shaken from losing out to the Japanese in the mid-1980s. Growth in regional manufacturing jobs, which had been steadily increasing between 1972 and 1984, declined almost 1 percent per year between 1984 and 1991.

In the late 1980s, the region began to experience competition from other technology centers such as Austin, Texas; southern Arizona; and Portland, Oregon. It lost out to Austin in 1988 as the site of the nation's advanced semiconductor research consortium, SEMATECH, and then seemed to lose out again when Applied Materials, Apple, and Cypress Semiconductor all decided within a few months of each other to build major new manufacturing plants in Texas. Reflecting on the emerging trend, T. J. Rodgers, Cypress Semiconductor's chief executive officer (CEO), said, "We have to wake up. Too many jobs are leaving the area, and that has to change" (Kaufman, 1992, p. 1F).

An April 1992 survey found that 80 percent of valley residents believed that there were fewer work opportunities in 1992 compared with 1987, and two-thirds believed there would be even fewer employment opportunities by 1997 (Gerston, 1992). Not surprisingly, it also found that 39 percent of valley residents would be willing to start elsewhere if they had the opportunity. "There was a growing impression among business leaders that there was something wrong with Silicon Valley," said Doug Henton, a consultant with SRI International. "There was a sense that the Valley had become a difficult place to do business."

Over the years, most observers point to the valley's extensive use of formal and informal networks as the most significant factor in its success. "It's not the entrepreneurs or the technology that make the valley go," Henton observed, "It's the networks." "The paradox of Silicon Valley," according to Anna Lee Saxenian, a professor at the University of California, Berkeley, "was that competition demanded continuous innovation, which in turn required cooperation among firms," a cooperation exemplified by their participation in networks (Saxenian, 1994, p. 46).

Surprisingly, the region's propensity to collaborate on a business level did not seem to translate to a community level. This might be laid at the door of the libertarian mind-set that permeated the thinking of many of the region's business leaders, who often regarded the market as a panacea for just about everything and rarely recognized the contributions of either the public or civic sectors. As a consequence, the rapid growth of the personal computer industry in the late 1980s generated a host of regional problems related to rapid growth, including municipal and state regulation, education, housing, transportation, and the environment. As difficult as these problems were, there is also no doubt they were compounded by the competing jurisdictions of various city and county governments that existed in such close proximity. With no available mechanism to deal with cross-regional concerns, issues were ignored or dealt with piecemeal. By 1992, this situation was creating significant additional costs for the area's companies just as the personal computer industry was maturing and cost cutting was becoming increasingly important.

"In the late 1980s and early 1990s there was a remarkable lack of consensus about how to deal with the region's problems," recalls Henton who is now president of Collaborative Economics in Mountain View. "A lot of people were blaming each other. As a community, we had failed to make the needed investments in our regional infrastructures that were relevant to our changing economic condition. Trust levels between business, government and the community were low. There was a lot of finger pointing." "Most important," Henton pointed out, "there was essentially no vehicle for creating a community-wide conversation."

## Making the Case for Collaboration

In May 1991, John Kennett, chairman-elect of San Jose's Chamber of Commerce, was particularly concerned about his members from the business services sector who seemed to be bearing the brunt of the region's economic downturn. The San Jose Chamber was by far the largest in Silicon Valley and tended to take a more regional perspective on issues. So out of need and with a spark of innovativeness, Kennett invited twenty-six representatives from the area's industry associations to dinner to discuss the idea of a common economic development agenda.

It was apparent from this meeting that the issues of concern—regulatory reform, education, housing, transportation, and the environment—cut across the region and could not be resolved independently by any local government or any of the associations. Subsequently, Kennett went to his board of directors to say that if they were really interested in improving the region's business climate, they would need to work with the other associations. Together they could apply pressure to the various local governments to create more regional programs and policies. Getting cooperation among themselves would be the first crucial step. He reminded them that catalyzing collaboration was a valuable role for the chamber of commerce, one that in fact was a part of its traditional role. The board agreed and, despite some initial misgivings, was willing to support a program of regional cooperation if it was separately funded and staffed. As a result, in the fall of 1991, the board formally adopted a coalition strategy, approving a framework for cooperation with the other associations called Joint Venture Silicon Valley.

In October 1991, Kennett invited the leaders of key associations—including the Semiconductor Industry Association, the American Electronics Association, the Building Industry Association, the Santa Clara County Manufacturing Group, and the San Jose Real Estate Board—to consider a working partnership. The idea of working together found a ready audience among the leaders of the valley's industry associations. "We weren't moving forward. We kept talking about the same problems, pointing the same fingers. Yet those of us who wanted to take action knew no one group could do it alone," said Kennett. The outcome of this meeting was an agreement among the associations to contribute members to a JVSV board of directors, a group that continued to meet biweekly until May 1993 and ultimately grew to fifty-three members.

While working together on regulatory reform or housing seemed eminently logical, from a practical standpoint there was a real question as to who was going to do the work. According to Kennett, "The consensus of the group was that 'somebody ought to do that,' "—meaning somebody else. Fortunately, the chamber was willing to act as the catalyst. Two of its members—Tom Hayes of Applied Materials and Brenna Bolger of PRx, a local public relations firm—took the initiative to create a structure for collaboration, while the chamber itself provided meeting rooms and support staff. Both Hayes and Bolger passionately believed in the potential for collaboration, a passion that enabled them to endure some of the harsher public criticism they ultimately received.

The group's first step was to assess the area's economic woes. Hayes suggested hiring the well-respected consulting firm SRI International to conduct an assessment. The JVSV board initially balked at SRI's cost of $75,000, but Hayes was able to persuade James Morgan, his boss at Applied Materials, of the value of such an assessment. Morgan immediately put $25,000 on the table, and Hayes committed to raising the remainder from other industry sources. Mollified, the board decided to go ahead. Hayes used Morgan's initial investment to leverage contributions from eight other valley companies, including IBM, Solectron, and Tandem Computers. Morgan himself assumed a further leadership role by forming a thirty-eight-person CEO advisory board to provide high-level corporate leadership and oversight. Yet despite the high level of corporate participation, JVSV was actually designed as a vehicle for broad-based participation. "Sure," Morgan once said, "a few of us could get together and develop a plan, but no one would believe us" (Joint Venture, 1995).

When the JVSV partnership was first publicly announced in March 1992, it was greeted with much suspicion. For some, the idea of businesses working together sounded a bit like collusion; for others, it smacked almost of corruption. "This pretense of cooperation makes me uneasy," said Timothy Taylor of the American Economic Association. "If it's not a pretense, I'm even more uneasy" (Elder, 1992, p. 7C).

In June, the SRI report, *An Economy at Risk,* was finally presented in a public forum. The report consolidated research conducted by a number of regional agencies, including the Centre for Continuing Study of the California Economy and the City of San Jose. It provided a diagnosis of the valley's woes and highlighted fifteen warning signs of future economic trouble, including declining new businesses, increasing bankruptcies, increased office vacancy rates, increased unemployment, and a growing number of local companies choosing to expand elsewhere. It laid blame for the valley's recent economic slump on the region's decreasing ability to compete with other regions in the United States and targeted a deteriorating local infrastructure as the cause.

Because of its high-profile corporate sponsors, the tabling of the SRI report was a major media event. Initially, only 150 business and community leaders were anticipated for the meeting, but over 1,000 showed up from around the region. "What I wanted to do was a barn-raising," said Tom Hayes, by then JVSV's new chair, "but first I had to draw a picture of a barn for this valley" (Elder, 1992, p. 7C). The picture was a broad overview of the economic and social trends in the valley, especially those that applied to its key industry clusters. The report's linking of the area's economic success with its collaborative capacity suggested that fixing the downturn was possible if community leaders worked together. The report was most critical of the region's culture of blame and proposed a cooperative strategy among business and government leaders.

The SRI report received mixed reviews. Some felt it distorted global economic realities and gave people unjustified hope for change. "This could be the economic rejuvenation of Silicon Valley," said Rob Elder, editor of the *Mercury News.* "It could camouflage a politically potent power grab. Just as easily, it could go nowhere" (Elder, 1992, p. 7C).

Working with local government was a key element of JVSV's collaborative strategy, but the relationship began poorly. Public officials were deliberately excluded from the analysis phase conducted by SRI. Although San Jose's mayor, Susan Hammer, had privately expressed interest, she did not attend the initial meeting. Her political advisers were convinced that the event would be just another business harangue. T. J. Rogers of Cypress seemed to affirm that view after his government-bashing comments at the meeting. As a consequence, JVSV remained primarily a business collaboration at this stage. According to Kennett, this exclusion was in part by intent until the area's business leaders found common ground to cooperate.

Subsequent to the June 1992 meeting, JVSV embarked on a collaborative problem-solving and opportunity-identifying process that continued until June 1993. Around 350 people from the initial meeting said they wanted to be involved, and an additional 300 responded to the media coverage. Fourteen working groups, comprising forty to seventy people each, were created to consider the implications of the SRI report and make recommendations for change:

| *Industry Working Groups* | *Infrastructure Working Groups* |
| --- | --- |
| Computers and communications | Workforce |
| Software | Technology |
| Semiconductors | New business formation |
| Space and defense | Regulatory climate |
| Bioscience | Physical environment |
| Environment | Tax and fiscal policy |
| Business services | Housing |

During the fall of 1992 and early winter of 1993, these working groups met three or four times to create a set of projects that might help to make a difference to the region. These open meetings generated a bottom-up type of feedback. SRI continued to work with these groups, facilitating their discussions and reporting on their results.

Morgan helped recruit other high-profile technology leaders from his extensive network of business contacts, many of whom did not even live in the area. Two of those he brought in were Lew Platt and John Young, the current and former CEOs of Hewlett-Packard, a company with a long history of civic involvement. Morgan persuaded several hundred CEOs to participate in JVSV's working groups. In this way JVSV also created a vehicle for a top-down type of feedback.

# No Champions, No Initiative

The key factor in moving from talk to action was JVSV's concept of champions. Its motto was "No champions, no initiative." Silicon Valley had a lot of strong entrepreneurial leaders, and JVSV wanted to use them to help make the necessary changes in the community. "We did not want to create another task force," said Henton. "We wanted to move beyond committees to creating active programs. In essence, Joint Venture became a network of action leaders."

Accordingly, JVSV appointed in September several highly respected Silicon Valley leaders to head the working groups, including Morgan, Winston Chen of Solectron, Yvette Del Prado of Tandem Corp., Ed McCracken, of Silicon Graphics, John Neece of the Building and Construction Trades Council, James Norton of the American Electronics Association, and Paul Locatelli, president of Santa Clara University.

JVSV also sought to balance the working group leadership with unlikely allies. For instance, the co-chairs of the Working Group on Physical Infrastructure came from the Building Industries Association and the Sierra Club. In return for support staff, recognition, and the opportunity to make a difference, the working group co-chairs provided leadership and lent their credibility to the process. They also met as a group, the Council of Co-Chairs, about three or four times between September 1992 and June 1993 to identify common issues and opportunities.

Through this process that involved public forums, the working groups, the Council of Co-Chairs, the CEO Advisory Board, and the Joint Venture board itself, JVSV established its mission—to develop and launch a collaborative strategy to compete in the global economy and create balanced economic growth, increasing individual prosperity, and a high quality of life—and achieved a level of public recognition independent of a simple chamber initiative.

In October 1992, it began soliciting broader community input into the problem-solving process with a visioning conference at Santa Clara University that was attended by over four hundred community leaders. Taking advantage of world-renowned futurists Alvin Toffler and George Gilder to help generate possible visions, together with leading business guru Tom Peters and economist Kenneth Courtise of Deutsche Bank, JVSV kick-started a very open, consensus-building process to define its future goals and directions.

During that same period, behind-the-scene discussions between Hayes and Mayor Susan Hammer convinced her, against the advice of her staff, of the value of cooperation. Her simple wisdom was in realizing she could not fix things on her own. Certainly part of her willingness to cooperate may have been due to the huge budget deficits she had inherited when she took office; nevertheless, she recognized that her city's priorities of jobs, schools, and youth would not be accomplished without enlisting the help of business leaders. Similarly, JVSV's objectives would not be realized without local government support. According to Kennett, Hammer took a significant political risk by embracing JVSV and deserved "a great deal of credit" for helping to overcome the traditional adversarial roles between local government and the business community.

The initial meeting got the attention of local government officials throughout the region. During the fall, public administrators began interacting and developing relationships with JVSV groups on several fronts: the building permit process, taxation and budgeting, and lobbying state government on local issues. With Hammer's encouragement, they even formed their own allied group, the Public Sector Roundtable, to discuss regional economic issues and contribute to the Joint Venture process. "Who would have thought [this would happen] last spring," reported the *Mercury News*, "when the private sector launched the problem-solving venture in a frenzy of local government bashing? But when public officials joined industry leaders at the table, things changed" (Vroman, 1993, p. 7C).

This process of airing and sharing ideas was immensely valuable in moving people away from the culture of blame. Business leaders learned that many of their problems originated not locally but in Sacramento or Washington. Similarly, public officials learned that business leaders wanted more streamlined regulation and less duplication, not less regulation.

Said columnist James Mitchell, "[Joint Venture has] created a mechanism that prompted people from all three sectors to set aside their differences temporarily, to understand each other's problems and, wherever possible, to develop solutions that help everyone" (Mitchell, 1993a, p. 1E). Reflecting this reciprocity, Hammer recommended in her January 1993 State of the City address that San Jose earmark $500,000 in each of the next two years as seed money for Joint Venture (*San Jose Mercury News*, 1993, p. 7B). The new willingness to collaborate had become evident to all.

In April 1993, JVSV's credibility and the integrity of the collaborative process were once again questioned after its attempt to build a consensus on housing failed. But, said Kennett, "The housing issue was just too complex, too big. It had too many constraints, too many players and too many rules. We learned a very important lesson nonetheless. We learned that there were some things we could do and other things, despite our best efforts, we couldn't change. We decided to concentrate on the things we could influence."

## Joint Venture Takes Shape

The housing failure notwithstanding, by spring the original working groups had generated forty-three specific initiatives from their activities. Some were solid and actionable; others were less so. Therefore, within the constraint of limited resources, someone had to choose which initiatives to pursue. That task fell to Joint Venture's Leadership Council, comprising the board, the CEO Advisory Council, the Public Sector Roundtable, and the Council of Co-Chairs. The Leadership Council required that each initiative had to demonstrate

- Broad support within the working group
- Commitment from champions
- A reasonably well-developed business plan
- A potential to make a significant difference to the valley's economic vitality

Cognizant of the pitfalls of trying to implement forty-three projects, the Leadership Council also imposed the further requirement for a solid implementation plan as a criterion for becoming a Joint Venture initiative. The forty-three preliminary initiatives were aired in a public briefing forum at the San Jose Convention Center attended by over two thousand people, and with input from this forum, the Leadership Council approved a final list of thirteen initiatives in April:

| *Major Regional Objective* | *Initiative* |
| --- | --- |
| Develop specialized infrastructure | Smart Valley, Inc. |
| | 21st Century Education Initiative |
| | Silicon Valley Technologies Corp. |
| Reduce cost of doing business | Regulatory Forum |
| | Council on Tax and Fiscal Policy |
| | Health Care Task Force |
| Retain and expand existing industry | Defense/Space Consortium |
| | Silicon Valley Global Trading Centre |
| | Economic Development Team |
| Support growth of new industry | Environmental Partnership |
| | Software Industry Coalition |
| | The Enterprise Network |
| | New Business Incubation Clusters |

In addition to being a decision-making body, the Leadership Council provided a mechanism for horizontal exchanges between working groups that proved essential in consolidating overlapping plans. The need to spark K–12 educational reform, for instance, was identified by five working groups: computer/communications, software, workforce, semiconductor, and business services. Jointly, the groups came up with the 21st Century Education Initiative. Similarly, the need to create business incubators and an environmental industry forum led the new business and the environmental industry groups to propose the Environmental Partnership.

In May, Joint Venture was organized as a nonprofit trade association: Joint Venture Silicon Valley. No longer just representative of industry, its new twenty-six-member board reflected the broader range of constituencies that had become participants of the Joint Venture process. Hayes withdrew as chair in order to de-politicize the new organization and diffuse some public criticism that he was using Joint Venture to advance his own agenda. Susan Hammer and Jim Morgan became the new co-chairs, although Morgan agreed to chair only on an interim basis.

The initiatives were divided among thirteen organizations, each with its own paid staff and board of directors. Each of these organizations had to have a champion for leadership, measurable objectives, a funding plan, and a business plan. As might be expected, not all initiatives were at the same stage of development. Roughly half still needed support and encouragement from the core group.

Each organization arranged memorandums of understanding (MOUs) with Joint Venture and reported to it. Nesting the initiatives in Joint Venture would ensure that the new initiatives did not lead to fragmentation. More important, the Leadership Council, fresh with the experience of successful collaboration, wanted to ensure that the organizations would retain this memory and operate within an overarching forum of regional exchange.

Armed with the initiatives and a strategic plan for Silicon Valley to implement them, JVSV went public in June with a major media campaign centered on its new strategy document, *Blueprint for a 21st Century Community*. Over fifteen thousand copies of the plan were distributed throughout the region. The launching of the *Blueprint* and the celebration of the more than one thousand area leaders who participated in creating it culminated in an hour-long television special.

The publishing of the *Blueprint*'s recommendations represented "a turning point" in JVSV's history, according to Kennett: "Confronted by a series of initiatives that were supported by thirteen organizations that had specific plans, targets, and credible champions, Silicon Valley leaders of all stripes—business, government or civic—could no longer ignore Joint Venture or write it off as a community lightweight." Although some among the press, local government, and academe had criticized JVSV in the past as having too narrow a business focus, the wide range of initiatives presented in the *Blueprint* made that charge insupportable. The co-chair arrangement between Susan Hammer and James Morgan and the leadership of the Public Sector Roundtable put to rest the idea that Joint Venture was purely a business organization. With the publication of the *Blueprint*, the focus of public debate shifted from whether collaboration would make a difference to how best to implement specific collaborative ideas.

The working groups and publications required resources. In 1992 and 1993, the process led by Joint Venture was funded by eighty-four companies and associations that contributed approximately $1.2 million. Hayes, Morgan, Joint Venture board members, and many chamber board members as well participated in the fundraising process. The funds were spent on consulting and facilitation, public relations and communications, and the visioning conference. Yet despite this successful fundraising, by the time the working groups had finished and made public their recommendations in the *Blueprint*, Joint Venture was in the red for almost $100,000.

## Sustaining Collaboration

Over the course of the summer of 1993, two critical events took place that ensured Joint Venture's successful transition from a good idea to a credible working concern. First, Joint Venture recruited a new CEO, California senator Rebecca Q. "Becky" Morgan, wife of James Morgan. She was a credible and well-respected member of the state legislature and an icon of state politics, and the community responded enthusiastically to her appointment.

The second event was the investment of $250,000 by the Bank of America to support funding for Joint Venture. This seed money leveraged another $350,000 from industry and local government. This large infusion of support put to rest any public fears of impending insolvency or unprofessional management. More important, along with Morgan's appointment, it helped to instill a great sense of public confidence in the organization.

By the end of summer 1993, JVSV had successfully put together a package of everything it needed to achieve its goals: strategy, leadership, money, initiatives, and, from its stakeholders, a thorough commitment to cooperate. In doing so, they had raised the public's expectations of what should be delivered. Columnist James Mitchell echoed that sentiment: "If by this time next year the organization can't point to significant, concrete achievements—such as the creation or retention of hundreds of jobs—[Joint Venture] won't receive the support it needs to solve some of the community's long-term problems" (Mitchell, 1993b). Clearly, the community was demanding results, not just talk—a desire further evident the following February, when the *Mercury News* marked Joint Venture's ten-month anniversary of incorporation by creating a report card to assess its progress.

The community did not have to wait long. By the fall, it began to enjoy a quick succession of Joint Venture achievements. Ed McCracken, one of the most highly regarded executives in the valley, was appointed co-chair to replace James Morgan. In addition, Smart Valley, one of Joint Venture's initiatives, announced a new telecommuting project involving more than a thousand people in eleven companies and that ultimately produced more than a 15 percent improvement in productivity. It also received an $8 million grant from the federal government to build a high-speed digital network to link area businesses, government agencies, and community organizations.

The U.S. Display Consortium (USDC), a federally funded research group supporting the development of flat-panel computer screens, announced that the region would receive a $20 million investment. Although only six new jobs were created by the USDC investment, the psychological impact of this investment was huge because the valley had outcompeted Austin and Ann Arbor, Michigan, largely on the strength of Joint Venture's partnerships. Finally, the Enterprise Network, the support network for new technology start-ups, began offering its services to area entrepreneurs.

In a number of different ways, JVSV was beginning to build momentum, establishing Silicon Valley as a place where people could work together. Peter Mills, the president of the USDC, underscored this change in his remarks about why San Jose was chosen over other locations. Mills, who had previously presided over the SEMATECH decision to locate in Austin, was blunt: "Before, California did not have its act together. Now it does" (Joint Venture, 1995, p. I-9).

At this stage, JVSV evolved a hub-and-spoke governance structure that remained in place until 1995. "It was very much a matrix organization," said Becky Morgan. At its periphery were the eleven initiatives (two of the thirteen were dropped in December 1993), five of which were entirely independent not-for-profit organizations: Smart Valley, the Defense/Space Consortium, the Global Trading Center, the Environmental Partnership, and the Enterprise Network. These five developed their own funding strategies and identities and appointed their own directors. Over time, all were spun off but Smart Valley, which wound up its activities in 1998, with its mission accomplished. The other six initiatives operated more closely under the incorporation of Joint Venture, which provided administrative support and staffing and brought them closer to its core networking activities.

At its center, Joint Venture's core activities included the coordination of communications and fundraising for all the initiatives. Because of the organization's strong orientation toward action over administration and the documenting of results, it developed and continues to produce an annual assessment of the region's economic and social progress, the *Index of Silicon Valley*, first produced in January 1995. "What you need in any situation of collaborative activity are indicators of progress," said Henton. Far from a vehicle for public criticism, the use of the progress indicators proved to be an essential tool for sustaining dialogue among the diverse members of the network.

This focus on documenting results went beyond the *Index* to the cultivating of a close relationship with local media. "In order to raise money for the initiatives," said Becky Morgan, "we needed to generate some positive press. . . . Knowing for instance that the education initiative would produce results only in the long term, we needed to provide the press with indications of our ongoing progress."

Joint Venture learned early to involve the press and keep them on its side. For example, Jay Harris, the publisher of the *San Jose Mercury News,* was eventually persuaded to become part of Joint Venture's board. "We learned," said Morgan,

> that we needed to invest time in cultivating relationships with the press on an ongoing basis. We tried to meet with the editors of the key papers once or twice a year to give them an update and progress report. The media never seemed to be able to absorb too much at one time, so we always tried to help them write the headlines and the highlights of each event. Because they were not always interested in the same things we were, we often needed to simplify things for them. What was important and exciting for us was the process of bringing people together and implementing big ideas but the media weren't interested in process, only results.

Joint Venture's core organization also provided a mechanism for inter-initiative benchmarking through its quarterly reports and progress updates. This allowed the different initiatives to integrate their activities and take advantage of overlapping interests and opportunities.

Finally, the core provided and continues to provide a forum for the identification of new regional issues. If this resulted in a need to add or drop initiatives, the MOU relationship offered the flexibility to make that change without seriously affecting the nature of Joint Venture's overall organizational capacity or its reputation in the community. The MOUs also reduced the confusion about expectations between the periphery groups and the core and satisfied community stakeholders about an initiative's accountability.

Of the thirteen original initiatives that began with the *Blueprint* under Joint Venture's umbrella, some, like Smart Valley, achieved their objectives and were wound down. The Enterprise Network was eventually spun off. So too was the Global Trading Centre. Others ceased to be relevant or capable of sustaining commitment. It became a matter of pride within the organization that Joint Venture was able to end a number of projects.

There were some failures along the way. The Workforce Working Group had to be reinitiated because the group was not able to develop consensus on an effective work plan or get industry and educational leaders excited. However, instead of abandoning it as it had the housing issue, the Leadership Council felt that K–12 educational reform was too important to walk away from. New co-chairs were brought in and an entirely new process begun, which eventually developed into one of Joint Venture's most successful and highly regarded programs, Challenge 2000.

The Silicon Valley Global Technologies Corporation and the Software Industry Coalition never got off the ground and were dropped in December 1993. The Software Industry Coalition was put forward as an association of the region's software community. But according to Henton, "the people never seemed to be right. They weren't industry people. They were primarily consultants and lawyers who wanted access to the industry. It all seemed very self-serving. At Joint Venture, we felt there needed to be more of a civic component in what they were doing and when it didn't fly, we weren't surprised."

This willingness to let go illustrates a key cultural characteristic at Joint Venture: its adherence to an entrepreneurship style that allowed some projects to succeed while recognizing that others would not.

## Generating Results

In the beginning, the directors of some of the initiatives felt a tremendous pressure to produce results quickly, so much so that they did not always invest the time in relationship building that might have produced greater long-term results. Taking the time to think things through and build support proved to be an essential element in all the initiatives, especially when problems were complex and multiple authorities existed. The experience of the Workforce Working Group bore this out. Yet over time, the Joint Venture–sponsored dialogue and cooperation produced outcomes that far exceeded the cautious expectations that greeted its launch in 1992.

In October 1994, the 21st Century Education Initiative and Smart Valley jointly launched Challenge 2000 as a major school improvement effort. Its goal was to raise $22 million for a community fund to spark systemic educational reform in curriculum, staff development, assessment, and technological capacity within local schools. In all, nine school teams received support from the Challenge 2000 fund, which eventually raised over $20 million from area businesses and government.

In its first year, Joint Venture's Economic Development Team assisted five companies with expansions, helped to retain four firms in the region, assisted in three relocation efforts, and resolved six regulatory issues for companies. Significantly, in July 1994, it seemed to come of age with a $2.1 million grant from the U.S. federal government to help ease the regional transition from defense-based industries. In 1997, the team eventually became part of the region's Economic Prosperity Council.

The Enterprise Network helped spawn hundreds of start-ups, including eBay, iPrint, and Xros. It was spun off in June 1996 and continues to support new entrepreneurs to this day.

Joint Venture's Regulatory Streamlining Council helped three cities, one county, and a county water district to reengineer their permitting processes, reducing the process in some cases from 110 steps to 36 and allowing 95 percent of permit applications to be processed in one day. By August 1995, the same group had prodded city officials from around the region to adopt a uniform building code—a feat unthinkable even a half-decade earlier. The move eliminated all but eleven of the four hundred various code amendments adopted by the region's twenty-seven cities and two counties, further streamlining the permit process for the roughly thirty thousand commercial projects and sixty thousand residential jobs that were proposed annually. "With this change," said Christopher Greene, a building engineer who worked to streamline the regulations, "I think the local permit process goes from being a hindrance to actually being an advantage, because no place else in the country is doing this" (Schwanhausser, 1995, p. 1A). Like the Economic Development Team, the Regulatory Streamlining Council became part of the Economic Prosperity Council in 1997.

The Global Trading Centre, in cooperation with the U.S. Foreign Commercial Service, helped fifty-four companies export into 158 new markets in its first year of operation. It was merged with the San Jose office of the U.S. Export Assistance Center in 1996.

Smart Valley's mission was to serve as a catalyst for applications of network technology, getting the projects started and then finding an appropriate home for them. In the end, its projects involved more than fifteen thousand volunteers and one hundred companies and leveraged $4 million of membership funding into more than $100 million in projects. The results were that 85 percent of valley schools were wired and connected to the Internet, nine thousand computers were placed in the hands of teachers by 1998, public Internet access became available at all public libraries, and Silicon Valley led the nation in the deployment of telecommuting. CommerceNet, one of Smart Valley's first initiatives, is still thriving as an international advocate of on-line commerce.

At the Silicon Valley Environmental Partnership, the focus was on efforts that bridged tensions between the environment and business and on demonstrating that goals of both can be achieved in a sustainable fashion. Through it, the nation's first incubator facility for the environmental technology industry was established, a move that eventually inspired eleven others in the Bay Area. In 1999, the Environmental Partnership created the first regional environmental index and a computer recycling directory.

"What I loved most about Joint Venture's success," said Kennett, was the psychological shift in people from competition to collaboration. For example, at one point, each of the valley's twenty-seven communities had its own economic development officer and its own economic plan. They were constantly bickering with and poaching off each other.

With the advent of Joint Venture, one of its first outcomes was the production of a common Silicon Valley brochure aimed at attracting companies to the region, not to a specific community. The communities worked together with business to produce it. True, it included inserts on each community at the back, but it focused on the benefits of living and working in Silicon Valley. The brochure was the product of a new understanding that if we could cooperate to get a company to settle anywhere in the valley, it would be good for everyone.

By far the most important and fundamental new capacity that emerged from Joint Venture was a regional capacity for structured, action-oriented collaboration. In all of its results and at every stage, collaboration was the common denominator. Joint Venture's leaders recognized early the potential competitive advantage inherent in the valley's rich mix of companies and people. "Our diversity provides us with a real asset for competing globally," said Rebecca Morgan. "In our vision, Silicon Valley is a community collaborating to compete" (Morgan, 1994, p. 7C). Joint Venture's actions seemed to stimulate a more cooperative governance style within the region, one that AnnaLee Saxenian had identified as essential for regional economic growth (quoted in *San Jose Mercury News*, 1994, p. 10B). What is important, she said, was to have "regional policies [that] catalyze and coordinate, rather than directly manage collaboration among the many actors that populate a regional economy."

Because its actions represented a consensus among a wide variety of Silicon Valley stakeholders, Joint Venture became a credible vehicle for the identification and discussion of regional issues. For example, it played a key role in convincing state legislators to give companies a 6 percent tax credit when they buy new manufacturing equipment.

## Sustaining the Momentum

The release of the *Index of Silicon Valley* in 1995 did more than just provide feedback on Joint Venture's progress towards its goals. In a fundamental way, it helped increase local awareness of the socioeconomic context in which regional decisions were being made. Public reaction to the *Index* reflected concerns that the valley could grow into a bifurcated society of haves versus have-nots and the position that social equity was equally important to economic development. This was a theme that would be echoed in each subsequent annual *Index*. As a consequence, it opened the door to a subtle shift in Joint Venture's focus: from creating a better business climate to developing people and a more balanced community.

As the continuous stream of Joint Venture projects developed, the organization began to garner national attention. Joint Venture teams lobbied in both Sacramento and Washington for a variety of industry and educational purposes, ultimately catching the eye of the White House. In August 1996, President Clinton pointed to Joint Venture as a model of business-community partnership, and in particular he praised the joint efforts of educators and Silicon Valley business leaders to reform education.: "I want every person to know that you can have all the national initiatives, but unless you have true Joint Ventures like here in Silicon Valley, you can't do it" (*San Jose Mercury News*, 1996, p. 14A). That the success of Joint Venture Silicon Valley had catapulted it onto a national political stage would have long-term implications.

By 1997, the growing social divide in the region was increasingly apparent. Silicon Valley was the epitome of economic success. It had created more than 130,000 new jobs since 1992, and workers' incomes averaged $45,000 annually, the nation's highest. It was the country's second largest regional source of exports and the home of hundreds of new and expanding businesses and the largest single destination of technology investment in the world. Yet as area municipalities encouraged the creation of six jobs for every unit of housing between 1992 and 1997, housing prices soared, and transportation was becoming increasingly congested. The area's affordability to workers and companies was declining faster than the increases in wages. "I still think people are going to be flocking to this area and commuting an hour and a half or two hours each way, because this is where the new and exciting jobs of the 21st century are," said San Jose Mayor Susan Hammer. But, she added, "I couldn't imagine making a commute like that. . . . I don't think it's a real super quality of life" (*San Jose Mercury News*, 1997, p. 1E).

The quality-of-life issue gradually gained ground as an umbrella issue for all the things that were not right with the valley even as it was clearly on top of the economic and technology worlds. Affordable housing, clogged traffic, overcrowded and poor-quality schools, and an increasingly unequal sharing of Silicon Valley's wealth from the knowledge economy now became targets of Joint Venture's activities. Many valley leaders came to believe, along with Noble Prize–winning economist Robert Solow, that "livability is an economic imperative" (Henton and Walesh, 1998, p. 15).

In response, Joint Venture initiated in June 1997 a year-long consultation effort, dubbed Silicon Valley 2010, to engage various community stakeholders in a visioning exercise for the valley. Although initially resistant, maybe because of JVSV's earlier difficulties with its housing initiative, Morgan was eventually persuaded by the board's commitment. A twenty-seven-person vision and leadership team was created to conduct a consultative and collaborative process to "create a vision, benchmarks, and commitments to action." That decision seemed justified by the January 1998 *Index* and a report by the South Bay AFL-CIO Central Labor Council, both of which pointed to many of the same troubling social trends: low education levels, high dropout rates, and relatively poor health care, especially among Latinos (*San Jose Mercury News*, 1998a).

From the fall of 1997 until the spring of 1998, the Vision Leadership Team analyzed the valley's strengths and weaknesses, consulted experts and focus groups, and conducted an eight-hundred-person survey in order to draft a vision for Silicon Valley. In April and May 1998, Joint Venture invited citizen feedback through a series of ten open community forms. It went directly to citizens to discover what they thought about what was right and wrong about the valley and what direction they thought the region should develop in. They sought input from people across all sectors: business, government, education, and the civic sector.

The Vision Leadership Team learned that most prized was the character and diversity of the people (their spirit of innovation and entrepreneurship, their ethnic and racial diversity, and their ability to get along with each other) and the opportunities for growth that stemmed from those qualities. Not coincidentally, what people did not like were the problems associated with unsustainable growth and the presence of too many people living too close together (too many cars; not enough homes, parks, or open space; and the ever-increasing cost of living). People and growth were both the most *and* the least desired elements of the community.

With a lot of fanfare, Joint Venture released its vision document in October 1998, *Silicon Valley 2010*. The report, which began with a friendly "Dear Neighbor," focused on four strategic directions for future development: promoting an innovative economy, creating a livable environment, ensuring an inclusive society, and building regional stewardship and shared solutions. The report identified the challenges associated with each direction (see Table 11.1) and then outlined the Vision and Leadership Team's commitment to working with the community to meet the challenges and actualize the vision. "We believe," said the report, "this framework is a promising starting point for broader debate and we are committed to engaging in that debate and to realizing this vision. . . . We hope this document will be used for helping to reshape public debate, for outlining shared responsibilities, and for developing policies and actions that allow future generations to experience

## TABLE 11.1. STRATEGIC DIRECTIONS AND CHALLENGES, SILICON VALLEY 2010.

| Economic Challenges | Environmental Challenges | Social Challenges | Stewardship Challenges |
|---|---|---|---|
| Employment growing faster than population, with increasing demand on labor market | Urban sprawl | Balancing work and family life | Coordination among the three distinct Silicon Valley communities |
| Rising household income inequality | A ratio of jobs to households at 5:1 | Access to employment opportunity hindered by a lack of the right skills, distance to work, and a lack of connectedness to people | Erosion of local control over local spending |
| A declining proportion of women and invisible minorities among top-income jobs | Minimal use of public transit and other alternatives to automobile transportation | Geographically concentrated areas of poverty | State tax and fiscal incentives discourage sustainable land use and encourage commercial over residential development |
| An increasing share of working-poor households | Air and water pollution | | |
| A bifurcated labor force of knowledge workers and low-skill service workers | Maintenance of wetlands and natural habitats | | |

economic prosperity and a satisfying quality of life" (Joint Venture, 1998). Specifically, the team committed to the following action steps:

1. Gain public commitments from the region's business, government, and community leaders to support the broad vision of Silicon Valley 2010 and then begin with them the process of developing regional solutions.
2. Catalyze action toward the establishment of a regional civic action network.
3. Measure progress toward the vision as a guide for decision making among Silicon Valley leaders.

Rather than trying to impose its solutions on the community, the team took its cue from John Gardner of Stanford University, who wrote in the foreword to *Boundary Crossers*, "What we need, and what seems to be emerging in some of our communities is something new—'networks of responsibility'—drawn from all segments coming together to create wholeness that incorporates diversity" (Peirce and Johnson, 1997, p. iii).

"Joint Venture's visionaries have made an excellent start in several important ways," responded the *Mercury News*. "They have recognized the many different factors that go into the creation of a sustainable region. They have integrated these factors with some new, creative concepts and with ideas from more than 2000 area residents. And they have not tried to dictate how the goals are to be achieved, *leaving that, as they should, to the region's residents to decide* [emphasis added]" (*San Jose Mercury News*, 1998b, p. 6B).

The *2010* report ignited the region in a way not seen since Joint Venture was created in 1993. Said Nick Bollman of the Irvine Foundation, "With Joint Venture's release of *Silicon Valley 2010,* the Valley once again demonstrates its well deserved reputation for innovation and leadership. However, this time the Valley is an innovator for better communities rather than for another microchip. . . . In short, the *2010* vision argues for a more integrated approach to creating a more livable region, one that is sustainable in both the short and long run, based on an understanding of the interdependence of economic vitality, environmental quality and social well-being" (Bolman, 1998, p. 7P).

For Joint Venture, the *2010* experience was the culmination of many of the important lessons it had learned in the previous six years. Those lessons were collected in two reflective volumes, *Lessons for Regional Rejuvenation,* in which the organization assessed its strengths and weaknesses, what worked for it and what did not. In the second volume, JVSV's leaders revealed "an important reality of a regional collaborative: it is about learning. The capability a region develops to learn about and characterize itself, to distribute this information to a broad regional audience, and then to use this understanding to create experimental initiatives helps a region develop and prosper" (Joint Venture, 2000, p. 44).

Joint Venture had a clear sense of its role as a catalyst for that learning and as an incubator of "new approaches to regional revitalization. Because it chose not to own these efforts and not to create long-term organizations around them, a natural cycle time began to evolve—a year or two to determine if an idea was viable and three to five to get up and running—and then, for many, out the door" (Joint Venture, 2000, p. 37).

There was no fixed time constraint on any activity, but because of limited resources, both financial and human, Joint Venture could support only a few initiatives at a time. It was therefore constantly in the position of having to choose among opportunities based on changing trends in its environment. Yesterday's issues could easily find themselves being displaced by today's more pressing ones. As described in *Lessons 2*, "This may mean leaping to a new set of goals before the existing set is fully accomplished and before adequate resources have been identified for addressing new challenges" (Joint Venture, 2000, p. 39).

As 1998 drew to a close, Joint Venture was well armed to meet a new set of long-term challenges. It was equipped with a new vision. It had significant financial and reputational assets along with a rich store of knowledge capital. It had also established a solid history community cooperation and the commitment of many local leaders to work together.

## Passing the Torch

On December 4, 1998, Becky Morgan had indicated to the board her desire to retire. She was still interested, however, in continuing to work to implement the *2010* vision or retain a leadership role as a member of Joint Venture's board. In an unusual move, however, given her previous contribution and her connections to many of the elite of Silicon Valley society, the board denied her request, citing the constitutional rules of the organization. This was a logical move that would have provided a freer rein to her successor, but it wounded Morgan deeply, as well as many of the staffers she had brought into the organization. Despite this, she was committed to leaving Joint Venture secure in its direction and with the full benefit of the corporate memory she had acquired. The *Silicon Valley 2010* document and *Lessons* 2 were therefore her last major contributions.

To replace her, Joint Venture chose former San Mateo County supervisor Ruben Barrales and a member of JVSV's board. Interestingly, Morgan had been developing Connie Martinez, JVSV's vice president and director of Economic Development, as her successor until what some insiders referred to as a palace coup took place. That coup was orchestrated by Condoleezza Rice, the provost of Stanford University, then a senior area Republican and today the national security adviser in the Bush administration. Barrales was considered by many to be her protégé. Although Rice, who had joined the Joint Venture board in 1997, had not been one of JVSV's more active directors, she invested a lot of energy to get Barrales elected CEO.

Many openly questioned whether Barrales, bright and articulate and clearly one of the region's rising young stars, would retire from partisan politics. Morgan had done just that in 1993 when she retired from her job as a California senator, but she was already a seasoned politician at that time. Barrales was just beginning his political career. The boundary-crossing job of CEO at Joint Venture required nonpartisanship. Barrales agreed to put politics aside, but scarcely six months later, he accepted the position as co-chairman of George W. Bush's California exploratory committee. After a few days of intense pressure from JVSV's board, which felt it inappropriate for the head of Joint Venture to be in such a politically activist role, Barrales stepped down from the Bush campaign.

The appointment of Barrales also raised the question whether his selection indicated a fundamental organizational shift to a more politicized Joint Venture. JVSV had originated as a collaboration of business interests. Although it had gained public sector allies and a political profile as an advocate of regional interests, a political Joint Venture would be less likely to command attention among the valley's more libertarian thinking business leaders. Joint Venture had become successful because all segments of the community felt ownership in it. If it were to anchor itself to a single sector, it would risk losing its credibility as neutral broker.

Barrales had set about to refocus the organization's activities in a narrower range, specifically education, and extend the reach of Joint Venture's activities beyond schools or boards. JVSV's original mandate covered many bases, from smart permitting to economic development to environmental and educational reform, but over the next few years, much of its efforts centered around issues related to the workforce and the digital divide separating those with high-technology skills and acumen versus those without them. This shift had as its basis the growing importance among local firms of developing, attracting, and retaining talent. Yet as Joint Venture defined its role in these areas, it would be much less interventionist because other organizations would deliver the programs. Barrales described this approach as one capable of having greater scale and leverage of resources to achieve more far-reaching regional impacts. However rational this may have appeared, this change would be wrenching for the organization in terms of its reputational assets and staff.

In 1999, JVSV achieved several significant milestones. It published a study with AT Kearney that examined the workforce gap, which, according to Barrales, "confirms that the area's high-tech industry was not growing as fast as it could be because there simply are not enough skilled people to fill the jobs" (Joint Venture, 1999). In addition, the Challenge 2000 Multimedia Project and the Smart Permit project received recognition as best practice models in education and e-government, respectively. Finally, Joint Venture convened a blue ribbon panel to begin addressing concerns about the inequities generated by the digital divide.

Against a background of rising criticism about the valley's deteriorating quality of life, including the 1995–1998 indexes of Silicon Valley and a 1999 study by IntelliQuest that showed the valley with the greatest percentage of unhappy people and the highest cost of living of any comparable U.S. technology center, Joint Venture announced the creation of the Silicon Valley Civic Action Network (SV-CAN), making good on its promise in the *2010* report (*San Jose Mercury News*, 1999, p. 1E). Henton remarked at the time that in the competitive high-tech world, "those places that already rank among the top tier of innovative regions are concerned about the sustainability of their success. They are realizing the importance of quality of life as an innovation asset" (Henton and Walesh, 1999). Although Joint Venture had always recognized that world-class companies required world-class communities, the new focus of SV-CAN on talent issues also precipitated a philosophical change in the organization from quantitative growth (more jobs, more consumption, more business friendly environment) to more qualitative growth (better jobs, better use of resources, more people-friendly environment)—what is now referred to as smart growth.

SV-CAN was also an explicit attempt to reorient Joint Venture from a network of leaders to a more grassroots organization. This change was crucial to the organization's renewal because many of Joint Venture's original champions began moving on to other areas or interests or retiring. Jim Morgan, Ed McCracken, Lew Platt, and eventually *Mercury News* publisher Jay Harris took their leave. Attracting new leaders of their caliber and communitarian vision proved increasingly difficult. The Internet excesses of the late 1990s had created a regional value system with a false sense of invincibility, entitlement, and self-reliance. The new dot-com business leaders created role models from the likes of Larry Ellison of Oracle, who could be described as mercurial, rather than Dave Packard of HP, viewed as steady-handed. So conscious of the big shoes that needed filling, Barrales attempted to substitute the reputational assets of JVSV's network of leaders with a more populist appeal for the organization. SV-CAN became a vehicle to engage Silicon Valley residents more directly to achieve the *2010* goals through new forms of civic engagement and special projects, along the themes of "bridging the digital divide" and "promoting smart growth." "SV-CAN was and is about creating a network of regional stewards," said Henton. But clearly SV-CAN was repositioning Joint Venture into the civic space rather than an economic one.

In the process, Joint Venture seemed to lose touch with its base of business community support. Even as the overall size of Joint Venture's board declined 22 percent from 1996 to 2001, the proportion of business representation on the board declined an additional 15 percent, replaced by representatives from education and the community. According to Becky Morgan, "Joint Venture lost the connection with business leaders by focusing too much on community issues that had good political profile but that did not interest too many people in the business community." Seeing an opportunity, the Silicon Valley Manufacturing Group led by Carl Guardino, a past JVSV board member, increased its scope of activities from simple industry advocate to champion of broader issues of transportation, housing, energy and power, tax policy, government relations, environment, and education—much like Joint Venture had been. It even picked up several Joint Venture board members, including Jay Harris.

JVSV did not stop dealing with business issues. Rather, it seemed to vacate the business issues space in favor of more peripheral business concerns. It led a regional dialogue around e-commerce issues and the reform of Internet tax regimes. In October 2000, it published *Internet Cluster Analysis* with AT Kearney, which examined Internet technology location factors and the valley's global competitiveness. It sponsored the Silicon Valley Technology Fast 50 along with Deloitte & Touche to recognize the achievement of the region's top companies. Along with the American Institute of Architects, JVSV has encouraged broad participation in smart growth urban design to help local decision makers deal more effectively with growth and to promote a new public attitude of regional stewardship. All the same, the relevance of Joint Venture to the business community seemed to decline.

That decline in relevance was also reflected in an almost 100 percent staff turnover in the first two years of the mandate of Barrales. In 1998, Joint Venture had put together a team of dedicated staffers and civic entrepreneurs who could catalyze, facilitate, and support collaboration on a variety of issues. By the fall of 2000, almost all of these people, even Challenge 2000 director Tim Cuneo, had left Joint Venture as strategy shifted from being a program deliverer to program broker. Among the doers and civic entrepreneurs at JVSV, this was anathema.

By the fall of 2001, this transition was complete. Of the four JVSV initiatives listed as current—SV-CAN, the Tax and Fiscal Council, Smart Growth, and the Economic Development Roundtable—none seemed to be doing anything beyond engaging stakeholders and providing forums for discussion.

With the ascension of George W. Bush to the White House and his appointment of Condoleezza Rice as his national security adviser in December 2000, it was less than two months before Ruben Barrales was asked to join the Bush team in Washington. However, since February 2001 when Barrales resigned as Joint Venture CEO, the board has been unable to identify a successor. Given the recent radical turnaround in the valley's economic fortunes, it seems to be struggling to find a new mission and invent a new reason for its existence. In May 2001 JVSV announced:

> Joint Venture: Silicon Valley network will be a regional, non-partisan voice and a civic catalyst for solutions to problems, which impact all sectors of the community. The boards of directors and activities of Joint Venture and its Civic Action Network (SV-CAN) have been merged. We must rekindle our passion for a better community and our compassion for . . . our fellow citizens. An economic slowdown, lack of affordable housing, traffic congestion, educational shortfalls, the income gap, and power crisis raise new concerns about the quality of life and the continued attraction of Silicon Valley for residents and businesses. This year, Joint Venture will focus sharply on just three regional goals: broadened prosperity, livable communities, and civic engagement [Joint Venture, 2001, p. 1].

Can Joint Venture reassert its relevance across the broad cross section of Silicon Valley stakeholders? Its lack of success in finding a replacement for Barrales suggests an organization without a rudder, unsure where it wants to go. Although its new goals are laudable, they are also bereft of the practical entrepreneurism and zeal of previous civic entrepreneurs. Where does Joint Venture go from here?

It is easy to say that Joint Venture was steered down a political path inappropriate for the collaborative role it had originally staked out for itself. In fact, given Barrales's eagerness to return to the political ring, it is hard not to think this. Yet one cannot forget the natural changing of the guard that left Joint Venture seeking replacements for its champions among a generation of business leaders who were much less communitarian. It is also clear that the issue of talent in the valley's knowledge-based economy would inevitably surface as the central regional concern in both the short and the long terms. It is equally clear that addressing the talent question in a manner that would have significant regional impacts would require more than the type of pilot programs generated by Challenge 2000 and significantly more resources. Therefore, Barrales's decision to move to a more grassroots, broker style of organization seems not only logical but also necessary.

Barrales, however, never seemed successful at engaging business leaders and getting them to take the lead. He was not at home with the technology movers and shakers of Santa Clara County in the same way Morgan was. So without short-term practical benefits to sustain their involvement, his theme of "education, education, education" was a tough sell for the business community. As the organization refocused itself, the business community seemed to lose its sense of ownership and then its interest. In an almost prophetic editorial, the *Mercury News* in 1998 cautioned against putting too much attention on education: "Education and workforce training have been *among* [emphasis added] Joint Venture's interests but by no means the only ones" (*San Jose Mercury News*, 1998c, p. 6B). In a collaborative environment, win-win benefits have to be present for partners in both the short and long terms; otherwise, the partnership risks losing the participation necessary to get it to the long term. Therefore, although Barrales was successful at bringing to the table key stakeholders from education and the community, his failure to sustain the level of enthusiasm of the private sector was problematic. As a boundary-crossing initiative, Joint Venture may have been diminished as a result.

In the end, the critical and originally unique value JVSV contributed to the valley was the provision of a vehicle, or more precisely several vehicles, for disparate parts of the community to engage in conversations and dialogue on issues of common concern. Those conversations were conducted not just in words but in deeds. They produced targeted outcomes with real commitments ensuring that the forums did not degenerate into empty talk or finger-pointing exercises. In order to come up with concerted action plans, the participants had to listen to each other. And in listening, they learned from one another. What Joint Venture established was a mechanism for learning by doing. The quality of that learning was tested by the success of its initiatives, the *Index,* and local media feedback. In the process, it became difficult to entertain narrow viewpoints in the face of the broad perspectives provided by Joint Venture's stakeholders. Therefore, as much as Joint Venture has been a collaborative vehicle for fostering change, it has been equally a means of fostering social learning and a more distributed system of regional governance.

As a spillover effect, the frequent instances over the years of successful collaboration have encouraged a more cooperative mind-set within the community generally, which has raised the standard of behavior between organizations and sectors. This mind-set has increased the demand for new collaborative vehicles (Joint Venture competitors) and the need for more insight into the mechanics of partnership. An increasing number of these partnership-styled competitors, including the Silicon Valley Manufacturing Group, TechNet, and the Alliance for Regional Stewardship, have emerged in recent years to help satisfy the region's need for collaboration. Although Joint Venture has regularly partnered with many of these organizations on various issues, each has tried to maintain its own separate niche. For organizations that function largely on the basis of intangibles, this was essential to maintain their own stocks of reputational assets in the community. Today, however, that differentiation is getting harder to make. While this may be good for the region, it may not bode well for Joint Venture.

Although imitation may be one of the best compliments, it is also the best test of the value of an innovative idea. So regardless of whether Joint Venture Silicon Valley can remain the vehicle of choice for collaborative community action, its legacy will always be that it did it first, showing the rest of us the way.

Since the preparation of this case study, Joint Venture Silicon Valley Network seems indeed to be reinventing itself. In the economic downturn of today, Silicon Valley appears to be coming full circle, with the need for cooperation again becoming paramount. Through collaboration JVSV's leadership is working to realign the region's economic and social infrastructures. Their willingness to take on this challenge is evident in their latest publication, *Next Silicon Valley: Riding the Waves of Innovation* (Henton and Walesh, 2001).

A new generation of business and civic leaders have joined with the initial group of regional leaders, who helped start Joint Venture a decade ago, in the Next Silicon Valley project to address the new challenges facing the region. This time the regional leadership knows that promoting social innovation in the workplace, education, and quality of life will be as important as the Valley's technology and economic innovation.

CHAPTER TWELVE

# TRANSFORMING CIVIC CULTURE

## Sitka, Alaska 1999–2001

David D. Chrislip

*The Sitka story chronicles recent events in a historically divided community. The Island Institute in Sitka has played the lead role in developing strategies to transform the town's civic culture by working on parallel tracks at multiple levels. In order to begin moving toward collaboration, the institute conducted an analysis of Sitka's civic culture and used this to convince others that new approaches to public issues should be tried. In partnership with the city, the U.S. Forest Service, and other organizations, the institute sponsored several leadership development workshops for citizens. As participants became more knowledgeable about collaboration, they began to consider how to apply the new skills to particular issues. An extensive collaborative process to address Sitka's municipal waste problems emerged from these conversations.*

*Concurrently, other intermediary organizations began to take leading roles in convening and catalyzing collaborative initiatives in new arenas. In partnership with the University of Alaska and the Turning Point organization, the institute wants to develop a long-term investment in civic leadership development to support future collaboration.*

*The Sitka story incorporates a number of aspects of successful collaboration. The initial assessment using individual interviews provided an accurate picture of Sitka's civic culture. This assessment helped focus the initial effort on helping Sitkans understand the promise of a collaborative approach. Out of this understanding, a number of citizens lent their credibility to help initiate the municipal waste collaboration. This convening group helped identify and recruit stakeholders, design a constructive process, define information needs, select a process expert, find content experts, and gather the resources necessary to move forward. During the process, stakeholders learned new ways of working with written and technical information, engaging with each other through dialogue, deciding by consensus, and developing a strong rationale for their recommendations. A carefully conceived outreach plan helped stakeholders communicate their work to elected leaders, city staff, and the community.*

Steep, mountainous, and heavily forested, Baranof Island in southeast Alaska is home to more brown bears than people. Sitka, the island's most populous town and only incorporated area, occupies a small, rocky outcropping on its western edge. Place matters here. The island's insistent and compelling beauty attracts both visitors and more permanent inhabitants. For many years, logging and fishing lured hard-working folks and those seeking to make a quick buck before moving on. Sitka's fortunes historically followed the boom-and-bust pattern of a resource-based local economy.

From about 1960 until the early 1990s, the town enjoyed an unfamiliar stability when a large Japanese-owned pulp mill became the mainstay of its economy. During these years, environmentalists battled timber interests over the environmental impacts of the mill and other timber-related activities. That battle, says one Sitka citizen, "pitted neighbor against neighbor and created a deep festering wound in the community" (Servid, 2000, p. 178). The closing of the Alaska Pulp Company mill in 1993 ended Sitka's reliance on large timber-related industry but not the controversy between the two sides.

The polarization and extremism of those earlier days still haunt Sitka's efforts to cope with civic challenges. In the fall of 1998, Sitkans voted overwhelmingly against a proposal to build a deep-water dock to accommodate large cruise ships near the downtown area. The town's elected leaders and businesspeople expected easy passage because of the shifting economic base. But citizens were more concerned with Sitka's quality of life than its economy and voted two to one against the dock. The failure of the ballot proposal left elected leaders and citizens deeply divided and distrustful of each other. Many citizens wonder whether it would be possible to find the common ground necessary to preserve the beauty, quality of life, and civility of the place.

In response to these challenges, one organization, the Island Institute, became a catalyst for transforming Sitka's civic culture. The mission of the institute recognizes the dynamic tension between human social and economic systems and the earth's natural systems. By integrating the humanities with specific programs exploring community values, it invests in social capital. It serves as an intermediary organization to help transform Sitka's civic culture and, ultimately, that of the region and the state.

Historically, Sitkans tended to identify the institute's interests in human relationships with the natural world with environmental advocacy. For some time, this perception limited its ability to serve as a catalyst and convener of collaborative action. In order to build trust, the institute has deliberately avoided taking positions on controversial issues. Through constant effort and attention, it has become a trusted civic organization in the community.

Instead of taking public issues head-on and looking for magic answers, the institute works to build the capacity of the community to address them in constructive ways. By taking the time to understand how civic cultures change and identifying the civic challenges facing the community, the institute has crafted specific strategies for addressing Sitka's civic needs.

## Understanding Sitka's Civic Culture

The Island Institute's efforts to transform Sitka's civic culture began in February 1999 with an assessment of the town's civic culture. It conducted a series of interviews with a cross-section of Sitka citizens (see Chapter Six for a description of the interview protocol). A series of open-ended questions uncovered various perspectives about how citizens experience Sitka's civic culture.

The responses described a troubling dynamic (see Figure 12.1). A high level of mutual distrust existed between citizens and those identified as the town's leaders—elected leaders and some businesspeople. Citizens viewed the leadership group as exclusive and concerned with its own narrow agenda rather than that of the broader community. Elected leaders and many businesspeople considered citizens reactionary, fragmented, and driven by extremes. The public outreach activities of Sitka's city council, the Assembly, commonly led to increased hostility and divisiveness. Citizens comfortable with strident advocacy confronted public leaders to get their perspectives across. Extremists often drove local politics. The animosity between elected leaders and more vocal citizens left many in the middle alienated and unengaged unless directly affected by public decisions.

The Tlingit Indian community, about one-quarter of Sitka's population, remains isolated from much of public life in Sitka. For good reasons, the Native community turned inward to meet its needs. Increasingly self-governed and independent, the self-containment of the Native community exacerbates the separation from the non-Native community.

Most Sitka citizens recognized their inability to act unilaterally. Virtually no one, including the Assembly, was in a position to act without eliciting a strong reaction from others in the community. This situation left many people frustrated with politics as usual yet uncertain about or unaware of possible alternatives. Many citizens wondered whether constructive civic action would ever be possible.

## Building Civic Capacity

With little knowledge of alternative approaches to public issues, few Sitkans were ready to try anything new. More people needed to understand different approaches and be prepared to play new leadership roles in order to move forward. In October

# FIGURE 12.1. THE CIVIC CULTURE OF SITKA, ALASKA.

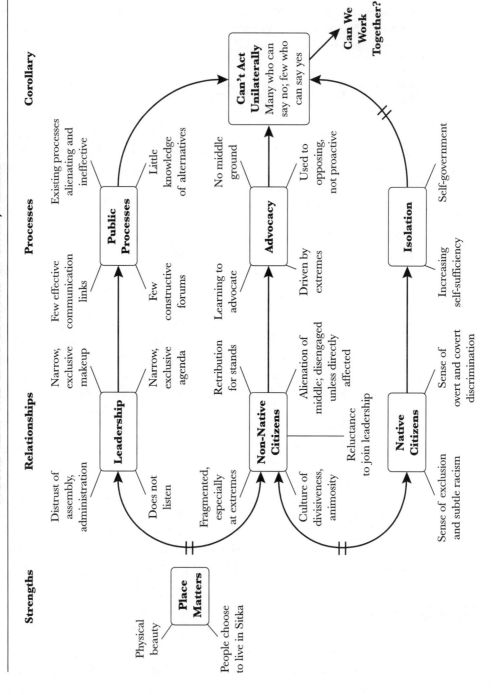

1999, the Island Institute organized two three-hour public meetings and a number of smaller meetings with other groups to help educate citizens about collaborative approaches to public problems. More than 130 citizens attended the public sessions, including Assembly members, city staff, business leaders, Native and minority community members, educators, retirees, and workers from all parts of Sitka's economy. The purpose of these workshops was to build a broader understanding of the critical elements and roles necessary for successful collaboration. As a result of these sessions, several citizens and some Assembly members and business leaders began exploring how these concepts could be applied to specific issues in Sitka. Because of a growing controversy over a local landfill, long-term planning for dealing with solid waste surfaced as an issue that could be addressed in a collaborative way.

Building on the October workshops, the institute organized a two-day intensive skill-building program in December 1999 for Sitkans to learn how to design and initiate a collaborative process. More than forty people participated, including three members of the city's Long Range Planning and Economic Development Commission (LRPEDC), responsible for developing long-term strategies for dealing with solid waste. The workshop prompted the LRPEDC to recommend using a collaborative approach to address this controversial issue.

# From Theory to Practice

In mid-1999, the Assembly, Sitka's elected governing body, announced its intent to reopen a long-closed section of an existing landfill. Part of a fifty-year-old landfill, this section had been closed and capped for several years and converted to softball fields. Temporarily reopening the landfill would help Sitka meet short-term needs for waste disposal until other alternatives could be developed.

Kimsham landfill sits in a residential part of town, adjacent to its largest educational facility, Verstovia Elementary School. The school and many nearby residences had been built several years before with the tacit understanding that the remainder of the landfill would be closed when it was full. The Assembly's announcement to reopen Kimsham caught many residents by surprise and sparked a hostile and heated reaction to the decision.

The debate over the landfill rapidly got out of hand as residents protested the decision while the Assembly defended its position. In recent years, citizens have regularly accused the Assembly of not listening to them. This time it failed to notify the school system and the people living in the neighborhoods adjacent to the landfill, yet it had consulted business and environmental interests. The furor over the decision quickly led to a formal decision by the school board to oppose the decision of the Assembly. With two powerful governing bodies at odds and neighborhood residents poised for battle, the city prepared for the worst.

Gaining support for a collaborative process in the face of these challenges was no easy task. As one of the Assembly members said, "The city doesn't have a history of long-range planning—a lot of things we do are knee-jerk reactions to what people want" (Haugland, 1999, p. 1). Commissions like the LRPEDC had never been used for engaging the public other than in the usual public hearing format. The combination of long-range planning and a collaborative public process offered the promise of a closer link between the public and the Assembly that might improve these relationships, but some Assembly members were wary that events could slip out of their control. From the public's side, citizens expressed fear that the Assembly would not heed the LRPEDC's recommendations. Lingering distrust between the public and the Assembly would continue to haunt the effort.

To complement its work with the Assembly, the commission began to build public support for a collaborative process. At a November 1999 public forum, more than fifty citizens turned out to help define what a successful process would look like, define the scope of the solid waste issue, identify who should be involved, and decide how to keep the public informed about the issue. The meeting ended on a promising note: participants began to see themselves and other citizens as responsible for addressing the issue rather than looking to the Assembly and city staff for guidance.

With its increasing support, the LRPEDC moved into an active planning phase. At a key meeting with the LRPEDC in late February 2000, Assembly members aired concerns about accountability and reservations about collaboration based on past less successful experiences. By the end of the meeting, they were generally supportive of a collaborative process and could see benefits for endorsing an alternative approach.

The same evening, the LRPEDC held a public meeting to help citizens understand how the solid waste issue would be addressed. The unusual meeting in Sitka's experience clarified expectations of what a collaborative process could do. Billed as an opportunity for citizens to address the solid waste issue, many people came expecting another confrontation with Assembly members and city staff. Instead, the meeting focused on how the issue would be addressed—the process—with elected leaders and city staff participating as peers with citizens. A neutral process expert facilitated the meeting. City staff reviewed how short-term issues would be managed, and the chair of the LRPEDC outlined the collaborative process for addressing the long-term aspects. More than 150 people attended the meeting. Although some were disappointed with the lack of conflict, most appreciated the opportunity to interact with public leaders in a different way and enthusiastically supported LRPEDC plans. With widespread public support and the open endorsement of the Assembly for a collaborative process, Sitkans prepared to try a new approach that might bring the community together rather than tear it apart.

Over the following two months, the LRPEDC recruited a convening group and began the detailed planning work. It particularly wanted "people who are involved and respected in the community and have the ability to draw a wide range of perspectives into this process as stakeholders." The convening group developed a statement of purpose, clarified the work of the convening group and the stakeholder group, and identified an initial list of stakeholder perspectives and experiences. At subsequent meetings, the group put together a design for the process (see Figure 12.2), made an initial cut at information needs, defined critical roles, and completed the stakeholder identification process. Soon after, the Assembly and city staff allocated several thousand dollars to support the process. These funds allowed the convening group to hire a facilitator and begin inviting and recruiting stakeholders for an initial meeting in May 2000.

Disposing of waste in Baranof Island's fragile environment tops the list of Sitka's perennial problems. With little open land and few viable sites for landfills, other options would have to be considered. The heated controversy over the expansion of the Kimsham landfill in the town itself made talk of a new one even more difficult. Most stakeholders entered the process with firm positions on landfills. Some opposed any landfill for environmental reasons yet could offer no viable alternative for disposing of solid waste. People living near the existing landfill wanted a new one so the one in town could be closed immediately. Others thought the town needed a landfill because residents should be responsible for disposing of the waste they create rather than shipping it off-island to other states. It would take a long time to soften these positions.

The initial stakeholder meeting, the first experience of collaboration for many participants, broke new ground. A skilled local facilitator, Mary Therese Thompson, kept the meeting focused on building understanding of the process. Jill Hanson, the chair of the LRPEDC, the primary convener for the process, explained the concept of collaboration, defined the role of stakeholders, and described the process that participants would engage in. The city's public works director, Hugh Bevan, outlined the city's short-term plans for dealing with Sitka's waste. Using this information, small groups of stakeholders began to identify areas of concern. As one observer put it, "The meeting went superbly well . . . people even clapped at the end." Perhaps another way of engaging would be possible.

The initial educational phase helped shift perspectives about the solid waste issue. Stakeholders analyzed existing waste streams and the current means for dealing with them. City staff prepared and presented this information. The credibility of the city's public works director helped stakeholders learn to trust city staff.

# FIGURE 12.2. SITKA MUNICIPAL WASTE COLLABORATION.

| Phases \ Tracks | Orientation | Education | Define Problem | Alternatives • Solutions • Strategies | Reaching Out |
|---|---|---|---|---|---|
| 2 to 3 hour sessions | May 18 | May 25; June 1, 8 | June 15, 22 | June 29; July 13, 27; August 10, 24 | |
| Stakeholders | • Introductions<br>• Overview of process<br>• Purpose, outcomes, time lines<br>• Define roles<br>• Guidelines<br>• Begin building relationships | • Municipal Waste 101<br>• Sitka's waste streams<br>• Status of current projects<br>• Understanding of where we are<br>  - Information sources<br>  - Operations and players<br>• Build agreement on facts and documentation | • Identify dimensions of problem<br>• Build agreement on problem | • Identify options and alternatives<br>• Develop criteria for choosing alternative solutions<br>• Narrow focus<br>• Research and information gathering on potential options<br>• Close in on solutions<br>• Build understanding and agreement on solutions and strategies<br>• Draft recommendations | • Engage Assembly<br>• Reach out to community<br>• Finalize recommendations |
| Steering Group | Information and public sessions will be scheduled throughout the process to keep the community, including the Assembly and city staff, informed and involved | | | | |

*Sitka Municipal Waste Collaboration Mission Statement:*

*The Municipal Waste Stakeholders Group will develop recommendations with a long-term (50-year) view:*

- *including consideration of all waste streams*
- *exploring alternative scenarios with consideration of the latest technology, current recycling successes, waste reduction, and regional efforts*
- *educating the community toward a better understanding of the current operations and the potential alternatives*

*The stakeholder group's scope of work will include*

- *reviewing all credible materials on current waste stream operations*
- *researching alternative scenarios including transition feasibility; cost estimates, rate structures/alternative funding streams; level of community interest*
- *making recommendations based on consensus*
- *following recommendations through to implementation*

Other experts educated stakeholders about solid waste issues. The stakeholders learned how to use the skills of dialogue to explore content issues. Instead of attacking each other over differing perceptions, participants developed a shared understanding of the information. Initial discussions mixed facts about current efforts with new perspectives about future possibilities. Stakeholders learned to distinguish the two and defer talk of possible solutions until they fully understood the facts. They identified six waste streams as priorities and developed a range of questions that would need answers to guide their work. The questions set parameters for choosing among options.

This work took several weeks. Hanson said that "the real reason it took so long is that municipal waste is a huge, complicated issue. Most people don't go exploring the municipal waste in their town, and it's not something that the average person knows anything about" (Bernard, 2000, p. 1). A group of citizens had made themselves experts, creating the beginning of a credible constituency for change.

With the education phase behind them, stakeholders began to consider options for dealing with the city's waste. Using a brainstorming process, they developed an extensive list of alternatives. Task groups in four areas—municipal solid waste; reuse, recycle, and reduce; biosolids; and fish waste, used oil, and hazardous waste—educated themselves about the options and began to narrow the list of possibilities. The task groups regularly reviewed their work with the larger stakeholder group to keep others informed. As their work progressed, each group evaluated alternatives against criteria developed from the original list of questions. Considerations included capital and operating costs; impacts of transfer, collection, and disposal sites on surrounding areas; impacts of handling and transportation; environmental and public health effects; minimizing the waste stream; increasing recycling; and impacts on future generations. Each group took responsibility for choosing strategies that best met the criteria and developed a rationale for their choice. By now, a new landfill was just one option among many.

By the fall of 2000, stakeholders had an initial set of recommendations and were ready to present them to the Assembly. A work session held in December brought together stakeholders, Assembly members, and city staff to review progress. Hanson reviewed the makeup of the stakeholder group and identified the people who were participating. One of the Assembly members appreciated the credibility of the stakeholder group, commenting, "It's not one special interest group." In each of the four areas, stakeholders presented their ideas, providing an overview of the information they considered, the options they evaluated, and their rationale for choosing a particular strategy.

The stakeholders' plan called for "the strategy of first resort": reuse, reduce, and recycle. Any effort to reduce or recycle waste would minimize the need for other waste disposal strategies. Residual municipal solid waste and construction and demolition debris would be shipped off-island to a permitted, environmentally sound site. The Kimsham landfill would be kept open but dormant except in extreme emergencies. In the longer term, Sitkans would explore opportunities for joint solutions with other communities in southeast Alaska. Several other recommendations addressed smaller waste streams, such as biosolids, fish waste, used oil, and hazardous waste. The stakeholders concluded that a comprehensive municipal solid waste plan would work best to meet Sitka's needs rather than a piecemeal response to problems as they arise.

Some stakeholders described the shifts they had made in their thinking. One of them, Tom Hart, had come into the process firmly convinced that the Kimsham landfill should be closed. After struggling with the issue for several months, he decided that "based on the information we considered, I've changed my mind. We can keep Kimsham open indefinitely with minor use for emergencies." Solid waste would be shipped off-island to locations that were more environmentally suitable for a landfill. This would avoid the need for a new landfill and maintain the existing landfill only for emergency use. The group knew what they were talking about. One Assembly member acknowledged that "the amount of information gathered [by the stakeholders] definitely allows us to make much more informed decisions."

After this meeting, stakeholders continued to work with city staff to clarify cost issues, coordinate long-term strategies with short-term actions, and refine their recommendations. In August 2001, the city administrator, the public works director, and the stakeholders took the recommendations to the Assembly. A majority of Assembly members were encouraged by the stakeholders' progress and looked forward to gaining a better understanding of their work. Two others remain hesitant to embrace the recommendations and express their support for the work. A controversial proposal for a ballot initiative asking voters if they conceptually approve of incineration was defeated, in part because of the stakeholders' concern that this would divide the community without educating them about the broader aspects of addressing the solid waste issue. Sitka's history of polarization still shadows the way it deals with public issues. Old ways die hard.

The Assembly now has the benefit of a well-thought-out set of strategies for dealing with a controversial issue and a credible constituency to support them as they begin to implement long-term strategies. Some of them remain wary of accepting the stakeholders' work but are beginning to recognize the political costs of failing to acknowledge the work of the stakeholders. The stakeholders continue to reach out to educate the community about the more controversial aspects of their plans and to build a broader constituency. Whether the current Assembly acts on the recommendations or not, the solid waste issue and the work of the stakeholders will influence the results of future elections and what Sitkans choose to do about solid waste.

## A Promising Legacy

Through persistence and hard work, a committed group of stakeholders has provided Sitka with sound strategies for dealing with solid waste. When the issue emerged, a number of citizens were ready to take on new leadership roles. Jill Hanson and Jim "Stef" Steffen, as strong, facilitative leaders, kept the initiative moving. Their persistence helped stakeholders sustain hope in the possibilities of collaboration, and their credibility compelled the attention of city staff and Assembly members. Members of the steering committee put in long hours communicating with other stakeholders and preparing the report of stakeholder recommendations. Mary Therese Thompson's facilitating skills ensured that stakeholder meetings achieved the desired outcomes. The stakeholders took advantage of a number of credible sources to learn about Sitka's waste streams and alternative ways to cope with them. City staff as well as other experts were drawn into the conversation. By the time the initiative was wrapping up, a wide range of Sitka citizens had a comprehensive view of the town's waste problems. Regular links with the Assembly kept elected leaders apprised of the progress and direction of stakeholder recommendations. Outreach to the community brought others into the process, encouraging them to learn more about the solid waste issue. Both the Assembly and others in the community have a better understanding of the influence of a credible stakeholder group in a collaborative process.

A growing number of citizens with experience in collaboration provide the beginnings of a new and less divisive civic culture and hope for constructively addressing future concerns. The Island Institute continues to foster this transformation. With the support and encouragement of the institute, Sitkans took the time to educate themselves about collaboration and to build necessary skills before addressing a particular issue. With this preparation, the solid waste process progressed much more smoothly than it would have otherwise. Emerging issues such as tourism and coastal resource management offer opportunities for continued learning and practice. Turning Point and the Alaska Marine Conservation Council serve as intermediary organizations, extending the use of collaboration to new arenas such as community health and marine conservation. The University of Alaska-Southeast, Turning Point, and the Island Institute are exploring longer-term civic leadership development initiatives. With time and help from intermediary organizations like the institute, Sitkans may yet transform their civic culture.

# CHAPTER THIRTEEN

# NEIGHBORHOOD ACTION INITIATIVE

## Engaging Citizens in Real Change

### William R. Potapchuk

*The Neighborhood Action Initiative in Washington, D.C., has perhaps engaged more citizens at one time than any other collaborative initiative. In part, use of skillful process experts and new technologies for instant feedback made this possible. By using collabora-tion at several levels—citywide, neighborhood clusters, interagency, and intra-agency— the initiative helped rebuild trust between citizens and government and helped reinvent government structures in ways that respond directly to citizens' desires and needs.*

*Mayor Anthony Williams, who took office in 1999, used his credibility as the former chief financial officer of the District to catalyze the initiative in the first few months of his administration. The initiative relied on citizen engagement to help set direction and strategies for the city. As the resources of city government were used in new ways, effective partnerships with citizens emerged to address the challenges of an urban inner city with wide disparities in income and education.*

Powerful images of Washington, D.C., reside in our collective memory. The White House and the United States Capitol are not only well-known build-ings; they are icons for the principles of our country. History happens in Wash-ington, D.C. It is where Dr. Martin Luther King, Jr., told us, "I have a dream," and President John F. Kennedy said in his inaugural address, "Ask not what your country can do for you, ask what you can do for your country."

Washingtonians share these images, but their daily lives and experiences away from the federal city reflect contrasting images. A Washingtonian recalling pow-erful images of notable streets might visualize Fourteenth Street after the riots in 1968, along with the extraordinary Embassy Row on Massachusetts Avenue. Images of neighborhoods might focus on Deanwood and Anacostia with their

---

Thanks to José Sueiro, Ward 1 neighborhood service coordinator, for his story in this chapter about Ward 1.

all-too-many abandoned houses, along with Georgetown and Chevy Chase with multimillion-dollar homes.

Contrasts also surround local notions of democracy. Washington, D.C., is simultaneously a global capital and the only place in the United States that does not have a voting representative in Congress. Federal intervention in the affairs of the District of Columbia is a prominent part of the political landscape. Members of Congress oversee the budget, review locally enacted laws, and on occasion insert unwanted restrictions on policy and budget.

Limited home rule has existed only since 1974, when residents first elected a mayor to provide executive and administrative leadership for the city. A large majority of residents believe that they have been denied full citizenship and continue efforts to make the District a state. This tension between home rule and federal intervention came to a boil in 1995 when Congress, driven by a sense that District government was out of control and quickly going broke, appointed the five-member Control Board with the powers to oversee the District's budget, veto legislation, and appoint senior officials. Longtime Mayor Marion Barry's erratic leadership and questionable personal behavior exacerbated congressional concerns about the district. Although many African Americans viewed Barry as a local hero, Congress did not hesitate to act.

The Control Board wasted little time in appointing well-respected public administrator Anthony Williams as chief financial officer (CFO). Williams, the former CFO at the U.S. Department of Agriculture, could not have been more different from Barry. The bow-tied, conservatively dressed Williams seemed more comfortable with numbers than politics, while the colorful Barry was the man of the people.

While the performance of others on the Control Board was disappointing, in 1997, Williams led the District to its first balanced budget in years. Because he improved tax collection and gained control of dysfunctional finance offices, admiration for Williams grew while Barry's star waned.

Against this backdrop, longtime community leaders—black and white—saw an opportunity to change the face of the mayor's office and began a campaign to recruit Anthony Williams to run for the office. Williams resisted at first, but slowly came around to the idea and started a low-key campaign. He started by attending gatherings over coffee in every corner of the District to hear what residents had to say.

On January 4, 1999, he was sworn in as the fourth mayor of the District of Columbia. He came to office with several clear perceptions. Citizens echoed his sense that the city's systems were profoundly broken. More disturbing to him was the profound distrust citizens had for District government. Many had lost faith in the possibility of fixing the government.

A larger need was also clear to Williams: the District must once again assert its ability to be a self-governing jurisdiction in order to remove the shackles of the Control Board. This meant maintaining a balanced budget as the statute defined while rebuilding congressional faith in District government to manage its own affairs. The District of Columbia needed to focus on the basics—collecting garbage, removing snow, and eradicating day-long waits at the Department of Motor Vehicles, among others—while improving the government's capacity to tackle larger tasks, such as revitalizing neighborhoods, reforming dysfunctional regulatory structures, and rebuilding public infrastructures. To be successful, city government needed to engage citizens to establish direction and set priorities and then work with them to achieve the goals.

One of the formidable challenges facing mayors and other chief elected officials is balancing planning, citizen engagement, and action. On the one hand, without enough planning, actions often fail to achieve intended results. Without appropriate and meaningful citizen engagement, citizens continue to distrust government and oppose plans in which they had no part. On the other hand, too much planning and not enough action usually means that elected officials are looking for work after the next election.

When Mayor Williams was elected, he announced a sixty-day plan of quick interventions designed to address long-standing citizen gripes. The initial set of thirty-three promises ranged from opening a long-closed section of Massachusetts Avenue to holding a summit to address the surge in the rat population due to poor garbage collection. While committing to take action on these complaints, the new mayor knew that his government would have to undergo fundamental change before it could address residents' needs in a comprehensive and sustainable manner. He also knew that he would have to rekindle citizens' belief in government in order to achieve his goals.

In his inaugural address, Williams committed to transforming the way the District government works and proposed a major new initiative: creating a planning and budgeting process that would engage citizens directly in the governance of their city, enable them to hold public officials accountable for improving services, and involve them in improving their own neighborhoods. These ambitious goals required a partnership.

## Transforming the District's Governance

To assist him in making his vision a reality, Williams partnered with AmericaSpeaks, a national nonprofit organization dedicated to developing innovative methods for large groups of diverse citizens to play a meaningful role in public life. The founder of AmericaSpeaks, Carolyn J. Lukensmeyer, brought an extensive background in large-scale systems change, along with a passion for empowering citizens and healing the nation's democracy. Lukensmeyer and AmericaSpeaks had recently completed a two-year project, funded by the Pew Charitable Trusts, to engage citizens in a national nonpartisan deliberation on the future of social security. Americans Discuss Social Security served as a groundbreaking laboratory for integrating face-to-face dialogue with technology that enables thousands of citizens to join the debate on a critical public policy issue. Three live two-way video teleconferences across ten cities, each with three hours of dialogue with citizens and elected officials, including the U.S. president, capped this innovative effort.

Williams challenged AmericaSpeaks to adapt its methods to local government to help create a new cycle of governance integrating cross-agency citywide strategic planning with broad-based citizen engagement. Williams knew that if he was to transform District government, citizens had to feel ownership of critical decisions and be willing to work as partners with the government in bringing about the needed changes. The partnership with AmericaSpeaks provided the means for achieving these ends. The mayor called the new effort the Neighborhood Action Initiative and committed himself and his administration to its bold slogan: "Come Together, Work Together, Succeed Together."

## Citywide Strategic Planning and Meaningful Citizen Engagement

Neighborhood Action's deep commitment to bringing together citizens to help set the District's priorities and strategic direction required new approaches. In most large jurisdictions, citywide citizen engagement is perfunctory at best. Numerous practical challenges for dealing with large numbers of people limit possible approaches. Smaller events held in various parts of the city raise concerns that citizens from different backgrounds do not meet. Activist groups often co-opt these kinds of events for their own purposes. Large citywide events often operate by invitation only as a means for limiting numbers. Those excluded often oppose proposed actions. Despite a sincere commitment to meaningful citizen engagement, the practicality of engaging large numbers of citizens too often precludes real engagement.

Neighborhood Action broke through these traditional challenges to meaningful citizen engagement with its Citizen Summit, a large-scale, technology-enabled deliberative conversation about future priorities and strategies for the District. Using a process designed by AmericaSpeaks and its model for citizen engagement, thousands of citizens from every walk of life and every neighborhood in the city shared their values and vision and expressed their collective desires for the future of the city.

Once the decision was made to hold the summit, it took six months to make the event happen by tackling countless logistical, financial, and political challenges. District staff and AmericaSpeaks shared the leadership and management tasks for this effort. Managing the event like a large political campaign, the organizers used frequent strategy sessions; a changing mix of staff, consultants, and volunteers; and a zeal for success to tackle the challenges. They raised funds from local companies and foundations. They consulted numerous community leaders either individually or through an advisory board and conducted aggressive outreach efforts through churches, neighborhood associations, and community-based organizations. They identified the Convention Center, a site that would accommodate several thousand participants, for the summit. They hired technology partners and recruited and trained facilitators from the District and elsewhere. They prepared a forty-page detailed agenda and engaged volunteers to make telephone calls, stuff envelopes, and prepare packets.

The idea of strategic planning was as new to the District as the summit was innovative. Over time, the District had developed a multiplicity of agencies, each with a separate plan along with numerous other plans for specific areas or issues. These narrow and more focused plans provided a foundation for the strategic plan so Neighborhood Action would not be seen as reinventing the wheel. A loaned executive from the World Bank reviewed and summarized each of the previous plans. This review, combined with a distillation of citizen concerns and requests that were received by the new administration, provided the background material for a mayor's cabinet retreat that launched the Citywide Strategic Planning Process. At the retreat, cross-agency teams were created to develop draft strategic plans for six priority areas: Building and Sustaining Healthy Neighborhoods, Investing in Children and Youth, Strengthening Families, Making Government Work, Economic Development, and Unity of Purpose and Democracy. Over several months, the cross-agency teams worked with community stakeholders to develop the draft plans. The organizers summarized these drafts into a four-page easily understood newspaper for use at the Summit.

## Citizen Summit I

On the morning of November 20, 1999, organizers wondered anxiously whether enough residents would participate to make the event truly significant. As the morning progressed, a trickle of citizens turned into a stream of citizens from every part of the city. Over three thousand citizens came, demographically reflecting the composition of the city.

The use of small groups and technology helped the organizers manage a public conversation of unprecedented scale. Citizens sat randomly at ten- to twelve-person round banquet tables in the largest room at the Convention Center. Each table had a trained facilitator, many with long years of experience and well-honed skills (all three hundred had received three hours of training on the specifics of this event). The facilitators helped make participants comfortable and introduced new arrivals to their tablemates. Each table was equipped with a laptop computer as part of a roomwide wireless network. Each participant had a wireless polling keypad. Looking something like a television remote, these keypads allowed instant voting—much like the "audience lifeline," which connects the audience with the participants, on the television show *Who Wants to be a Millionaire?*

This combination of technology and process expertise was important. Lead facilitator Carolyn Lukensmeyer framed and defined tasks from the main stage. Following the opening, the facilitators guided a table conversation. One person at the table was responsible for gathering what citizens had said and typing it into the computer. This information was instantly transmitted to a "theme team" responsible for identifying common threads and themes. The emerging themes could then be used to frame questions for the audience to respond to using their polling keypads. The keypads allowed the mayor and the summit's facilitator to poll citizens throughout the program on questions ranging from demographics to policy priorities to their satisfaction with the event. The results of each poll appeared instantly on large screens at the front of the room. Williams could respond to the themes and preferences voiced by citizens in real time, letting citizens know their voices were being heard.

Citizens spoke clearly. They showed overwhelming support for the themes of Investing in Children and Youth and Strengthening Families and urged that they be combined into a comprehensive strategy. They expressed their exasperation, pain, and anger at the abysmal performance of the schools. At the conclusion of the summit, using their polling keypads, 94 percent of the participants said they had the opportunity to "fully participate," 91 percent of the participants rated the summit as "excellent" or "good," 96 percent said the technology added value to the forum, and 99 percent said Neighborhood Action was an important program.

## Processing Summit Results: Finalizing the Strategic Plan

The organizers collected over three hundred pages of ideas, concerns, and affirmations from citizens at the summit. Additional information was provided by a Neighborhood Action Web page, a discussion guide that was published in the *Washington Post* and *Washington Times* with a feedback form, and telephone lines available to citizens watching the summit live on cable television. A team of fifteen staff people analyzed and organized this information into common themes, presented a report of citizen priorities to the mayor's agency directors, and sent copies to every participant from the summit. At a cabinet retreat in December, senior officials used citizen priorities articulated at the summit to modify the City-wide Strategic Plan.

A Neighborhood Action Forum on January 29 brought citizens back together to assess the changes to the strategic plan and to have focused discussions about issues in their neighborhood. Despite being rescheduled from January 27 because of snow, more than fifteen hundred citizens came to the gymnasium at the University of the District of Columbia on a Saturday morning to join the conversation. Participants received the revised strategic plan as well as a document describing how the plan connected to citizen priorities. Once again, citizens participated in facilitated round-table discussions with wireless polling keypads.

Using input from the January 29 forum, the mayor and his agency directors finalized the citywide strategic plan in February. Aspirations and actions in the plan framed changes to the mayor's budget for fiscal year 2001. They earmarked over $700 million to match program priorities to citizen priorities in the mayor's budget request to city council. Following budget approval by the council, staff summarized the strategic plan into a twenty-eight-page citizen friendly report showing how it responded to citizens' desires.

## Implementation and Action

Citizens for the most part wanted profound and deep change—a transformation of dysfunctional systems that were no longer productive. Schools, human services, and regulatory functions were the main targets. Citizens also wanted improvements in their immediate environment—their neighborhoods.

The District adopted a multifaceted implementation plan. Early activities focused on the schools. The importance of schools in the minds of citizens defined a significant portion of the mayor's agenda and emboldened him to tackle governance in the District of Columbia Public Schools (DCPS).

Although DCPS was separately governed, it also was subject to Control Board intervention. The Control Board sharply restrained the school board's powers, naming advisers to a school committee to provide policy guidance and appointing senior administrators for the system. The mayor decided to tackle the issue of school governance by proposing an appointed board, a path taken by other big-city mayors. The proposal was met with substantial resistance because it limited local democracy. The mayor argued that well-qualified citizens tended not to run for school board. He actively and visibly negotiated with the city council, the school board, the Control Board, and the community on his proposal ultimately reaching a political compromise. A half-elected, half-appointed school board would now have full control over the schools.

The implementation of the strategic plan included a series of robust initiatives along with programs and actions linked together to work toward its goals. Two new initiatives—the Neighborhood Planning Initiative and the Neighborhood Services Initiative—joined with the Office of Neighborhood Action to create what is informally called the Neighborhood Action triangle. The Neighborhood Planning Initiative engages citizens in every neighborhood in the District to develop short- and medium-term action plans for improvements to their neighborhoods. The Neighborhood Services Initiative, using multiagency teams of employees works with citizens to tackle persistent problem areas.

## The Neighborhood Services Initiative

The Neighborhood Services Initiative (NSI) assumes that ward-based, cross-agency teams working together with the community will be far more effective in resolving issues through joint understanding and trust building than through traditional service delivery systems with little or no engagement with the neighborhood. In other words, a staff team drawn from different agencies working in partnership with neighbors to solve problems will be more effective than a single staff person working alone. Working collaboratively with neighborhood residents would require changes in the organization and its systems.

Simple in its principles but radical in its significance and ambitious intent, the NSI changes how the city does its business. Its approach is in stark contrast to the autonomy and independence enjoyed by agencies in prior years. NSI requires partnerships and places employee accountability at the ward level. The initiative has a profound impact on the way work is done inside the District government as agencies work to ensure that citizens receive the services they need. NSI intentionally embeds a new approach within the organizational culture that also can be used to tackle other complex problems.

The cross-agency Neighborhood Services teams primarily focus on persistently problematic areas registering high levels of community concern and interest, such as drug activity occurring in abandoned buildings or the spillover effects of poor apartment building maintenance in a neighborhood. These chronic problems absorb a disproportionate level of effort and resources amid few signs of progress. Neighborhood Services teams zero in on these problems, developing and implementing work plans in partnership with residents to help reclaim and stabilize their neighborhoods.

## Handling the Tough Problems and the Everyday Problems

One of the continuing challenges for government is balancing the tension between a desire to engage citizens in responding to specific challenges against the desire of citizens to find someone who can fix their problems. To combat this challenge, the NSI partners with the Customer Service Initiative (CSI), featuring a call center with a central number for all citizen requests. Each caller receives a tracking number for his or her complaint. The Call Center notifies the agency responsible for action and tracks the resulting actions. The Call Center focuses on common citizen-generated single-agency requests. A single request might identify the need to pick up a large item of trash or for trimming a tree or inspecting a problem property. Some requests appear to be directed toward a single agency yet require a multiple agency response. For example, in some neighborhoods, abandoned cars are used by drug dealers to stash their drugs so they cannot be arrested for possession. If the Department of Public Works tows the car, dealers quickly move another in to take its place. Only a coordinated response between the police department and public works can fix the problem.

A review of the number of citizens requests and the District's responses illustrates the challenge. In 1999, the Mayor's Office received nearly 440 requests for agency services each day (13,200 a month), the majority of which (61 percent to 75 percent) were misdirected or unfulfilled. Many requests remained outstanding for more than ninety days as unaccountable agency contacts and unreliable or nonexistent systems precluded follow-up. Few constituents were contacted during these ninety days, whether action was taken or not. Not surprisingly, approximately 25 to 50 percent of requests were resubmitted by dissatisfied constituents. Citizens experienced the District government at best as unresponsive, ineffective, and uncoordinated and at worst as extremely frustrating. If effective collaboration with citizens were to occur, District government needed to become a reliable partner. The NSI and CSI formed the primary strategy for rebuilding citizens' trust in the ability of local government to deliver services.

## Developing Core Teams

In order to engage citizens where they live, District government staff had to meet them as real and worthy partners. District employees would have to become knowledgeable about neighborhoods and their service needs. Familiar faces needed to be able to deliver on commitments to make meaningful and tangible change in their neighborhoods.

Each of the eight wards now has a core team made up of seven to twelve front-line workers and program managers from agencies with the most-needed services for that particular ward. A Neighborhood Services coordinator guides and manages their work. The coordinators facilitate problem solving by the group, work with other core team members to engage residents, and monitor progress on problem areas across their ward.

Initially, the NSI teams focused on connecting agencies dealing with various aspects of public safety, public health, and cleanliness to provide readily visible differences in the neighborhood environment as a means of rebuilding trust in government. Goals related to economic and health issues will be added as the effort matures.

Each team tackles a workload of persistent problem areas throughout their ward. As staff are out on the street, they learn about other issues and attend to these as well. These services help stabilize a neighborhood but are not sufficient to revitalize it. This is the task of the Neighborhood Planning Initiative.

## A Week in the Life Neighborhood Services in Ward 1

On Monday, two police sergeants, a housing inspector, and a fire marshal meet in front of an illegal rooming house to decide what to do with a variety of housing code violations: a gambling parlor, brothel, and drug distribution center in the basement; a non-working fire detection system; defective smoke detectors; and only one point of egress for the entire building. As they check with each other and seek advice from their superiors, a Neighborhood Service coordinator (NSC) locates a city lawyer and briefs the city administrator's office as to what is going on at 1512 Park Road. Decisions are made on the spot, and the neighbors congratulate the team at their next community meeting.

That Thursday night at 7:30, the Ward 1 NSC is explaining to the Quebec Street neighbors all the steps that were taken to abate the problems on Hobart Place. As he finishes, the police sergeant chimes in, describing the work of the Police Department. The inspector from public works adds what she can do about the trash problems, and the ward planner explains what will happen once new development comes to that area. The successful transformation of the Hobart Place neighborhood creates enthusiasm and disbelief among the Quebec Street neighbors. The residents resolve to organize, and the meeting ends with renewed hope and optimism. The NSC promises he will be back.

On a wintry Saturday morning, a seven-year-old boy finishes a street football game on Hobart Place as curious neighbors wonder why there are police officers, fire fighters, and Recreation Department workers right on the street where there used to be drug dealers. The seven year old finishes the game and tells the NSC that he is ready to help clean up the empty lot. The neighbors, many of whom have never met before, bring out doughnuts and hot chocolate while approximately twenty youths from seven to seventeen years of age sweep, shovel, and pick up a dozen bags of trash. A crew from public works chips in with a pick.

This is a brief snapshot of the weekly schedule of an NSC and his team. The ward-based, cross-functional, interagency, holistic approach to problem solving is slowly but surely turning around people's perspectives, changing the negative paradigms, and allowing citizens and front-line workers to see, hear, and participate with each other in cooperative and refreshingly unorthodox ways. A new city is at work.

## The Neighborhood Planning Initiative

In the late 1970s and early 1980s, neighborhood planning in the District of Columbia served as a national model for other cities. Over three hundred locally elected neighborhood representatives—Advisory Neighborhood commissioners—helped neighborhood planners develop ward plans: comprehensive documents informed by enormous data-gathering efforts and defined through a consultative process with citizens. By the time Mayor Williams took office, the Office of Planning, which once employed almost one hundred staff members, housed only eleven professional planners. Ward planning and neighborhood planning had become spotty and perfunctory. The District's neighborhoods paid dearly for the lack of thoughtful, strategic attention.

The Neighborhood Planning Initiative emerged from citizens at the summit and from the administration. Building on earlier successes at neighborhood planning in the District, it addresses three common shortcomings of neighborhood planning efforts both within the District and in other cities around the country:

- Different neighborhood planning efforts within the same neighborhood are often not coordinated with each other.
- Neighborhood plans are often not fully implemented.
- Neighborhood plans are often not connected to citywide strategic plans and budgets.

The design of the neighborhood planning process addresses the first shortcoming, and the linkages within the Neighborhood Action triangle largely address the next two. The linkage with Neighborhood Action provides a vehicle for carrying neighborhood issues and priorities forward to the citywide strategic plan and budget. The linkage with Neighborhood Services relates service interventions to longer-term planning goals. With these linkages, the Neighborhood Planning Initiative becomes a powerful tool for building and maintaining healthy, safe, and vital neighborhoods.

## The Scope of the Neighborhood Planning Initiative

Many cities that have initiated neighborhood planning programs do so by concentrating their efforts in specific neighborhoods and then expanding to reach most or all of the other neighborhoods. In Washington, D.C., the decision was made to work in all neighborhoods concurrently for two reasons. First, previous targeting decisions in the District had been made largely on political grounds, creating widespread distrust of the District's ability to select wisely. Second, and perhaps more important, if neighborhood plans were to become a major vehicle for driving the future budgets and citywide strategic plans, it would be unfair to be planning in some neighborhoods and not in others.

However, it was important to limit the reach in other ways. There are at least 120 named neighborhoods in the District. Creating a plan for each of them would be impossible. At the January Neighborhood Action Forum, planners floated a map grouping every neighborhood into one of thirty-nine neighborhood clusters. Citizens were asked to identify boundary issues at the forum, and planners then convened follow-up meetings to address them.

The Neighborhood Planning Initiative hired eight neighborhood planners—one for each ward—to staff the effort. Planners became partners with their respective NSCs on a variety of tasks. Operating on a very ambitious time frame, the planners had to complete the neighborhood plans prior to the next citizen summit in order to identify neighborhood issues to bring to the summit.

## Strategic Neighborhood Action Plans

Each neighborhood cluster completes a Strategic Neighborhood Action Plan (SNAP), with a profile of the neighborhood cluster, a citizen-developed vision for the neighborhood cluster that includes the essential ingredients for a livable community, and action plans for priority essential ingredients. Action plans include strategies for near- and medium-term improvements, as well as requests to be fed into the District's strategic planning and budgeting process.

Several structured workshops and a series of consultations with steering groups—some informal, some formal—in each cluster helped planners develop SNAPs. Through the SNAP development process, action plans begin to detail requests for specific agencies. Each agency must then review and respond to all of the requests. Agencies act on these requests when possible and provide a clear rationale when action is not possible. Certain requests require additional problem solving by agency staff, neighborhood planners, and the community. The SNAPs are finalized in a validation workshop with the community.

## Bringing New Voices to the Table

The first citizen summit largely reflected the makeup of the District in terms of representation by ward, race and ethnicity, and income level with one significant exception: youth. Significant parts of the strategic plan spoke to issues affecting youth, but few younger people were in the audience to share their perspective. Based on that recognition, the mayor committed to convening a summit for youth.

Youth do not do well in the District of Columbia. Sixteen percent of residents between sixteen and nineteen years old are not in school and not working compared to a national average of 8 percent and that of the worst state, New Mexico, at 13 percent. The rate of teen deaths by accident, homicide, and suicide is 159 per 100,000 teens ages fifteen through nineteen in the District. The national average is 54 deaths per 100,000 teens, with Nevada the worst state at 86 deaths per 100,000 teens (Kids Count, 1998). Other indicators confirm that youth do not do well in the District.

When approached about the possibility of a summit, young people were skeptical. Many felt that they had been used in the past by politicians to score political points without any commitment to change in return. They demanded a full youth-adult partnership through every phase of planning for the summit.

The administration worked with a design team dominated by young people. Focus groups with over four hundred youth participating helped the design team identify the issues to be discussed at the youth summit. Young people identified three principles that should guide planning for the summit:

- Genuine youth empowerment
- Youth-adult partnership in all phases, including the leadership of activities at the summit
- Commitment to real and tangible follow-through to ensure that systemic change would occur

They also insisted that they be able to walk away from the day having learned a skill or talked about something critical in their personal lives, as well as helping shape the city's policies and program for youths.

The event, The City Is Mine: Youth Summit 2000, took place on November 20. Fourteen hundred young people between the ages of fourteen and twenty-one had the opportunity to tell the community the problems they face while growing up in this city and what needed to be done to address these issues. They worked specifically on three major issues: safety and violence, education, and jobs and training. They also participated in workshops such as Joining Forces:

Youth/Police Relations; Bling, Bling: Real Life Success Stories; and Uncensored: The Real Deal about Sex, STDs, and Pregnancy.

In order to realize the promise of the summit, follow-up was critical. In December, 125 summit participants met with Mayor Williams and other city, community, business, and faith leaders to review the outcomes of the summit, suggest additional actions, and prioritize the recommendations. In February, 225 young people and adults gathered to hear the government's plans for responding to youth suggestions. Small group discussions provided input into the design of youth governance mechanisms and suggested ways to improve working relationships among organizations serving young people.

As a result of the summit, the city council created a permanent Youth Advisory Council. A number of young people visited Hampton, Virginia, and Portland, Oregon, to learn about their models and then formulated their own approach and lobbied the City Council to adopt it. The Youth Advisory Council gives youth in the District of Columbia an ongoing voice in budget and policy. In addition, the District realigned its budget to respond to youth priorities, and community-based organizations began to realign their work as well. Many of the youth who were trained to be facilitators at the Youth Summit went on to serve as facilitators for Citizen Summit II.

## Working Through a Strategic Management Cycle

Neighborhood Action's efforts to transform the District's governance are rooted in a strategic management cycle that holds government accountable for implementing the community's shared goals and priorities. The two-year cycle brings together citizen-driven planning—summits and neighborhood planning—with implementation and performance measurement tools. Each cycle informs the subsequent one, making it more comprehensive. The strategic management cycle include the following key elements:

> *Citizen Summit.* The summit and the follow-up forum drive the elements and priorities of the strategic plan. Summits are the capstone of the cycle, integrating past achievements with current aspirations and providing the core mechanism for citizens to drive the strategic plan.
>
> *Strategic plan.* The plan contains a vision, key themes, objectives, and action items for every objective.
>
> *Performance contracts.* Based on the objectives in the strategic plan, the mayor establishes a performance contract with every deputy mayor and

department head. The department heads extend these performance contracts to every member of management.

*Scorecards.* While performance contracts are increasingly common in government, few citizens know the content of these contracts. The District lifted the key elements out of each department head and deputy mayor's contract and printed scorecards. Each scorecard has a picture of the person and a checklist for his or her major performance goals for the year. The scorecards help keep the government accountable to citizens.

The first iteration of the cycle addressed each of these elements. As the cycle progresses, new elements emerge that inform the second iteration of the cycle:

*Neighborhood plans.* Draft SNAPs propose a series of action steps either for immediate action or to be included in the citywide strategic planning and budgeting process.

*Neighborhood Service resource needs.* Neighborhood Service work plans identify needs for which there are not sufficient resources. These needs then feed into the strategic planning process.

*Strategic plan and performance contract assessments.* The completion of the first round of the cycle yields data on how well the District performed in meeting objectives in the strategic plan.

## Holding the Second Summit and Moving into High Gear

Planning for Citizen Summit II provided an opportunity to learn from the first summit and to implement the citywide strategic planning process in the District fully. One of the shortcomings of the first summit was the lack of city employee involvement. Employees complained that they knew the District well and that since they would be charged with implementation, they should have a voice in the development of the plan. This time, five employee mini-summits were held, one for each theme in the plan. In addition, a special session brought in labor leaders who had been left out of major decisions. As a result of their participation, they were better positioned to become partners in the implementation of the plan.

In addition to preparing the draft plan, planners worked diligently to finalize and summarize the draft SNAPs for presentation at the summit. Designers struggled to find a balance between providing a performance report—which might be viewed primarily as public relations for the mayor—and finding ways for citizens to learn what was working and what needed improvement.

The world-shaking events of September 11 changed all the calculations. Three students from district public schools, winners of a contest sponsored by *National Geographic*, were killed with their teachers when their plane crashed into the Pentagon. As October 6, the day of the summit, approached, Reagan National Airport remained closed. Tourism had almost disappeared, and by some reports, as many as twenty thousand service workers had been laid off.

The agenda of the summit reflected the new times. The mood of the day was more subdued. An interfaith ceremony conducted by leaders of seven different faith traditions helped participants mourn those who died and to acknowledge their common humanity. While many were moved to tears, there also was a desire to get on with the business of the summit.

Indeed, while many at the first summit were intrigued by the technology, at the second summit, the technology just became part of the program as citizens came prepared to work. The rest of the day focused on two tasks. First, participants examined the draft 2002–2004 strategic plan, which reflected input from the first strategic plan and the SNAPS. Participants discussed how to improve the plan, using the same format as at the first summit. Then participants joined others from their neighborhood clusters. While in their cluster groupings, citizens reviewed priorities from their SNAP plans and discussed implementation ideas.

At the end of the summit, participants were of two minds. In part, they expressed frustration that there was not enough time to work on the plan because of the introductory interfaith ceremony. They also affirmed the need to recommit to the democratic process and strengthen civil society in the aftermath of the September 11 events.

Following the summit, staff again worked to digest the enormous amount of data generated. In addition, a further intensive effort combined the draft strategic plan, the data from the summit, the draft SNAPs, and priorities from Neighborhood Services into priorities for every neighborhood cluster in the District. These priorities will be presented to citizens in the form of a revised strategic plan at the follow-up Neighborhood Action Forum. Strategic priorities will then be reflected in the administration's budget request to the City Council several months later.

# The Path Forward

Neighborhood Action comprises a powerful set of ideas and actions focused on two critical objectives: deeply engaging citizens in the governance of their city and building a high-performance local government organization that responds to citizen needs and delivers on its promises. Both aspects are essential in order to rebuild trust between citizens and government.

Neither would have been possible without the leadership and the commitment of Mayor Williams. His role in articulating the felt need and core values was essential for moving forward. Similarly, the effort would not have moved far without the framework, process expertise, and technology provided by AmericaSpeaks and the desire and endless energy of a set of core staff members.

This partnership allowed the District of Columbia to engage citizens in the development of a strategic plan perhaps more deeply and effectively than any other jurisdiction in the country. Numerous other forums offer citizens opportunities to participate in governance. Citizens who want to work in their own neighborhood can join hands and tackle problems with the Neighborhood Service Initiative, or they can engage in the Neighborhood Planning Initiative, developing and driving the strategic agenda for their neighborhood. Every two years, citizens can participate in the Citizen Summit, setting the overall direction for their community.

The District still has a long way to go. Distressed neighborhoods, the disturbing statistics on youth, and dysfunctional regulatory systems will not be changed in a year or two. But the District has put in place an effective model for collaborative change that puts it on the path toward true self-governance and transformative long-term results. The anachronistic Control Board put in place in 1995 has long since shut its doors.

CHAPTER FOURTEEN

# EQUAL PARTNERS, SHARED VISION

## The Colorado Partnership for Educational Renewal

Carol A. Wilson

*The following story describes a long-term collaboration between school districts and universities and its efforts to build a broader constituency by working together with citizens. Over more than a decade, the Colorado Partnership for Educational Renewal (CoPER) built its credibility by bringing together unlikely partners and engaging them in constructive dialogue about educational renewal. Because of this credibility, the partnership has become an important stabilizing element for state educational policy in a highly charged, fast-changing political environment.*

*The Colorado Partnership illustrates several essential elements of long-term collaboration. Strong, facilitative leadership from both the staff and the governing board kept the organization focused on its essential role as a convening organization. The working relationships built among leaders from school systems and higher education over an extended period of time helped CoPER extend its credibility to new arenas such as state educational policy. It hosted a series of constructive forums over the years that led to a number of innovative responses to educational challenges. The combination of good information and a constructive process helped diverse stakeholders work through controversial issues in ways that led to results. Persistent and engaging outreach to educational leaders and policymakers established CoPER as a prominent convening and problem-solving organization in the educational arena.*

During the mid-1980s wave of criticism and heated debate about the public schools, significant collaborative linkages began to form between public schools and higher education. The impetus for these linkages was the vast research, experience, and practical insight of educator John I. Goodlad. Completing the most extensive study of schooling to date, Goodlad put forth the reasonable and somewhat revolutionary idea that schools and universities should collaborate for their mutual benefit (Goodlad, 1984).

Although the connection may seem an obvious and natural one, in reality a huge chasm existed between the public schools and the colleges and universities that prepare teachers for those schools. Perpetuating and exacerbating the chasm, educators in the schools and universities engaged in ceremonial finger pointing, characterized by comments such as, "Those public schools should just do their job and send us better-prepared students," and "Those college and university professors haven't stepped foot in a classroom for decades. How can they presume to know how to prepare teachers for the real world of teaching!"

Despite such obstacles, in 1983, Calvin Frazier, Colorado's commissioner of education, invited John Goodlad to the state with a view toward creating school-university clusters to address particular themes and issues similar to Goodlad's earlier work in California. This began a relationship that eventually led to the formation of the Colorado Partnership for Educational Renewal (CoPER) following Goodlad's 1985 founding of the Center for Educational Renewal (CER) at the University of Washington. Through the CER and with funding from several national foundations, Goodlad launched a comprehensive school-university partnership initiative focused on renewing schooling and the education of educators. This effort led to the creation of the National Network for Educational Renewal (NNER), a network of the school-university partnerships. Because of Goodlad's prior association with Colorado, he invited interested Colorado superintendents and deans to form a partnership and apply for membership in the NNER, which was to have twelve partnership settings.

After numerous meetings and discussions, leaders of seven school districts and two universities created a formal partnership in 1986. Membership in the NNER required meeting several minimum essentials addressing the school-university partnership concept, purposes, agenda, and structure. The minimum essentials called for a formal, mutually beneficial, interinstitutional relationship, accompanied by processes and structures "through which each *equal* party to a collaborative agreement will seek to draw on the complementary strengths of the other *equal* parties in advancing its self-interests" (Sirotnik and Goodlad, 1988, p. 26). It was to have a governing board, preferably composed of superintendents and deans, a modest secretariat including an executive director and support services, an operating budget, institutional endorsement, and task forces or work groups, among other requirements.

## Building a Partnership of Equals

In the beginning, an astute observer may have noticed signs suggesting that it would take time for the equal aspect of the partnership to take hold. In meetings with potential partnership settings, Goodlad had warned of the long-established attitudes of higher education "going out to help the unwashed" when working with public schools. He noted the sentiment of "noblesse oblige" on the part of university faculty and the acquiescence of public school educators in acting as receivers of knowledge that had been created at the university (Goodlad, 1990). This may reflect a perception held more broadly in society. A false dichotomy has long existed, assigning the creation of knowledge to the university and the use of that knowledge to the public schools. Much earlier and along these same lines, John Dewey noted the separation of "head" and "hand" in American educational institutions and the damage this does to learning, when the reality is that each informs the other and cannot stand apart.

Goodlad, as did Dewey, pointed to a fuller view of knowledge creation and use. He suggested that all educators be involved in the creation of knowledge that was useful and that this be done through inquiry into the circumstances of the school and what might be done to improve learning for all students.

The idea of simultaneous renewal of schooling and teacher education implied that both institutions look critically at what they were doing. Because the superintendents and deans together decided to form the partnership, the perceived attitudes about the university and school relationship were not so apparent in their interactions but became obvious in the way the agenda began to play out. As the initial working agenda emerged, attention became focused on the public schools. There was an assumption on the part of higher education that the universities were functioning quite well and what really required attention was the public schools. The public debate about schools gave support to this somewhat one-sided perception, and activity began.

Initially working through special projects and initiatives, CoPER's efforts did indeed focus on school renewal. The projects were not seen as ends in themselves, but as "starter kits" for ongoing renewal. They were ways to develop and cultivate relationships between and among schools and universities over the long term, along with some short-term successes, thereby laying the foundation for continued efforts in identified focus areas.

In 1990 and 1991, three influences interacted to expand the singular focus on school renewal to simultaneous renewal, that is, to include teacher preparation at the university level. One influence was the reformation of the NNER and its accompanying requirements, which essentially asked that participating universities fully engage in the simultaneous renewal agenda, that is, attend also to renewing teacher education. CoPER's focus on school renewal was the common experience across the country, and Goodlad thought it essential to draw attention to the full meaning of "simultaneous renewal." Accompanying this phase of work was a clear explication of the moral dimensions of teaching in our democracy. The Agenda for Education in a Democracy, outlined in *The Moral Dimensions of Teaching* (Goodlad, Soder, and Sirotnik, 1990), expanded and deepened the original issues undergirding the NNER.

Goodlad and his associates clearly delineated the public purposes of schooling in and for democracy and the responsibilities of educators in those schools. Four themes emerged that were to ground the work of NNER school-university partnerships:

> *Enculturating the young into our social and political democracy.* Children and youth need to learn what it means to function as citizens of the United States, as well as learn about the country's undergirding principles, history, documents, and structures.
>
> *Access to knowledge.* All students should benefit from equal and excellent education, which should enable them to participate in the human conversation.
>
> *Nurturing pedagogy.* Teachers must acquire a repertoire of teaching practices that will enable them to nurture every student's learning.
>
> *Stewardship of the schools.* Educators are concerned about all students in the school and about the school as a learning community. Educators continually inquire into the circumstances of the school and its students, working with colleagues and others to renew the school as a normal part of their responsibility.

A second influence was Colorado's Educator Licensing Act of 1991, which included standards for programs preparing teachers and placed new requirements on the universities, including expectations for closer ties with the public schools. Several of CoPER's leaders served on the newly created Professional Standards Board, bringing issues of democracy and the importance of simultaneous renewal to bear in the larger context.

The third influence was new leadership from the universities in the form of three new deans of education. These leaders, in concert with several strong superintendents on the governing board, saw the possibilities in CoPER's mission, and especially in the light of the needs reflected in the licensing policy, and they began working earnestly to realize that potential. The combined nudge from the larger context—the NNER and the state—and the fresh and potent leadership invigorated CoPER and brought the partners to a new level of understanding of simultaneous renewal and its promise.

## Layers of Collaboration

A salient vehicle for simultaneous renewal in education is partner schools: public schools that join with teacher education programs to help prepare new teachers, provide ongoing professional development for faculty in the school and the university, engage in inquiry and research that lead to improvement of the school and the teacher education program, and most important, provide exemplary education for all students. The union between schools and teacher preparation programs for several of these purposes is also often referred to as a professional development school. The concept of partner schools goes further by grounding this work in understandings of what it means to teach and learn in a social and political democracy. Partner schools also share a commitment to renewal through ongoing action-oriented inquiry and reflection.

A few universities worked closely with their school partners to create and nurture partner schools. During this time, CoPER secured several large grants to support partner schools' work, and it was then that the complexities of pair-wise partnerships within the larger partnership began to emerge. A basic principle of CoPER and the NNER was that the school is the unit of change and analysis, which meant that those in the school (and, in partner schools, those in the school and the university partner) identify their needs and find appropriate ways to address them. Sometimes "alternative drummers," people outside the school who could bring different lenses through which to view the school and its issues, could help, but the work was of the school community to be done by the school community. The common bond was commitment to the need for simultaneous renewal and the grounding in democratic principles.

To balance the focus on individual schools with their larger context, the school district rather than the individual school made the commitment to CoPER, for two reasons. First, unless the district provided support for individual schools that were recognized for various forms of excellence, those schools would become targets, and progress would not be sustained. Second, schools engaged in various endeavors were learning useful lessons, and it was important to share these lessons beyond the individual school. The hope was that the district as a whole would benefit from what was learned and gained at individual schools.

For the university's part, Goodlad recognized that the responsibility for preparing new teachers went beyond the college of education, especially when one considers the amount of time prospective teachers spend in general studies and their academic majors. This work called for collaboration within the university between colleges of education and colleges of arts and sciences, something that was even rarer than collaboration between schools and teacher education programs. Asking colleges of education and colleges of arts and sciences to collaborate with the school, thereby forming a tripartite relationship, gave the two university-based partners neutral ground on which to create new ways of working with each other and with their school partners.

As partner schools developed, the partners began to notice disparate levels of resources directed to the work. Two universities moved to base their entire teacher education programs on partner schools, while others paid minimal attention to their development and use. Some school districts invited and encouraged more participation than others. Those who put more energy into them were concerned that the idea would be diluted by the "low-energy" partner schools, particularly as CoPER began to realize the policy implications of partner schools. Successful efforts could lead to state funding streams in support of partner schools that required more resources and were perceived to produce better results. In addition, policy support in terms of reward structures for university faculty had to be examined, because current policy did more to inhibit than promote university faculty involvement in schools.

As a way to help the partners develop a shared vision of partner schools beyond the initiating concept, CoPER staff facilitated a series of discussions and examinations of the partner school concept, and over the course of two years, they developed a set of characteristics or criteria for partner schools. These were approved by the board after many discussions and published in a document for use across CoPER. The "pair-wise partnerships" found the document useful for established partner schools, as well as for those that were just forming, because it provided a common goal toward which all were moving, albeit at different paces and in different ways.

## Connecting with and Influencing the Larger Community

Because CoPER was the only organization in the state representing both schools and universities, its leaders found themselves on a wide array of committees and task forces in various state-level initiatives. Of primary importance was membership on the newly established Professional Standards Boards, created by the 1991 Educator Licensing Act. One board was to address teacher and special services provider licensing and the other principal and administrator licensing. These boards were appointed by the governor, confirmed by the Senate, and served as advisers to the State Board of Education.

When the Professional Standards Boards were formed, several CoPER leaders were nominated for the Teacher and Special Services Professional Standards Board. Nominating and confirming these leaders' membership on the board seemed an acknowledgment that the ideas and principles CoPER represented were coherent, positive, and systemic as they encompassed teacher education and schooling. The nine-member board, consisting of educators and community members, was charged with fleshing out the Licensing Act for teachers and special service providers, developing standards, and then developing the rules and regulations by which Colorado teachers would be licensed. Essentially, the profession was given more self-responsibility.

The CoPER and NNER ideas found fertile ground as the working framework was developed and the standards explicated. Especially promising was the initial response to CoPER and NNER's moral grounding in democratic principles and the role of schooling in a democracy. One of the five licensing standards required teachers to understand and also engage in democratic practices in their classrooms. While this standard was not as far-reaching as it might have been, it expressed and represented an essential idea that has long been neglected in public education. As the board reviewed standards developed by prestigious national organizations, it noted an absence of explicit statements having to do with a public school educator's role in a social and political democracy.

The board also began to fill several other voids, suggesting that school professionals be stewards of their learning communities and school professionals serve as links to the larger community, including higher education. Regarding approval of teacher education programs, the board sought legitimate ways of promoting school-university collaboration, and also collaboration between teacher education and the arts and sciences. Thus, the Professional Standards Board was in a position to encourage simultaneous renewal through the standards for school professionals and through the teacher education program approval standards. Doing so not only allowed others beyond the Colorado Partnership access to these principles but also strengthened the work within CoPER, as the larger community verified the significance of the partnership's work.

Many of the fundamental ideas, such as school-university collaboration, found strong support at the state policy level in recognition that the existing fragmented approach to education was undermining progress. Colorado values the local nature of decision making on important issues in communities, but also suffers from the accompanying fragmentation. For several years, various organizations had held summits and other forums seeking more coherence and collaboration among the myriad groups working on educational reform. Furthermore, there was broad consensus that while standards could be used punitively and counterproductively, if used constructively, they could be a galvanizing force for advancing educational reform. Standards forced statewide discussion about what is important in teaching and learning. Most important for CoPER, it was seen as a legitimate and viable effort to reduce the traditional competition among the institutions of higher education themselves and between those institutions and school districts.

Educators Calvin Frazier and David Imig note, "Ideally, in the field of education, local and state policy making should reinforce each other in the search for effective strategies to enhance public goals" (Frazier and Imig, 1999, p. 9). Moving toward coherent and compatible programs, several CoPER universities, in collaboration with their school partners, brought together the hopes and requirements of the new licensing standards with their deeper grounding in the shared CoPER and NNER agenda. These renewing programs had the dual motivation of commitment to the simultaneous renewal agenda and consistency with state requirements. CoPER found opportunities to convene discussions about various aspects of the policy work underway, sometimes to share information about current successful practices that might inform policy, sometimes to share concerns and work through difficult issues.

More recently, other educational reforms have come to Colorado, bringing a policy environment less supportive of education. Consequently, CoPER's governing board decided to use regular board meetings to address policy concerns and develop appropriate responses. Program and operations oversight were assigned to the program committee, and the board began focusing on policy-related issues of common concern. With support from two local foundations, the Rose Community Foundation and the Denver Foundation, a governing board task force developed a policy matrix to guide reflection and analysis of district, college and university, and state policies to determine their contribution to or impediment of progress on the CoPER and NNER agenda.

During the two years of discussions, as issues and agreements emerged, the board formed creative and productive responses. Individual district and university issues could be addressed by the respective sites. Collectively, CoPER gained further insight into its functioning, particularly as a citizen organization in the state. In the light of a stewardship role regarding the state policy environment, these steps included having op-ed articles published in key state newspapers to broaden the public dialogue about the purposes of schooling in the United States; convening a team of school and university leaders who visited another state to talk with school, university, and state leaders about the statewide testing program and its accompanying information infrastructure, and also inviting that commissioner of education to Colorado; and creating a broad-based policy committee that included legislators, school board members, business leaders, the media, public school leaders, and university leaders, who in turn carried CoPER and NNER principles into their respective arenas.

The work, which continues, has evolved into a set of themes, guiding continued inquiry by the board, its policy committee, and other pertinent groups:

- The nature of quality teaching and appropriate ways of evaluating it
- The role of partner schools in teacher education
- The characteristics of a fair and effective accountability system
- Finding a common focus and means of balancing perspectives for the decision-making framework for public education
- The public schools' unique role in serving the public good

Using these themes as guides and Frazier and Imig's characteristics that good policies in a democratic society "must be people sensitive and recognize the worth of the individual" and "must recognize the importance of accountability in terms of the stewardship of the resources and advancing the public purpose," CoPER participants employ inquiry and reflection as essential components of policy renewal. Such a course offers a way for the collaborative to embody the approach it promotes for individual partners as stewards of educational renewal, that is, engaging in inquiry, reflection, dialogue, and action, thereby contributing to renewal in the state. It has also yielded synergistic and complementary strategies and outcomes, strategies illustrated by the governing board's way of working with policy issues, and outcomes illustrated by the following array of results.

## Communication

Layers of collaboration in and across school districts universities, and the broader communities, facilitate work on new initiatives, such as addressing the teacher shortage and galvanizing groups to respond to immediate issues, such as new requirements for teacher licensing.

## State Policy

CoPER leaders serve on key statewide committees, ensuring that more than the usual commentators and the usual issues are heard. Examples resulting from their participation include Senate Bill 99–154 on teacher preparation and licensing, which calls for closer linkages between teacher education and the schools, particularly in teacher candidates having extended, well-supervised field (school) experience, and closer collaboration between the arts and sciences and teacher education, thus encouraging partner school development. In addition, the democratic ideal, which forged new ground in earlier state policy development, remained in the new teacher licensing standards, despite attempts from some policymakers and others to remove it.

## Partner Schools

Agreed-on partner school criteria toward which to work, and which have helped inform state policy, serve to support and guide partner school development. CoPER's early research pointing to the efficacy of partner schools affirms its work, as do anecdotal reports from school principals and personnel departments concerning the quality of new teachers coming from partner school experiences. More than sixty well-functioning partner schools are educating hundreds of teacher candidates and thousands of public school students. Students in these schools say they benefit from having more adults (teacher candidates) to help them, and teacher candidates talk of the confidence they gain from the in-depth and far-reaching experience in authentic situations. Teachers in the schools speak of the new teaching approaches they learn from teacher candidates and a desire to evaluate their own practices. University faculty report a deeper understanding of the issues facing schools and the consequent reshaping of teacher education classes and programs.

## Teacher Recruitment

A scholarship program exists to recruit high school and community college students into teaching, with particular emphasis on underrepresented groups. More than eighty participants are now in partner universities' teacher education programs, and more will be recruited. In addition, a working group continues to develop and promote strategies for recruiting, such as the Teachers Recruiting Students into Teaching effort, which provides teachers with information and techniques for helping their students consider postsecondary education in general, and teaching in particular. CoPER educators have established or revitalized numerous Future Educators of America clubs in secondary schools and community colleges, bringing many young people into service-learning projects, as well as encouraging them to consider becoming teachers.

## Teacher Retention

With the view that appropriate support during a teachers' first teaching years will help them remain in the profession, all sixteen school districts participated in "critical friends" visits, with critical friends teams across CoPER reviewing each others' new-teacher induction programs and making suggestions for improvement. As a result and with CoPER grants, each district has strengthened its program, using best practices with their new teachers. Among these is the use of mentors and ensuring that mentors have the appropriate training. CoPER-wide training, as well as individual district training, helps mentors gain effectiveness.

## Diversity

Given CoPER's focus on democracy and educating all students well, a Diversity Cadre continues to expand and offer support to teachers, whole school communities, and teacher education programs. Educators in the cadre are selected for their recognized success in working with a broad range of student needs and student populations. More than sixty cadre members offer workshops, individual coaching, mentoring of new teachers, working with teacher candidates, assistance in teacher education classes, and much more.

## Leadership Development

A Teacher Leadership Initiative stimulated more than five hundred educators to examine their beliefs and understandings of their responsibilities for helping children and youth become participants in our democracy. They did this by working with state-mandated content standards and developing strategies to ensure that democratic practices and content were integrated into the standards. Called Finding Democracy in Standards-Based Education, this initiative helped shape meaningful responses to new state requirements that could have been treated as technicalities rather than substantive opportunities. Teachers and other educators see more clearly the critical connection between democracy and their roles, which has implications for how they teach, how they group students, which students get which materials, how decisions are made in the classroom, and other matters.

Participation in the Institute for Educational Inquiry's Leadership Associates Program and replication of that program in Colorado has brought school faculty and administrators, teacher educators, and arts and sciences faculty together to inquire into particular issues and develop appropriate responses. For example, one team evaluated the degree to which schools and the university were using democratic practices. The results were surprising, and changes in decision-making processes and curriculum soon followed.

## Professional Development

In addition to the professional development in many of these examples, CoPER provides professional development opportunities as particular needs arise and as interest dictates. One example is Socratic Seminars, which school, community college, and university faculty alike find helpful. The seminars promote careful reading, substantive discussion, and critical thinking. It is a specific strategy that works in the classroom, as well as for a group researching specific areas. Hundreds of CoPER educators have participated in Socratic Seminar workshops and now use this approach in their classrooms and other settings.

# Summing Up

CoPER's experience suggests lessons for both leadership and collaboration, many of which overlap. First, CoPER's success depended (and still depends) on leaders who understood the power of collaboration and were willing to step forward for the collective. These individuals could lead as peers and also follow as leaders.

At the same time, as a group, CoPER leaders had to determine goals that spoke to both their individual and shared interests. Essentially, broader goals responded more easily to parochial needs, allowing for individual circumstance and response. Balancing self-interest of an individual or particular institution and the common good provides an ongoing challenge, but along with inclusive leaders, experiencing success as a whole and garnering credibility from the broader public helps keep the seesaw level.

Leaders with credibility and positional power who will use these assets to move the organization and the work make a dramatic difference. These leaders manifest strategic, far-seeing qualities and strive for immediate results within the context of long-term, complex goals.

The importance of leadership at different levels cannot be underestimated. Superintendents and deans who were willing to step forward for the whole proved vital. Similarly, associate deans, assistant superintendents, curriculum directors, teachers, principals, and others provided leadership with peers and others on key initiatives and daily tasks, creating a web of support and accomplishment throughout CoPER. Another factor has been continuity in a director—someone who can work with schools and universities, has credibility in both, is willing to work as both a convener and catalyst, and will do so for the long term.

At the same time, leadership from the national level—John Goodlad and the NNER—reminded CoPER members they were part of something larger yet and shared the values that are the very essence of democracy.

For the collaborative, one overarching lesson is that CoPER's work must both respond and contribute to the realities of its context. This is an essential part of the stewardship inherent in its agenda. In order to do so, CoPER must sustain and continually renew a viable structure and a deep understanding of and commitment to the substance of the work itself.

CoPER's position allows it to work in the larger context, informing state policy, because of its history and credibility. The diversity of its membership reflects the broader community. School districts, universities, and community colleges of varying size, demographics, and locales, joined together over time sharing a vision respecting individual differences, bring a potent voice to the dialogue. Such a partnership cannot be easily dismissed as a single interest group advocating narrow responses to complex issues or as a group reacting to particular policies. Rather, with well-developed relationships and the ability to convene groups across school districts and higher education institutions, CoPER and organizations like it can serve as a credible source of ideas, articulating its moral grounding in ways that help inform policy and practice.

Changes in political leadership and corresponding changes in policy direction bring opportunities and challenges. Because of its makeup and credibility, CoPER, along with other organizations with similar concerns, helps provide a steady focus on the public purposes of education, transcending the vicissitudes of political leadership. This network of associations—a central aspect of a healthy civil society—plays an essential stabilizing role at both state and local levels.

Much remains to be done. The democratic process itself relies on informed voices willing to remain in dialogue. The tensions and pulls will not cease, but there is reason to hope the dialogue can move to increasingly higher levels. It is critical to create and sustain opportunity for broad—and deep—dialogue. With this in mind, given CoPER's membership, history, and sense of purpose, it can, in John Gardner's words, act as a "constituency for the whole."

CHAPTER FIFTEEN

# SCENARIOS

## Catalysts for Civic Change

David D. Chrislip, James Butcher, Adam Kahane

*The forecasting denoted by* chih *involves two essential activities. First,* chih *involves the bringing into focus of selected possible future events along with the conditioning features of the past and present that form the context out of which these events may emerge. Secondly,* chih *entails a casting of the form of the future in such fashion and with such persuasive authority as to invite sympathy and participation.*

DAVID L. HALL AND ROGER T. AMES (1987)

*Scenarios provide a powerful artifact for enhancing strategic planning and visioning. When groups have a deep understanding of possible future contexts, they are better prepared to develop robust and well-grounded visions and strategies, and beyond that, to influence their future for the better. A number of American communities and regions have used civic scenarios to help prepare for an uncertain future. Missoula, Montana, used them to help with land use planning and population growth management. The Central Carolinas region used scenarios to launch a major initiative—Voices & Choices—to address quality-of-life issues associated with population growth and urban sprawl. The Boston region used scenarios to help prepare its nonprofit sector to meet future challenges in the human services arena.*

*Although scenarios provided a central element for each of these initiatives, other aspects of collaboration contributed to their success. Each example began with a broadly credible convening group willing to use its influence to encourage collaboration and bring others to the table. A carefully designed process and skillful process experts helped guide stakeholders through difficult and controversial points. New relationships and skills for working together brought strength and credibility to the immediate results of the collaboration (Missoula) and to future initiatives emerging from these efforts (Voices & Choices, Boston).*

Since the early 1990s, countries, regions, and communities have used scenario thinking as a tool for effecting societal change. In a civic scenario project, a group of citizens and civic leaders, drawn from a broad range of sectors and organizations, works together to understand what is happening, what might happen, and what should happen in their area. They then act together on that shared understanding and vision.

One of the early applications of scenarios as a tool for societal problem solving took place in South Africa in 1991. During the tumultuous transition away from apartheid, the Mont Fleur project brought together a range of stakeholders from across South African society, including community activists, conservative politicians, African National Congress officials, trade unionists, academics, establishment economists, and corporate executives. They came together to develop a set of alternative stories about South Africa's future in order to provoke debate and encourage progress in the country (see Figure 15.1).

The "Ostrich" scenario pointed out the risk and futility of the white government's trying to prevent or avoid a negotiated settlement with the black majority. A second scenario, "Lame Duck," envisioned a prolonged transition with a constitutionally weakened government. Because the government "purports to respond to all, but satisfies none," investors hold back, and growth and development languish in a mood of deep uncertainty. In 1991, the majority political parties were working toward a coalition government. The Lame Duck scenario allowed people to see the potential dangers of coalition governments and decide how to mitigate them. Another scenario, "Icarus," suggested that a black government could come to power on a wave of public support, embark on a huge, unsustainable public spending program, and consequently destroy the economy. This was the first time that a team including prominent left-wing economists had discussed the possibility of a new government's trying to do too much. Finally, the "Flight of the Flamingoes" scenario outlined a positive and successful transition: everyone in the society rises slowly and steadily together.

The Mont Fleur process, together with countless other projects, workshops, and meetings, helped provide the foundation of relationships for the "miraculous" 1994 shift to majority rule. The project contributed to the building of a common language for talking across groups about the opportunities and challenges facing the country, and, hence, about a way forward. In the fearful and confused South Africa of the early 1990s, the Mont Fleur team's message that a positive Flight of the Flamingoes future was possible had a strong impact. One of the team members said, "We mapped out in very broad terms the outline of a successful outcome, which is now being filled in. We captured the way forward of those of us committed to finding a way forward." Mont Fleur contributed to the way in which South African political parties approached the pivotal and ultimately successful

### FIGURE 15.1. MONT FLEUR SCENARIOS.

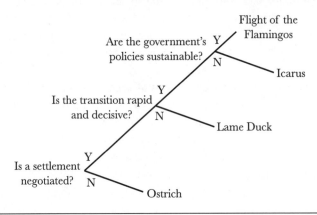

constitutional negotiations as well as to the surprising shift in economic policy of the victorious African National Congress. In 1999, eight years after the scenario project, one of the members of the Mont Fleur team, on being appointed governor of the South African Reserve Bank, referred to the scenarios' work: "We will not be an Icarus."

Since Mont Fleur, scenarios have been used in many settings, both national and international. Civic scenario processes have helped reframe mental models, develop shared commitment through dialogue, and regenerate energy and optimism for collective action (Kahane, 2001).

## Using Scenarios in the Civic Arena

By making different yet plausible assumptions about important but uncertain factors affecting the future, stakeholders construct a series of stories—scenarios—about how the future might unfold. These provocative, divergent, and relevant stories expose challenging dimensions of possible futures that communities and regions may face in coming years. By developing a deeper understanding of possible future environments, communities and regions can make better, more grounded, and more realistic decisions.

Communities and regions use scenarios in two ways: as a catalyst for working together and for decision making. As a catalyst for collaboration, scenarios offer a means for creating a common agenda for moving forward. Mutual learning and exploration build shared understanding of possible future environments. In the Central Carolinas region, Voices & Choices, a civic organization, used scenarios to set a regional agenda for dealing with the impacts of population growth and urban sprawl and as a catalyst for collaborative action. Stakeholders in Missoula, Montana, used scenarios to make decisions about land use and community planning strategies for dealing with population growth. In the Boston region, the Goldberg Seminars brought together a wide range of stakeholders to develop strategies for coping with revolutionary changes in state and federal funding of human services (see Figure 15.2).

## Voices & Choices: Scenarios in the Central Carolinas Region

"Is Charlotte doomed to copy the urban sprawl that characterizes Atlanta? Will Rock Hill and other cities ringing the Queen City retain their unique identity and charm, or become ozone-choked bedroom communities?" These were some of the questions Voices & Choices, the Central Carolinas' regional civic organization, hoped to answer in a regional summit to be held in November 1998. Recently completed civic scenarios provided the tool for getting at these questions.

That first regional summit was the culmination of years of analysis of the region's problems and the first major initiative of Voices & Choices. Between 1990 and 1998, the region's population had grown by 14 percent each year. Recent forecasts

## FIGURE 15.2. USING SCENARIOS IN THE PUBLIC ARENA.

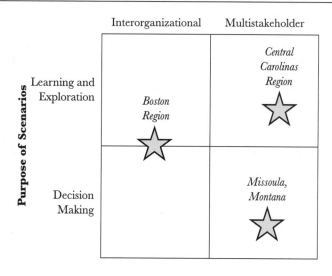

indicate another 300,000 residents will be added to its current 1.8 million by 2010. The rapid growth has brought prosperity and problems. Ozone levels exceeded federal clean air standards. New development devoured large tracts of rural open space and agricultural land. The region's water quality deteriorated as erosion and pollution increased. Traffic-clogged freeways and feeder roads slowed traffic, creating transportation bottlenecks. To top off these challenges, the region had no history of planning or concerted regional action. Persuading fourteen counties to work together seemed like herding cats to many regional leaders.

Voices & Choices had been formed specifically to address these issues by four influential regional organizations: the Foundation for the Carolinas, *Charlotte Observer*, Carolina's Partnership, and the Urban Institute at the University of North Carolina Charlotte. By engaging citizens across the region, Voices & Choices hoped to build a consensus on a regional vision that would lead to action on the region's major problems.

As a first step toward a vision, Voices & Choices decided to use scenarios as a catalyst. By exposing possible futures, citizens could begin to identify characteristics of the region they considered positive and those they wanted to avoid. In the summer of 1998, Voices & Choices organized a working group to develop the scenarios. More than forty people from all sectors and from throughout the region gathered to create three provocative stories about the future of the Central Carolinas Region.

The scenarios workshop began with the identification of ten driving forces, defined as the most significant, and unpredictable, factors affecting the future of the region. These driving forces ranged from the impacts of the global economy, to the nature of government policy, to the willingness of citizens within the region to work together.

## Driving Forces: The Future of the Central Carolinas Region

- Rate and nature of population change
- Degree to which credible information sources (about regional issues) and delivery mechanisms exist
- Strength and regional effects of global economy
- Regional capacity to attract and retain business, industry, and employers
- Willingness of citizens to change, lead, and serve
- Nature of, availability, and willingness to embrace application of technology
- Willingness to work together as a region
- Direction and level of government regulatory and tax policy
- Attitudes toward education (willingness to invest)
- Capacity to match, govern, and maintain infrastructure and land use and development

By making different assumptions about these factors, the scenarios working group developed three stories they believed would stimulate the thinking of the region's citizens and, they hoped, provoke new responses. The first scenario, "Whatever Will Be, Will Be," describes a region that rests on its current success. But current success without foresighted action ultimately leads to deterioration. Economic growth levels off, environmental problems spiral out of control, new development squeezes out farmland and open space as land prices skyrocket, and progress in transportation comes to a dead stop as bickering regional entities stall action. Charlotte looks more and more like Atlanta, with its traffic-clogged highways and urban sprawl.

The second scenario, "As Good As It Gets," portrays a very different world. Because of strong regional organizations and active civic engagement, the region learns to manage new growth and development in ways that enhance its environment and quality of life. New transit taxes lead to new solutions in rapid transit. A regional environmental authority manages land, air, and water. Although schools continue to decline in the first few years, lottery funds eventually help improve education. By 2015, the Central Carolinas region has become a shining success and a model for other regions in the country.

In "If Not for Bad Luck," the third scenario, what can go wrong does. A severe drought beginning in 1999 spells the end for local agriculture. Air quality warnings become routine and bring an end to federal highway money. War in the Middle East exacerbates these problems as oil prices skyrocket and the national economy heads into a deep recession, with the Dow dropping more than 1,000 points in one week. Utility bills go through the roof. The region's powerful financial sector goes into freefall as the global economy collapses. It takes years for the region to regain some stability in its economy. The one positive aspect about this story is the growing appreciation for the natural environment as the economic problems backhandedly restore a better balance between human action and the natural world.

Once the scenarios were completed, a series of town meetings in the fall of 1998 prepared the way for a regional summit in November. The scenarios made the region's problems real to many citizens and sparked a wide-ranging discussion about the region's future. Voices & Choices funneled the information and input from these meetings into the visioning and strategy work that would take place at the summit.

The summit brought together more than five hundred people from across the region, shocking them into concerted action. Using the scenarios as a starting point, participants identified six priorities: land use, transportation, open space, water quality, air quality, and resource recovery and recycling. They defined the current situation in each of these areas, specified the desired future for each, and identified strategies for moving ahead. Over the next year, action teams continued the work developing specific action plans that were taken to citizens and civic leaders in early 2000. These action steps led, in part, to a two-year process beginning in 2001 to integrate planning for open space, transportation, and land use. Other initiatives, such as the Catawba River Basin Conference, focus on water quality and quality-of-life issues. Finally, the Central Carolinas region had a common agenda and the formidable regional organization it so badly needed to energize action.

## The Missoula, Montana, Scenarios Project

Population growth and its consequences challenge many communities in the Rocky Mountain region. Growth and development issues paralyze local political initiative as interest groups hamstring decision making by public officials. Suburban sprawl and industrial development interfere with the desire for a more livable community. Private property rights conflict with broader community values. Trade-offs between environmental amenities and new job creation become divisive. This multilayered conflict is mired in decades of community history. Old patterns of development are difficult to change.

In the early 1990s, Missoula, Montana, found itself in similar straits as bedroom communities and strip development threatened its spectacular mountain setting. Angry citizens and frustrated elected officials failed to cope with these challenges. Every citizen, it seemed, defined the problem of growth in a different way and fought for different solutions. Planning and development experts could not solve the problem for the community. Without the broad civic will to address these issues, there would be no political will to implement solutions.

In order to create civic will, Missoula used a new approach: collaborative scenario-based planning. Civic leaders chose this approach based on similar successful experiences in other communities. An inclusive, collaborative approach could build the civic will, and scenarios could challenge traditional assumptions about how the future might unfold. By creating provocative new stories about the future, Missoulians could break down paralyzing mental maps that limited creativity. Instead of being stuck in historical responses to problems like growth, citizens could create a viable, coherent vision for Missoula and develop new and innovative responses to growth management.

The primary goals of the project were to identify and explore alternative futures for the Missoula Valley, develop a vision for the region supported by the broader community, and identify policies and management tools that would lead to the vision. In order to do this, the process needed to engage a broad cross-section of the region's citizens. It had to be credible, open, and well informed. The collaborative effort had to create a broad constituency to act in order to make progress.

Missoula's Growth Management Task Force (GMTF), the convening body for the initiative, recognized early on that the only way to be successful in addressing the challenges of growth was to build a broad consensus about how Missoula should evolve. This unique committee of elected officials from the city and county, business representatives, and neighborhood council representatives invited a team of citizens to help address the emerging issue of growth within Missoula Valley. Fifty-four individuals from government, business, interest groups, and academia and citizens from throughout the region were selected to serve as stakeholders. They reflected a wide variety of perspectives and experiences, from affordable housing to outfitters. The GMTF designed a three-phased process to engage and educate the stakeholders (see Figure 15.3).

In Phase I, stakeholders developed four scenarios about how the future might unfold. Each presented a plausible narrative of how important and highly uncertain factors affecting Missoula's future might play out over the next ten years. These stories captured, in fictional form, the hopes and fears of the region, which informed the vision. "Status Quo Vadis" told a story of current trends rolling forward with political leaders unable to cope with the divisiveness in the community. Without effective planning, the city evolved into one of the "new gentry cities" in the West with a high cost of living, sprawl, and a high rate of migration. "A Not-So-Grimm Fairy Tale" (or "A Carousel IS Missoula") portrayed a shift from city-wide planning to neighborhood planning with a high level of trust and cooperation among citizens. In the third scenario, "Field of Dreams," three major high-technology firms moved to Missoula, permanently transforming the region's economic base. With a growing economy, new infrastructure needs challenged local officials to stay ahead of the growth curve. New developments and a younger population forced many older residents to move out as the cost of living increased. The "Grapes of Missoula," the final scenario, told an opposing story as a downsizing federal government gutted public sector jobs the region depended on. Population plummeted, and it would be years before the region regained a reasonable level of economic self-sufficiency (see Figure 15.4).

In Phase II, stakeholders created a vision of a desirable future for the Missoula Valley. The scenarios provided a solid foundation for developing the vision. By identifying the aspects of each scenario that appealed to or repelled them, stakeholders clarified their thinking about the vision. Ultimately, they defined ten critical aspects of a desirable future for the valley.

These ten dimensions provided an interconnected, holistic vision to guide future development. The economy and the built environment would complement the natural environment. Education and the arts and culture would help enhance

# FIGURE 15.3. MISSOULA, MONTANA, SCENARIOS PROJECT.

| Phases / Tracks | Phase I — Scenario Development | | Phase II — Vision and Policy Development | Phase III — Vision to Action | |
|---|---|---|---|---|---|
| Growth Management Committee | *May 25, 3 hours* | *June 9–10, 2 days* | *July 28–29, 2 days* | *October 20–21, 2 days* | *November 15, 3 hours* |
| Scenarios Stakeholder Group | **Initial Meeting**<br>• Purpose<br>• Introductions<br>• Overview of process<br>• Roles and ground rules | **Develop Scenarios**<br>• Identify and understand the focal issue and agenda<br>• Identify key driving forces<br>• Create scenarios | **Create a Vision**<br>• Incorporate public review comments in scenarios<br>• Vision<br>• Characteristics<br>• Assess current reality, gap analysis<br>• Begin developing strategic priorities | **Vision to Action**<br>• Review questionnaire<br>• Narrow strategic priorities<br>• Develop policy recommendations for Growth Management Task Force | **Vision to Action**<br>• Finalize policy recommendations |
| Community Outreach | *July 17–19*<br>**Public Review** | | *September–October*<br>**Land Use Questionnaire** | | |
| Outreach to Formal Organizations, Authorities | | | | | |

Missoula, Montana, Scenarios Project

## FIGURE 15.4. MISSOULA SCENARIOS.

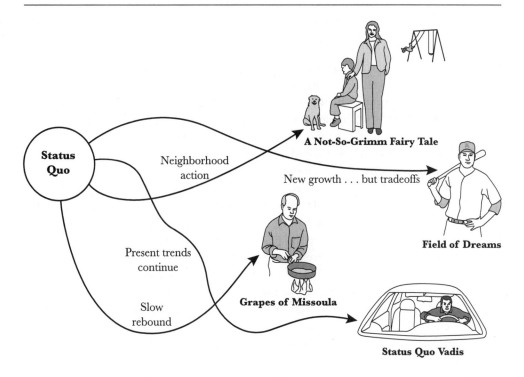

Missoula's already strong sense of community. Collaborative decision-making processes, durable partnerships between sectors and empowered, and inclusive government would build a healthy social climate or civic culture.

Phase III focused on strategy and policy development. A thorough analysis of Missoula's current status for each of these aspects identified key gaps between current reality and the vision. Stakeholders then brainstormed more than one hundred strategic possibilities for bridging these gaps and achieving the vision. Seven priorities emerged from the dialogue:

1. Designing and implementing appropriate land use and planning tools
2. Protecting the natural environment based on carrying capacity
3. Institutionalizing community information and problem-solving processes
4. Encouraging the development of community and neighborhood councils
5. Seeking legislative changes at the state level to give local government more power on development-related issues

6. Removing jurisdictional boundaries for neighborhood planning and city and county collaboration

7. Encouraging environmentally friendly economic development and above-average-wage job creation

An extensive education process about each of these priorities helped stakeholders define four specific recommendations for moving from vision to action that they would take to the GMTF. First, the city should establish a bottom-up neighborhood-based approach to city planning rather than the current developer-down approach. Second, neighborhood planning efforts should be guided by wider agreements about community design standards and coordinated with infrastructure development. Third, the city and county should adopt a set of land use and planning tools congruent with the vision. These tools would provide for education to support planning efforts; comprehensive planning, including fair share concepts; and appropriate regulation, incentives, and financing. Fourth, community information processes and neighborhood councils should be established to support inclusive, collaborative, consensus-based efforts to guide Missoula's development.

The GMTF, with its diverse membership, took the recommendations to Missoula's city council and county commission. Subsequent legislative action touched on all of the recommendations. Neighborhood councils and planning processes were established and are now up and running. An urban development plan was adopted to guide neighborhood planning efforts. New growth was tied to infrastructure development and capital planning. Elected leaders unanimously voted to change the comprehensive plan and associated zoning regulations consistent with the recommendations.

None of these actions would have been possible without the engagement of the stakeholders. Because of the nature of the process they had been through, the stakeholders represented a constituency to act crucial to the success of this effort. Elected officials now had the support they needed to move ahead in addressing growth management issues. They had commissioned the work, sat in on the stakeholder identification process, and observed the work. They had become convinced that the work of the stakeholders reflected the will of the community. They now had concrete, well-conceived recommendations when nothing coherent existed before. With a credible group of stakeholders behind them, risky political action became possible. Missoula now had the impetus to control its own future.

## The Future of the Nonprofit Sector in the Boston Region

In the 1990s, changes in federal and state policy regarding welfare and social services forced nonprofit organizations across the country to reconsider strategies and programs for meeting human service needs. The Greater Boston region, a broad landscape of urban and suburban areas with multiple and overlapping jurisdictions, was hard hit by these changes. As federal and state devolution progressed, several questions dominated the agenda. To what extent would local demand for human services increase as clients' benefits are cut? How would block grant accountability measures affect service delivery? Would block grant distribution favor large public institutions, cutting out small nonprofit service providers?

In 1995, the Boston Foundation and several local family foundations started the Goldberg Seminar on the Future of Boston Area Nonprofits to address these questions. Initially designed to explore the impacts of state and federal policy changes, the seminars evolved into an action group ready to consider revolutionary changes in the region's human service infrastructure. Stakeholders included representatives of nonprofit organizations, businesses, state and local governments, universities, policy institutes, and the media. Specifically, stakeholders needed to define the changing roles of governments, nonprofits, and businesses in meeting community needs; decide how to ensure community participation in decision making about block grants; build the capacity of Boston-area nonprofits to meet changing needs; foster collaboration and consolidation among nonprofits; develop public support for them; and improve accountability and evaluation.

Given the uncertainty about the direction and role of state and federal government policy in the human service arena, stakeholders would have to develop robust strategies for the nonprofit sector that would be viable in a range of possible future environments. Scenarios offered a tool for grappling with these uncertainties.

Participants in the scenarios working group identified nine driving forces—the most important and uncertain factors affecting the future of the nonprofit sector. These interconnected factors covered a range of considerations from the changing demand for service to the extent of polarization of race and class within the community.

---

## Driving Forces: The Future of the Nonprofit Sector in the Boston Region

- Changing demands for service (broader community needs)
- Willingness for consolidation and collaboration within the nonprofit sector
- Extent of collaboration across all sectors (government, business, nonprofit)
- Ability of the nonprofit sector to influence government decision making
- Adequacy of professional management capacity within the nonprofit sector
- Extent of polarization of race and class within the community
- Citizen participation in the community and political process
- Direction and role of state and federal government policy
- The impact of the global economy on our community

---

Each of the statements on the driving forces identifies the particular content of the driving force and defines the nature of the uncertainty (for example, willingness, extent, and direction). A wide range of plausible assumptions can be made about what may happen to these dimensions in the future. The interplay of differing assumptions about the driving forces leads to a range of stories about possible futures the Boston region might experience. The scenario working group needed to choose a handful of provocative stories in order to develop strategies that would help them cope with the uncertainties. The stories described both positive and negative futures.

---

# Boston Scenarios

## The City of Villages

A wave of immigration brought educated newcomers to Boston just as the city needed their language skills for its new role in the global marketplace. As a result, Boston's long-time anti-immigrant feelings began giving way to a new appreciation of people from other cultures. With high-paying jobs now available to people living in the city's neighborhoods, new prosperity and stability reigned throughout the city. Money has become available for community development, and judicious investment in decaying commercial centers has resulted in the revitalization of entire neighborhoods. Crime has gone down, the streets are safer, local politics have been revitalized, the schools—now decentralized—have improved, and the exodus to the suburbs of the previous century has been reversed. After a long history of taking second place to the interests of downtown, Boston's neighborhoods have developed a new economic independence, and Boston has become a city of villages.

---

Indicators (signs that this future is emerging)

- More newspaper advertisements in foreign languages
- Fewer empty storefronts
- More community-owned cooperative businesses
- More multilingual facilities

---

Newspaper Headlines (that might be seen if this future emerges)

- "Local Economy Boosted by Immigrants"
- "First-Generation Asian American Becomes Mayor"
- "School Committee Grants Autonomy to Neighborhood Schools"

## Tea Party II

Something very like a revolution took place in Boston in the year 2028. As with the first Revolution, this one too began with mounting hostility toward a government regarded as uncaring and remote. Anger and resentment toward the federal government gradually mounted in the years of devolution following 1997. When a young leader emerged who understood from her own experience both how beneficial government programs could be and how painful life in poverty was without them, she quickly developed an enthusiastic following. Further moves by the federal government to shed responsibility for the poor brought things to a crisis, and a near revolution took place in Boston. For a while, power was transferred to the people in a meaningful way. However, Boston's ethnic and racial groups, divided for so long, were unable, despite the opportunity of a century, to come together to create a new democracy.

### Indicators (signs that this future is emerging)

- Increased percentage of nonprofit budgets supported by individual contributions
- High voter turnout
- Large percentage of citizens involved in voluntarism
- Increased civility
- Increase in partnerships and collaborations

### Newspaper Headlines (that might be seen if this future emerges)

- "Power to the People"
- "America's Promise Realized"
- "Prison Construction Hits New Low"
- "Long Lines at Voting Booths Late into the Night"
- "Boston High School Students Playing New Roles in the Community"
- "Multicultural Festival Draws Bigger Crowds Than Bicentennial"
- "The New America in the New Millennium"

## Devil-ution

Bostonians seem less than appropriately enthusiastic about celebrating the four hundredth anniversary of the city's founding in the year 2030. Some of the great gathering places, including the Esplanade, have lost their old appeal, as the homeless population increases in the parks and squares and on the banks of the Charles River. People had not quite realized how essential the federal government's support had been to sustaining the city's poor. When a mild economic downturn occurs just as the cuts take their full effect, the nonprofit organizations that serve the poor are overwhelmed. Many close or consolidate. Only the very neediest are served; others are turned away. Meanwhile, downtown, the economy is booming. The rift between rich and poor has widened dramatically, and Boston enters its fifth century with a community that is deeply divided.

## Indicators (signs that this future is emerging)

- Increased sales and mergers of nonprofit organizations
- Increased percentage of population living in poverty
- Rising infant mortality rate
- Increased number of people uninsured
- High turnover rate in nonprofit management
- Voter registration down
- Falling newspaper readership

## Newspaper Headlines (that might be seen if this future emerges)

- "Columbia HCA Buys Partners"
- "Lowest Voter Turnout Ever in Mayoral Election"
- "Disparity Between Black and White Infant Mortality Rates Increases Dramatically"
- "Homeless Outnumber Tourists on Freedom Trail"

## To Hell in a Handbasket

Devolution has proceeded at a rapid pace for several years, uncorrected even by an economic downturn in the late 1990s that reveals the seriousness of unmet social needs under the "reformed" system. When the international economy crashes a few years later, hardship spreads through Boston and the rest of the nation. Diminished services are hardly able to dent the distress, but the worst effects of the new poverty are the conflicts it breeds first between the old and young and then between the suburbs and city, natives and immigrants, blacks and whites, middle class and poor. Boston in 2010 is a grim city, the only ray of hope being the revival of concern among a few religious and ethnic organizations, which, unfortunately, have scant resources at their disposal.

## Indicators (signs that this future is emerging)

- Stock market at all-time low
- Unemployment rising dramatically
- Six "Black Tuesdays" in a row

- Nursery school becomes halfway house
- Retirement age rises to seventy-five

---

**Newspaper Headlines (that might be seen if this future emerges)**

- "Gray Panthers Form Third Party"
- "Run on Hemlock and Ginseng"
- "Elderly Abuse Up 500 Percent"
- "National Guard Replaces Community Police Force"

---

Each scenario calls for different responses. "The City of Villages" suggests investments in local economies, technology, education, and youth services to enhance its positive aspects. "Tea Party II" demands effective cross-sector collaboration within the region in order to compensate for the federal government pullback and stronger roles for communities and clients in setting priorities for meeting human service needs and overcoming racial barriers. Similarly, "Devil-lution" requires decentralizing decision making in schools, economic development, and social services to respond to local needs and overcome the decline in federal support. Increased collaboration across sectors could help address the rift between rich and poor. Mitigating the egregious consequences of "To Hell in a Handbasket" calls for a wholesale revisioning or reengineering of the nonprofit sector. The social contract—the roles and responsibilities of government, business, philanthropy, and nonprofits—needs to be redefined. Nonprofits must develop a strong and coherent voice in the policy arena. All sectors need to learn to collaborate in order to make the most of limited local resources.

Because no one knows which of these futures will unfold, stakeholders identified robust strategies that would mitigate the effects of changes in government policy, strengthen the region in ways that prevent the worst consequences of these scenarios, and build on existing strengths. Specifically, this required increased collaboration among different sectors, a redefining of roles and responsibilities—a new social contract—and better communication and public relations to help the nonprofit sector develop political leverage.

Prior to the introduction of scenarios, participants tended to analyze needs and opportunities based on well-established assumptions and so considered a narrow range of fairly predictable responses. The scenarios helped open up people's minds, encouraging them to think more deeply and creatively about what futures might unfold. Specifically, the scenarios called participants' attention to the possible impacts of substantial changes in the population mix and to potential changes in policies, practices, and roles of the different sectors. By exposing these dimensions, the scenarios helped participants develop viable strategies for the nonprofit sector by challenging old assumptions and stale responses

The process as a whole proved valuable to the region. Several key participants in the initiative helped boost the quality and quantity of management support services available to nonprofits. The specific strategies for addressing the challenges of the nonprofit sector became a point of reference for many local organizations, helping them gain more support from their boards and constituencies. New working relationships emerging from the collaboration led to new partnerships between organizations from different sectors where none existed before.

## The Value of Scenarios

Scenarios help people face future challenges by surfacing provocative stories about the world in which citizens may have to live. They do not predict the future; rather, they identify hypothetical futures in order to make better decisions in the present. Instead of avoiding or denying potentially threatening futures, communities and regions can realistically consider plausible alternative futures and create strategies to prevent or mitigate their worst effects. Scenarios helped citizens and civic leaders in Missoula, Montana, and the Central Carolinas region confront their worst fear: collective impotence in the face of pervasive and potentially devastating population growth.

Scenarios challenge mental mind maps, which guide how people think about the world they live in. Sometimes these maps are accurate and helpful representations of reality. They can also be woefully inadequate, incomplete, inaccurate, and misleading. Scenario thinking helps improve the quality of mental models by giving voice to them, challenging them with different perspectives and models, and collaboratively developing alternative stories (scenarios) to expand them. Scenario work reframes mental models. The Boston scenarios helped stakeholders recognize a new world and prepare for a revolutionary restructuring of its nonprofit sector.

Collective action demands a strong measure of shared perspective: a common mental model, a shared vision, a jointly told story. Organizing scenario processes as open and constructive conversations among stakeholders helps build the mutual understanding, trust, and sense of community that make this possible. In the Central Carolinas region, little effective dialogue existed prior to the creation of Voices & Choices. The use of scenarios at the summit in 1998 stimulated conversation and the recognition that collaboration would be essential in order to move ahead on regional issues. The scenarios helped focus questions on both positive and negative aspects of possible futures, gave an idea of concerns people had, established a common agenda, and provided guidance on which directions to head in.

Ultimately, change requires not only new thinking and relationships but also new action. Moving forward together requires energy, which requires hope. Each of these examples included a positive scenario that inspired hope and provided insight into how significant challenges could be met. Rather than simply reacting to symptoms of public problems, the scenarios helped stakeholders imagine more systemic responses that would address root causes. Missoula's comprehensive response to growth management established a far more effective framework than the piecemeal reactions of the past.

The ultimate objective of scenarios is to provide a tool for engaging the hearts and minds of citizens in the process of creating a better future. These experiences demonstrate that civic scenario processes can help make this happen.

CHAPTER SIXTEEN

# BUILDING CIVIC LEADERSHIP
# IN PORTLAND, MAINE

Thomas J. Rice

*The Institute for Civic Leadership (ICL) in Portland, Maine, grew out of a collaborative process to address the city's leadership vacuum in 1993. The initial sponsors understood that any civic leadership development program would have to focus on building the collaborative capacity of the region. Congruent with this understanding, the design process itself was a model of what a collaborative process should be. The resulting program has helped transform the civic culture of the region.*

*At the time the ICL developed, few civic leadership programs had been designed and initiated in a collaborative way by the community or region itself. Most were either sponsored by a single entity (for example, a chamber of commerce or university) or were designed and delivered by an organization specializing in civic leadership development (for example, the American Leadership Forum). The design process reflected several key elements of effective collaboration. An initial assessment helped stakeholders understand the Portland context and its implications for civic leadership and sharpened the focus of the design task. The effort was inclusive in terms of a diversity of credible stakeholders, well informed by content experts in leadership and leadership development, and facilitated by skillful process experts. An effective outreach program helped generate the resources and support necessary to implement the program. The initiating work modeled the collaborative leadership capacities it sought to develop in the program itself.*

Visiting Maine in 1995, Charles Kuralt, beloved star of *On the Road* fame, gave voice to a common sentiment: "If I were going to choose an American city to live in, Portland would be on my list" (Kuralt, 1995, p. 168). It was high praise from a veteran chronicler of America's most attractive habitats.

Kuralt's impression echoes a chorus of other enthusiasts who shortened their list to one and acted on it. They find this old port city of about sixty-three thousand a marvel of livability, blending the best of small town civility with refined urban amenities. Driven by the economic prosperity of the 1990s and the freedom of telecommuting, Portland has attracted a diverse array of newcomers: immigrants, artists, new economy inventors, old economy investors, restaurateurs, and a host of civic entrepreneurs, making the region a model of creativity, energy, and possibility other cities can only dream about. It was not always so.

Portland's story strongly supports the adage, "no pain, no gain." In the late 1970s, the city was a case study in stagnation. With many other northeastern cities, including Boston, urban life cycle theorists wrote it off as a city that had outlived its usefulness. It was seen as beyond hope by the pundits, best left to fade away. They cited ample evidence: severe and rising unemployment, beautiful old buildings abandoned, shopfronts boarded up, locals leaving for more promising environs. It seemed that all of America was moving to the Sunbelt. Despair was closing in. Then the 1980s boom hit.

Portland rode the rising tide. With pent-up capacity—human and material— and a hunger for local opportunities, the city rebounded to heights "that exceeded the expectations and experience of most Maine people" (Cohen, 1993, p. 1). Job opportunities became competitive with the best national profiles, along with wages and benefit packages. Housing prices escalated, driven by the manic speculation in the Boston region and the northeastern real estate market. Bankers, real estate developers, investors, and political leaders basked in the glory of success.

## The Presenting Problem

In Portland's rollicking 1980s, an aura of invincibility prevailed throughout the region. Now that prosperity had arrived, the future was all upside until, as with all other business cycles, the bubble burst. Suddenly, things looked bleak again. As the downward spiral gained its vicious momentum, business after business folded; banks closed their doors; homes leveraged with jumbo mortgages were repossessed. Unemployment soared. And rainy-day government services suffered cutbacks.

Predictably, the spotlight turned on community leadership, which up to now had been taken for granted. An informal power structure—the Cumberland Club, an exclusive downtown dining club reserved mostly for Portland's business elite— had held sway for years, but it had disintegrated in the rough and tumble of bankruptcies, mergers and acquisitions, and absentee ownership. As the leadership vacuum became apparent, the questions—first insistent, then angry—started: How could this happen? Whose responsibility was it to see this coming? Why didn't the leadership warn us? What kind of leadership do we have here anyway? And, finally, what can we do about this mess?

## Key Players

To Jim Orr, the new CEO of UNUM Insurance, the leadership void was obvious, especially in civic engagement. He had no interest in playing the blame game, but he also knew the solution had to go beyond the chamber of commerce: "I just knew that the usual handful of CEOs who came together for lunch at the Cumberland Club were not going to be the answer. The world had changed too much; it was time to involve the fabric of the community in defining and solving the problems that we all shared."

As a former executive vice president of Connecticut Bank and Trust in Hartford, the insurance capital of America, Orr had moved to Portland in the late 1980s to assume the top job at UNUM. He had some experience with a new way of thinking about complex problem solving. As a participant in the American Leadership Forum (ALF), Orr had grasped the potential of new attitudes, skills, and behaviors to make real change in the way leadership is practiced. Urged by Janice Cohen, UNUM's talented director of corporate public involvement, Orr saw Portland's predicament as an opportunity to model a new kind of leadership. This meant resisting the traditional temptation to define the issues and drive the solutions that seemed obvious and in UNUM's best interest. With Orr's support, Cohen forged ahead. The stage was now set for the first phase of the collaborative process.

## Initiating the Collaborative Effort

Consistent with a disciplined effort not to just assume the problem existed, UNUM began with a series of questions. Is leadership a concern to the Greater Portland community? Is there a leadership vacuum? Is leadership a key ingredient in why public issues are or are not being resolved successfully? What are the leadership issues of the region? What is the need to help promote effective solutions to public issues? If it is important, how would we promote an ethic of civic involvement?

Armed with these protocols, UNUM hired The Philanthropic Initiative (TPI), a Boston-based nonprofit research group, to conduct interviews with a target population of key leaders in Greater Portland. They were looking for "leaders who had significant experience wrestling with public issues as elected officials, community representatives or corporate leaders and had demonstrated a high level of civic involvement" (Philanthropic Initiative, 1992).

TPI selected a first round of interviewees based on their potential to furnish insight on the issue. From there, the sample snowballed as each person provided new names until they tapped twenty-five leaders covering the three sectors. Not surprisingly, their findings provided strong affirmative evidence for concern with leadership at all levels:

- Lack of political leadership at the state level
- Lack of dialogue between special interest groups and less narrow constituencies
- Lack of common ground where solutions to issues can be hammered out
- No ethic of public service and civic leadership in the private sector except in a few sporadic cases
- Little or no sense of ownership of government and public issues within the private sector

In addition to these five substantive findings, the researchers found a pattern of civic neglect linked to several systemic concerns. The region's economic success drained corporate energy from civic participation. The press of business came first in the emerging global economy. Most CEOs could not afford the luxury of time and energy their predecessors had given to large-scale civic endeavors. Communication had also become a barrier: business, government, and the community sectors appeared to speak different languages, especially when the stakes were high on critical issues such as growth and development. All sectors feared the complexity of public issues. People seemed reluctant to get involved in what often proved to be an endless cycle of blame and recrimination without resolution. While the old model of corporate paternalism in public life seemed dead and gone, there were few opportunities for those who wanted to step up and fill the vacuum of leadership in civic life. All of these factors underscored the need for the creation of a new network of civic peers.

Given these findings, TPI outlined a framework for what a new leadership institute should address. Their recommendations were very specific: the creation of a civic leadership curriculum that would provide participants with sophisticated support in building skills relevant to addressing civic issues (such as facilitation and mediation), high-level briefings on the analysis of key problems that challenged the area's well-being, and actual collaborative problem-solving experience. Operationally, it would entail the recruitment of an annual class of relatively senior representatives from the business, community, and government sectors. This would require ongoing support for the civic activities and aspirations of the institute's graduates. Finally, the program would require the development of an academically connected database and research component that supported the training and public policy activities of the institute.

## Working Together: The First Test of Collaborative Acumen

Now came a critical juncture for UNUM's Orr and Cohen. Mindful of the need to transfer ownership with all deliberate speed, they invited a core group of stakeholders—some of them participants in TPI's interviews—"who had demonstrated a passion for effective leadership and a thoughtful approach to potential solutions" to form an advisory group (Philanthropic Initiative, 1992). Their mission would be to collaborate in designing a response to TPI's research findings.

Cohen consulted leadership experts of local, regional, and national stature: "We needed to know what was already being tried to develop the leaders for this more complex and diverse society, what leadership development programs actually resulted in improving community life, and what would we need to do if we were to go beyond training leaders to actually changing the leadership culture? What still seemed missing was the integration of the new leadership model into the community by reconnecting the leaders to the general citizenry and an infrastructure to support practicing leaders" (Cohen, 1993, p. 3).

Orr echoed this concern. He did not want to create just another leadership program that might benefit the participants or their organizations, but leave the community untouched. "We needed to provide some glue, something intense, like being trapped in an elevator together and coming up with the solution as a group. It had to be that visceral; it had to go beyond an intellectual exercise."

Cohen and the advisory group took up the challenge. Recognizing they had no time for missteps, they retained Interaction Associates, a consulting and training firm noted for expertise in collaborative leadership. David Straus, the firm's founder and lead consultant, brought a wealth of experience in designing and facilitating public-private partnerships in many cities. From the start, Straus operated from the premise that "if this is to be a collaborative leadership program, the planning process needs to model collaboration. The change you want is the change you start with."

Straus began with an education phase using basic principles of collaboration. He formed a small process design team—a subset of the advisory group, including Cohen—to plan a series of meetings with clear desired outcomes and supporting agendas. They developed a process map with milestones and agreements to be achieved along the way. In the end, they wanted a well-designed leadership institute and a solid foundation of agreements by consensus. They especially needed an answer to the question, How could Portland create a self-renewing civic leadership culture that would not peter out as soon as the external infrastructure that created it is removed?

After the first round of education sessions and preliminary alignment on the nature and scope of the program—its design specifications—the advisory group decided to bolster its content expertise in building the leadership curriculum. They turned to David Chrislip of the National Civic League, who brought his program design experience from his work with the American Leadership Forum (ALF). Orr had firsthand experience of ALF. Chrislip, a scholarly practitioner, had also been a senior consultant with Interaction Associates in the mid-1980s and had collaborated with Straus on several projects.

The advisory group now had the perfect mix of resources: generous sponsorship from UNUM, exceptional content and process expertise, and a genuine crisis—lack of respected civic leadership—to propel the initiative. The group had created an overall purpose statement that captured their strategic intent: "Create a network of leaders who can act on behalf of the shared concerns of the Portland region." By early May, Chrislip had a draft of the offering ready for the advisory group. Working closely with Straus, who brought Interaction's facilitative leadership practices and change management models and tools to the mix, the two had fashioned a uniquely rich offering. The draft proposal had all the specifics: outcomes, agendas, roles, and so on, complete with a transforming experience—four days together at Outward Bound. The product was worthy of all the hard work: a rigorous fifteen-day program based on the best existing practices with the unique quality of being collaboratively designed and integrated. Over time, if the theory was correct, it would add up to a large-scale cultural change in the civic leadership capacity of Greater Portland.

The advisory group welcomed the program outline with some relief, seeing for the first time how the fifteen-day program would unfold. They were delighted with the product, which exceeded their design specifications. It was distinguished in sophistication, creativity, and relevance to the challenge at hand. They had their program and more. (Appendix B provides an outline of the program curriculum.)

Still, a problem remained: the process and program was still strongly associated with UNUM. Everyone acknowledged that Cohen was the driving force that kept the initiative on track. The UNUM Foundation, of which she was director, provided all the initial funding to pay for consulting and research. It was time to transfer ownership to the broader community.

The core design group realized that their adoption of the program design would not be enough to ensure broader buy-in. UNUM, gracious benefactors to the end, hosted a luncheon presentation for civic leaders from throughout the region, including those who had been interviewed. It was a carefully orchestrated event, and it achieved its goals. In follow-up telephone calls, Cohen contacted each attendee and those invited but unable to attend and asked a series of questions: What do you think? Should we go ahead with implementation? Will you be willing to serve on the board of directors? Will you give us financial support to launch the program, including an $8,000 tuition grant for the first-year participation? The answers were positive, and they could finally move on to implementation.

The mantle of leadership had been passed on. It was now up to a broader base of community leaders to take stewardship of the region's destiny. Only time would tell if they would rise to the occasion. In the fall of 1993, after a long labor of love, Cohen took the long view as she submitted her summary report to the board of directors:

> A new culture of collaborative leadership will not be created in greater Portland simply by training 25–30 new leaders each year. Their commitment to civic life cannot be a ten month training program that ends with the completion of a "community project." Those leaders need to become practicing collaborative leaders in the community and in their organizations. They need to facilitate the involvement of the whole community in creating a collaborative culture and they need to integrate their own organization whether private, public, or non-profit into the whole fabric of the community [Cohen, 1993, p. 5].

## Outcomes of Collaborative Leadership

Given all the energy and resources that went into its creation and the flood of commitment it has taken to sustain the ICL, it seems fair to ask about impact. Did it realize the original vision? Is the civic leadership vacuum filled in Greater Portland? Is there tangible evidence that the investment was worth the return?

Three sources of data serve to answer these questions. One comes from an assessment commissioned by ICL's third executive director, Susan Clark, in 1999, the second from interviews conducted with a sample of alumni for this chapter, and a third from anecdotal accounts of participants and their colleagues over the past eight years. Each time the alumni come together—and that is quite frequently—someone has a new story to relate about the impact of the institute's program. The following examples illustrate the richness of its impact.

### Cruise Ships Coming to Portland Harbor

When she participated in the institute's class, Roxanne Cole of Ram Harnden Realty was already heavily committed to civic leadership as the chair of the board of the Chamber of Commerce of Greater Portland. Reluctant to undertake more civic responsibilities at that time, Roxanne was nevertheless haunted by an image of "ships of money" bypassing Portland for Bar Harbor and other New England destinations. With the help of Portland's director of waterfront and transportation, Tom Valleau, Cole agreed to chair a chamber of commerce committee to look at the opportunity. "With all my other chamber duties I never would have agreed to take this on," she recounts, "except for the insights gained at the institute training. Frankly, because of the institute training, I could see that I would be able to form the initiative, include future leaders in the original meetings, and that they would own the vision and ultimately bring the project to fruition."

That is exactly what happened, and today, with the help of leaders like David Swardlick and Jerry Angier (most recent chair of the Cruise Ship Committee), Portland is attracting higher-quality cruise ships and implementing a strategy to increase the number of military and cruise ships coming to Casco Bay.

The most significant symbol of the success of the initiative was the first visit of Holland America's most prestigious cruise ship, the *Queen Elizabeth II*, in 1996. In the summer of 2001, Portland hosted forty-five ships—well beyond the ambition of the original vision—including the *QE II*, which has returned every year since that first triumphant visit.

## Maine Environmental Priorities Project

Throughout the development boom of the 1980s, environmentalists, developers, and state regulators battled over the proper mix of development and preservation— what is now called smart growth—of Maine's natural resources. Tired of the combative approach, key representatives of each group came together in the early 1990s to find a better way. By early 1996, the Maine Environmental Priorities Project (MEPP) had identified and ranked the state's most urgent environmental issues. More important, because of the collaborative process that involved most of the key environmental stakeholders in the state, implementation of MEPP's recommendations proved relatively smooth.

Al Curran of Woodward and Curran, an environmental consulting firm and a member of the ICL class of 1994, was instrumental in the initial successes of MEPP, but he had a lot of help. Essential leadership was also provided by Evan Richert, director of the State Planning Office and former president of the institute's board of directors. Ted Koffman, state legislator and public affairs director at College of the Atlantic at Bar Harbor, active from the start, continues to hold the center for collaborative leadership in this project.

Other initiatives inspired by the MEPP model include Smart Growth, Indoor Air Forum, and the Water Monitoring Project, all of which focus on resolving issues of shared concern to every Mainer. These initiatives have in common the application of collaborative principles that all the graduates of ICL learn—such as stakeholder inclusion from the start; consensus-based decisions; balance results with a good, facilitated process and a relationship focus; and celebrate the little successes along the way.

## National Semiconductor Expansion in South Portland

In the fall of 1995, Greater Portland was buzzing about the decision of the National Semiconductor to expand its operations in South Portland. The project created hundreds of new high-paying jobs in construction and manufacturing and hundreds of spin-off jobs, which actually exceeded the number of new National Semiconductor positions as additional goods and services were required by the firm. How was Greater Portland able to land this prize? According to Laurenz Schmidt, managing director of National Semiconductor's operations in South Portland and a member of the ICL's class of 1995, Maine won over the company's site selection committee with a formidable display of civic will.

Relying on collaborative principles, a large group representing the multiple stakeholders in the project convened to pursue this regional development opportunity. There was no evidence of a leadership vacuum in that initiative. Potential conflicts were worked out in advance of the site selection committee's visit; National Semiconductor was offered an array of incentives, including the creation of a tax increment financing district, which put Maine ahead of even Sunbelt competitors that had been lavishly successful in the 1980s exodus from the Northeast. Speaking to the chamber of commerce, Schmidt cited the ICL as one of the key resources that allowed Greater Portland to muster the civic will necessary to achieve sustainable economic development in a globally competitive environment.

In 1997, Fairchild corporation acquired most of National Semiconductor, including many employees who are ICL graduates. In spite of an industry downturn and some painful layoffs, the firm is a solid contributor to the Portland economy.

## Boys' Conference: Getting at the Roots of Domestic Violence

It began with a "strategic moment," to hear Layne Gregory (a member of an ICL class and former co-chair of the ICL board) tell the story. As program manager of Family Violence Prevention Programs for Portland, Gregory had convened a group of about twelve men to respond to the question, "What do boys need?" This is a hard question that opens up all the explosive issues of gender, power, and responsibility for the problem of family violence.

It would have been easy to become defensive and seek to drive the answer. Instead, Gregory recalls, drawing on her ICL experience, she and Julie Schirmer (who had participated in an ICL class) took a process perspective. They convened a steering committee of sixteen men and two women to design a collaborative process that would ensure an open dialogue.

The upshot was a highly successful conference (350 people attended; another 250 had to be turned away), held November 4, 2000, focused on media messages of violence associated with masculinity, especially in musical lyrics and images. Annual conferences are planned for the future to keep these issues fresh.

## Youth Assets Builders

What can collaborative leadership contribute to the issue of at-risk youth, a national problem?

In the late 1980s, the Search Institute of Minneapolis, Minnesota, introduced a body of research to show that healthy youth need developmental assets if they are to reach their full potential. The institute created a method of determining the current state of these assets in a given community and made its approach available to concerned communities across the country.

Drawing on the assets builder's methodology, a Portland coalition led by John Shoos of United Way (who had participated in an ICL class) received a grant from the Governor's Office Communities for Children. Using the forty-asset framework to survey Portland, the coalition members conducted an intensive round of community conversations with both mainstream stakeholders and those typically excluded: homeless and incarcerated youth.

The ICL had a particular impact on the way the survey findings were presented to the community. The innovation in design took shape as an inclusive community forum. The sponsors facilitated a genuine dialogue using interactive exchanges to build shared meaning around the findings. Unlike the frustration of most public forums, the quality of the facilitation and the importance of a shared collaborative model was critical. "We had our usual struggles with balancing results, process, and relationships," Layne Gregory recalls, "But our ICL training helped us to keep going back to the mission and to maintain a discipline. Without that shared model in front of us, I don't think we would have been as successful in keeping inclusion at the forefront and ultimately creating a community more focused on the needs of youth."

Clearly, a process that honors stakeholder inclusion—however tempting selective exclusion may be—yields superior results in the long run.

## Other Success Stories

In addition to these highly publicized results, a steady stream of reports and accounts documents the wide-ranging impact of the ICL. A five-year follow-up study of alumni conducted in 1998 found a robust 95 percent of respondents (over 50 percent responded) rated the core program excellent, and many said it continues to affect their leadership styles and lives.

The Portland region now has a network of collaborative leaders who can approach issues from a similar mind-set and move things forward without the adversarial tangles of past efforts. Portland's former mayor, Ann Pringle, has this to say: "Take mental health issues. Rather than suffering through those deadly meetings in which nothing is accomplished, I can look around and see fellow ICL grads and say . . . hey, we don't have to put up with this. It was because of this common set of skills and mindsets we were able to succeed in setting up a local service network for mental health providers. We had learned a common set of dimensions at ICL around results, process, and relationships. This was invaluable, but it doesn't just happen. You have to call it up."

Consistent with the theory of the case, the new and expanding civic leadership of the region shows itself in a number of smaller, subtle ways. It is, as the founders intended, becoming embedded in the fabric of the community. Examples abound where the unique assets and values of the ICL are on display.

This new type of personal development, trusting relationships, and camaraderie—what Robert Putnam (2000) calls social capital—is rapidly becoming a differentiator between successful and lagging regions in the global economy.

One of the greatest benefits cited by graduates addresses the inner side of leadership. Dick Sawyer, a class participant and a financial planner, puts it this way: "I thought I would learn a lot of skills [at ICL] and form some new friendships. And I have. But what I never figured was the personal transformation it has wrought, especially from the dialogue on diversity. Far from being the end of something, this is just the beginning of a whole rethinking of who I am and what I'm about. It is the most powerful learning experience I have ever had."

## Reflections and Learnings over Eight Years

Since that first September launch in 1993, over 230 leaders have graduated from the ICL. The founders (Orr, Cohen, and the original advisory group of thirteen, as well as Chrislip and Straus) have detailed memories of the struggle and the rewards of launching what everyone agrees is a highly successful program.

Over the eight years since the first program was crafted, there has been a sea change in consciousness about civic engagement in America. Now, in the aftermath of the September 11 attack on New York and the Pentagon, this coming together has been massively accelerated. In response to these terrible events, an outpouring of ideas on revitalizing the human spirit, rebuilding community, and bringing diverse cultures together permeates civic dialogue. A vast literature has emerged documenting the rise of collaborative leadership, by any other name—civic entrepreneur, regional steward, servant leader. Indeed, this research emphasizes social capital—networks, norms, and trust, the essence of ICL—as the essential ingredient in economic development and civic engagement around the globe.

For all of the accounts of success, there remains considerable room for improvement. The region still faces some thorny issues that have not yielded to the collaborative ethos. Each year many of the same intractable concerns are being voiced by the new class of leaders—for example:

- The need for a more skilled, inclusive approach to the region's growing ethnic and racial diversity
- The increasing disparity between the haves and have-nots in socioeconomic standing
- Workforce education to meet the new economy requirements
- Affordable health care
- Sustainable—smart—growth and development

Over the eight years of its existence, the ICL has been a powerful lever for building civic capacity in Portland. Yet it is no panacea. Human institutions do not yield their ingrained habits easily. As with any other community in America, the future of Portland is a question of the character of the next generation of regional stewards in the region: Will they have the wisdom, the vision, the commitment? Will they have the generosity of spirit to put community first? To put compassion ahead of privilege? These choices will be made at the individual, organizational, and community levels, resulting in a civic life that either thrives or withers away. Whatever their choice, Portland's future leaders will inherit a solid legacy of social capital in the currency of collaborative leadership. It is a credit to the ICL that the leadership vacuum no longer exists. The ICL has realized the original 1993 vision of building "a network of leaders who can act on behalf of the shared concerns of the Portland region" that taps the power of collaborative competence to create a better future for all the residents of Greater Portland.

CHAPTER SEVENTEEN

# Building Leadership Capacity in a Socially Emerging Community

## Allan Wallis

*Historically, marginalized minority groups have had to be skillful practitioners of community organizing in order to assert themselves in the face of segregation and discrimination. In recent years, many of these groups have gained substantial legitimacy in the broader community. Unfortunately, many of them still rely on the confrontational strategies that got them to the public table in the first place. In Denver, one such minority community decided to broaden its repertoire of tools to include collaboration in constructive ways both within its own networks and with the broader community. This desire for a constructive role in public life led to the creation of a powerful civic leadership development program.*

*In keeping with its focus on collaboration, the initiative exemplified collaborative principles in its design and initiation. A convening group reflecting the diversity of the gay, lesbian, bisexual, and transgender (GLBT) community helped design the initiative. The diverse nature of this group lent credibility to the effort and provided the impetus for others to participate in the initial program and for finding the resources to support the effort. A carefully planned and facilitated design process led to a well-conceived program. Strong, facilitative leadership from a few people within the GLBT community kept the initiative moving. Outreach efforts to philanthropic organizations and the larger community helped establish the program within the larger community context.*

On the evening of October 26, 1998, a group of over 450 guests assembled for a reception in Denver at the mansion of the governor of Colorado. The mansion hosts many such receptions, but this one was arguably different. There were about an equal number of men and women, all well dressed as befit the occasion, all enjoying the opportunity to be in this special place. But most of the couples consisted of men accompanied by men and women accompanied by women. In fact, most of the participants were gay, lesbian, bisexual, or transgender.

They were gathered on this night to celebrate the beginning of a new initiative: a leadership development program designed to train current and emerging leaders of Colorado's gay, lesbian, bisexual and transgender community (GLBT). The goal of the community-building initiative, known as Leadership Challenge 2001: Connecting, Communicating, Collaborating, was to instill principles and practices of collaboration in the leadership ranks of this community. The hope was that their forthcoming training would allow the participants to become more effective in working with one another to strengthen their community and reach out to other communities.

Governor Roy Romer addressed the group:

> Ceremonies are important. They mark important moments in our lives—whether it is a graduation, a wedding or a first prom date—human society has always used ceremonies to put into memory the important mileposts in life. Unfortunately, the gay community has not always been welcomed to honestly and fully participate in some of the time-honored ceremonies that have evolved in our culture, so tonight I have been asked to lead you in a ceremonial affirmation of the purpose that drew us all together this evening. Whether you are participants in the class, or whether you are here to support the participants, please consider responding from your heart.
>
> To the participants, friends and colleagues and faculty of this initiative: You have all made a decision to participate in this program—some at substantial sacrifice. Tonight, you are asked to make this commitment:
>
> > To come to this experience with an open heart and an open mind—with a willingness to connect to others;
> >
> > To seek and accept the possibility of change in oneself and others;
> >
> > To persevere in times of challenge; and
> >
> > To put what you learn from this experience to work for others during and after completion of the program [Lundy Foundation, 1998].

## The Problem: Building Leadership in the GLBT Community

Being "closeted"—that is, being secretive about one's sexual orientation or identity—historically has been a major impediment in creating a GLBT community (Clendinen and Nagourney, 1999). People cannot begin to become part of that community until they make the decision to come out. Under such circumstances, the first feeling of community is having a network of support to salve the stigma that often accompanies the process of coming out. To become a leader in such a community involves not just coming out but a willingness to be "a public queer," an enormous impediment for many people.

The presence of a publicly visible, politically active gay community is a relatively recent development. Arguably, the 1969 Stonewall uprising in New York City marks the formal emergence of gay liberation (Duberman, 1993). Throughout the 1970s, gay culture became more visible and was embraced by many people, both gay and straight, as something positive rather than stigmatizing. But by the early 1980s, a new threat—HIV/AIDS—was becoming visible and starting to reshape the GLBT community. Because the vast majority of those being infected and dying of AIDS were gay white males, it soon became known as the "gay plague." For the better part of a decade, the federal government had stood by, largely ignoring the crisis, while zealots from the religious right labeled the epidemic "God's judgment" (Shilts, 1987). Being the object of bigotry, on the one hand, and death, on the other, can be a great motivator. A new level of activism arose in the gay community demanding recognition and support. New leadership was being bred by crisis, but it was also being killed off by it (Vaid, 1996).

The 1990 passage of the Ryan White CARE Act began providing significant federal funding for services supporting those with AIDS and HIV-related diseases. In 1992, the same year that the Denver metropolitan area became eligible for Title I CARE Act funding, an initiative was placed before Colorado voters—Amendment Two—that would prohibit local governments from enacting ordinances protecting the civil rights of gays and lesbians. The issue passed, throwing members of Colorado's GLBT community into a state of heightened mistrust, grief, and anger. It would take four years of expensive legal battles to bring Amendment Two before the U.S. Supreme Court, where it was declared unconstitutional.

Amendment Two, combined with the impact of HIV and AIDS on the gay and lesbian community, stimulated increased activism. New organizations, such as Equality Colorado and Ground Zero, formed to fight the perceived threat of bigotry. As the number and membership rolls of organizations grew, some collaboration occurred, especially around the fight against Amendment Two, but competition also developed, notably among HIV/AIDS service providers. A community, though attacked from the outside, still needs to learn how to collaborate from within.

# Key Players

Vic Dukay had been a community activist during the various crises affecting the gay community in Colorado. He was aware of the need for better community organizing and leadership and, as a member of several boards and advisory groups, had seen, firsthand, competition undermining collaboration.

In 1995, Dukay completed a doctorate in communications at the University of Denver. Studying under Carl Larson, a noted authority in the field of leadership development and team excellence, Dukay determined to do something with his degree that would serve the GLBT community as well as the community at large. He observed:

> There is a tremendous need for leadership development, especially leadership based on collaboration. Compared with the investment that the corporate sector makes in developing leadership to meet its needs, there is virtually no investment made to nurture leadership in the GLBT community or, for that matter, in the civic sector in general. In addition to dealing with the challenge of scarce resources, it is difficult for leaders to sustain personal motivation in an environment saturated with conflict and hostility. There are few rewards for taking on the role of leadership and unreliable support for those willing to do the job.

"Other marginalized communities face similar challenges," Dukay concluded. "Too often marginalized populations have been unable to maintain a coherent front within their own communities. The energy expended in internal conflicts precludes either meeting their own communities' needs or reaching out to form collaborations within the larger community. The challenge for leadership in marginalized communities is to learn how to advocate in ways that build and expand the network of allies. That's probably the surest route to furthering the goal of being legitimized as an authentic community in society."

Dukay had a vision of creating a leadership development program, but was unsure whether the existing leadership of Colorado's GLBT community would share that vision and help make it a reality. With joint support from the Lundy and Gill foundations, Dukay was able to put together a series of six half-day professionally facilitated meetings to discuss the concept of a leadership development program. An initiating group of seventeen individuals representing twelve different GLBT organizations in the state, as well as a cross-section of the community's diversity—including representation from the academic, business, philanthropic, human services, political, and religious sectors—participated in the sessions.

Dukay felt that it was essential that the initiating process employ a collaborative process. There was a broad range of power within the initiating group, vestiges of past confrontations, and a wide range of opinion about what was relevant to leadership training. Modeling collaboration at the outset was an important test of the principles that would eventually guide the training program. If this group could not form a strong consensus, then there would be no reason to go further.

By the conclusion of its work, the initiating group had identified substantive issues facing Colorado's GLBT community and specified desired shifts in attitudes and behaviors that they felt needed to be achieved. In addition, the group recognized some daunting challenges: how to overcome the lack of support for community leaders, the absence of any significant mentoring of new leaders, and the lack of norms and practices for working collaboratively. They examined what other communities had done to enrich their leadership resources, including traditional and more innovative models of leadership development. In the end, the group agreed to move toward a more innovative approach built on the idea of collaborative leadership that works to inspire commitment and action and focuses on bringing people together to solve problems rather than expecting leaders to take command of the situation.

As part of its work, the initiating group designed a preliminary curriculum, drafted a detailed first-year budget for the anticipated three-year program, and identified an administrative framework to implement what would become Leadership Challenge 2001. The group also decided that the entire initiative should be thoroughly evaluated so that if the pilot was successful, the training program could be replicated in Colorado and other parts of the country.

Each of the GLBT organizations represented on the initiating committee agreed to nominate two of its members (staff or board) to participate in the training program. A few of the committee members themselves eventually became program participants.

At its last meeting, the group selected the Lundy Foundation, headed by Dukay, to administer the project. This included raising the funds necessary for implementing the program. Fundraising efforts commenced immediately following the initiating process and have continued throughout the initiative. In the end, almost $1.3 million will have been secured to carry out the five-year initiative, including the initiating process and follow-up evaluation activities. Support came from a diverse group of thirty-nine foundations, corporations, and individual donors, including the Gill Foundation, Coors Brewing Company, AT&T, the Women's Foundation of Colorado, and the Denver Broncos Charities Fund.

## The Collaborative Project

Although the initiating group had developed the outline of a curriculum, there was no pedagogy to the program. Issues such as how it should be organized and taught, by whom, and in what sequence were turned over to the Lundy Foundation. Similarly, the initiating group had looked at models of leadership and leadership development, but it found that most were designed for the public or private sectors, not for the civic sector comprising nonprofits, community-based groups, and unaffiliated members of a community. Consequently, the pilot effort was expected to chart new territory in leadership training.

## Designing a Detailed Curriculum

In late spring 1998, Lundy convened a group of five individuals—curriculum designers and an evaluator—to develop the program. Leadership Challenge 2001 was designed as a three-year pilot project that would run fifty-seven days, including four retreat weekends. This relatively long training period was selected to allow participants to get to know one another, form interpersonal networks, and provide the opportunity to work in teams to achieve something of value in the community.

The curriculum was structured on four levels: (1) personal and interpersonal skills development, (2) team building, (3) skills needed to run organizations, and (4) techniques for community outreach and engagement. These levels were roughly sequential, but with a great deal of overlap. In fact, some focus on personal and interpersonal skill development was part of almost every session.

The curriculum development process had to address several difficult challenges. First, how could the curriculum design team balance the expectation of participants who might want primarily hard skills development (such as conflict management, decision making, and convening community) against those who are more interested in personal and interpersonal insights that might be regarded as soft skills (such as building trust, reflection, and ethics)?

Second, how could the curriculum encourage participants to address forces that divide the community? It is one thing for the GLBT community to be attacked from outside. Attacks such as Amendment Two can serve to unify the community against a common enemy. But it is quite another thing to address prejudices within the GLBT community. Bisexuals, for example, often are challenged (other members of the gay and lesbian community perceive them as straddling the fence), and transgender individuals are often perceived as pushing the envelope of society's acceptance even by the gay and lesbian community. Similarly, the GLBT community suffers all of society's other biases and forms of discrimination: racism, classism, and sexism, among others.

Finally, how could the curriculum instill the ethic and practices of collaborative leadership? Clearly this would require more than classroom instruction. All of the activities related to the program would have to embrace collaborative ideals. But what would collaboration between project administrators, facilitators, and participants look like? Would there have to be a point where participants began taking more responsibility for the direction of the curriculum? If so, when and how?

## Faculty

Lundy wanted high-quality faculty teaching in various areas of content expertise. That meant searching both within and outside the state. It also meant that the same faculty probably would not be used from module to module, so achieving continuity could be a challenge. In order to address this challenge, the role of integrating facilitator was created. This individual would be at all training sessions and would work with a pool of thirty-two content faculty to ensure that their sessions were appropriately integrated into the program.

The curriculum design team thought that it was preferable that the integrating facilitator be a member of the GLBT community, but that this was less important for content-area faculty. For the first year of Leadership Challenge 2001, the integrating facilitator was a gay man, but in the second and third years, a straight woman carried this role.

The Lundy Foundation, under the direction of Dukay, provided administrative management for the initiative and had visible involvement in the training throughout. In addition, members of the evaluation team were integral to the program, including involvement in curriculum design and ongoing assessment of project outcomes.

A collaborative approach guided the way instruction was delivered. For example, faculty, management, and evaluators met in the middle and at the end of each instructional module to discuss how things were working and brainstorm changes that seemed necessary. In the second year of the program, upcoming faculty were brought in to observe the work that preceded their own, so that they had an understanding of how the group dynamic felt and how the content of instruction was being delivered. During the second and third years of the program, several participants volunteered to be part of session debriefings.

## Choosing Participants

An important part of the design of the initiative was to bring together a truly representative cross-section of the GLBT community in Colorado. If members of this group could learn to trust one another, developing interpersonal networks and working collaboratively, they could serve as a model for the larger community.

Achieving the desired representation was a fairly complex process. The Lundy Foundation convened a seven-member selection committee to assist in recruiting and selecting participants for the program. In addition, a person-of-color outreach coordinator was hired to help ensure that targeted demographic goals were met: achieving a balance across age; race and ethnicity; geographical representation (rural and urban); gender; sexual orientation (including bisexuals and transgender individuals); socioeconomic status; ability and disability; education; sector of employment (public, private, nonprofit); and current versus emerging leaders.

In order to reach the desired diversity goal, the number of individuals who would be invited to participate in the program was increased from the original target of twenty-five. Ultimately, one hundred applications were submitted. The selection committee chose forty-three to participate. All but two accepted.

## Year One: Exploring Self and Others

A month and a half after the commitment ceremony at the Governor's Mansion, Leadership Challenge 2001 participants met again, this time with sleeves rolled up ready to work. Assembled in a large room were many of Colorado's current and emerging GLBT community leaders. Although some people knew one another, virtually no one knew everyone in the room.

The first year of Leadership Challenge 2001 included twenty-one days of training, about two days a month over a nine-month period, plus two retreats in the Colorado mountains. A central focus of the year was encouraging participants to explore issues that unite them as a community as well as those that divide them—an essential exercise in creating a culture of collaboration. These issues were addressed with an emphasis on personal development, including an assessment of leadership practices and interpersonal skills.

In the first session, considerable time was spent establishing ground rules for how the group would operate. In the second session, a simulation game, "Star Power," designed to help participants understand how power and privilege affect relations in society, provided a powerful learning experience, as participants found themselves acting out stereotypes of the roles they had been assigned, often contrary to the ways they perceive themselves acting in everyday life.

In general, the first year focused on skills training, especially related to the overt and covert dimensions of interpersonal communications, conflict management, facilitation, decision making, and team dynamics.

Participants developed a goal statement:

> The overarching goal of the Leadership/Community Building Initiative is to develop a statewide network of gay/lesbian/bisexual/ transgender (GLBT) leaders, to help these individuals increase their leadership capacities, and to encourage them to focus their collaborative energies so as to positively affect the quality of life in the GLBT community.

Running parallel to skills training was the equally, if not more, important work of developing a sense of cohesion and trust within the group. In a very real sense, the broad diversity of participants mirrored not only the diversity of the community, but also embodied the challenge of building bridges of trust across differences. The first real test of how well this part of the program was succeeding came toward the middle of the first year. During a training session, a facilitator checked in with the group, asking if there were any issues not on the table that needed to be there. What came forth, with little hesitation, was a challenge that the group had not explicitly addressed issues of racism.

In order to address this issue, much of the planned agenda for the next day was scrapped, and time was set aside to explore concerns. This was clearly something that could not simply be discussed and set aside. Facilitators and participants agreed to form a committee to help design a module (three-day session) for Year Two focusing on the ISMs, as the group came to call them—racism, ageism, sexism, classism, and other forms of discrimination.

Much of the second half of the year focused on understanding team dynamics and practicing skills in a team environment. By the end of the first year, participants were able to reflect on what they had learned and the time commitment required of them—for example:

> "The progress we have made, and the growth I have seen, have only increased my desire to see this through to success."

> "The curriculum has very real applications in my life, and experience has taught me that there isn't a way to get the complete picture if one doesn't put in the effort."

Participants also honestly reflected on the significant time commitment required of the program.

## Year Two: Developing a Vision and Working in Teams

The focus in Year Two shifted from learning and practicing individual and interpersonal leadership skills to an emphasis on working in teams. Whereas in the first year teamwork was based on classroom exercises, in the second year participants had to develop projects and test their learnings in the larger community.

The year began with several significant and unexpected challenges. The first three days were held at a mountain retreat. Early on the second day, three African American participants shared with the group their feelings of intense discomfort regarding the physical setting and negative associations that the setting provoked about the historic persecution of blacks. The unplanned discussion that followed was so powerful that the faculty and management team altered the agenda in order to accommodate some of the issues raised.

There was a constant underlying tension between what the group later came to call track one and track two issues—personal and interpersonal development work (internal) and team project work in the community (external). A difficult challenge throughout the program was simply keeping on track in the curriculum as originally planned. The next three days of training addressed racism and other forms of discrimination within the GLBT community. Although these sessions had been designed before the retreat incident, they dovetailed well with the challenges and concerns raised there.

In approaching the ISMs, it is clear that while pain can be an element that binds community, it can also divide (Collins, 1998). All participants identified with the pain of being ostracized for their sexual orientation. But each has multiple identities. Does an older lesbian black woman identify with her sexuality alone? Clearly not. So when sexual orientation is not an issue, those other identities—gender and color, for example—can come more significantly into play. They can have a greater effect of creating barriers between individuals and make developing a sense of community more difficult.

A clear precondition for the group to be able to address the ISMs was the development of a sufficient level of trust to allow participants to understand and appreciate one another's perspectives, especially when a perspective directly challenged their own. It is difficult to imagine these sessions occurring earlier than they did in the curriculum. An adequate foundation was needed before issues could be exposed and openly discussed. Consequently, at this point in the program, it was heartening to observe that Leadership Challenge 2001 participants were remarkably honest with one another. That they could engage in difficult conversations—some of them on a very personal level, but none of them so threatening as to break the bonds that had formed—speaks to the level of trust that had developed within the group.

After a holiday break and about halfway through the second year, the group spent two days developing a collective vision of what the GLBT community in Colorado might look like in the future. They began by developing a statement of purpose:

> United through individual responsibility, we pledge to serve, inspire and lead the GLBT community to realize a society that elevates the humanity of all, where justice and equality prevail.

Using a large sheet of paper, everyone employed color markers to leave his or her graphic "fingerprint" on a mural expressing their vision.

Participants then agreed on the following core values that would guide their interaction: service, courageous responsibility, social justice, respect, heart and soul, and integrity. With these values and vision in mind, the participant group was asked to define key leverage areas—places where they could focus action in order to affect long-term change in the GLBT community. These leverage areas would drive their project work over the course of the year. Eventually, participants selected five key leverage areas, self-assigned to project teams in each, and defined their missions:

- *Civic responsibility.* GLBT community members may serve in public positions, but if they remain closeted, their appointments do not raise public awareness of the positive contributions the community makes to civil society. The strategic issue that this team chose to explore was identifying ways to increase participation of GLBT community members on public boards and commissions in the Denver area. The team felt that appointments to such positions could serve as a stepping-stone to future elected office and increased political empowerment.

- *Internal communications.* Colorado has many GLBT organizations, but relatively limited networking among them. The strategic issue chosen by this team was to build a broad communication network, based on the model of collaboration created by Leadership Challenge 2001 and ultimately to conduct a statewide summit of existing organizations and interested individuals.

- *Building alliances in the larger community.* The strength of any marginalized community is limited; consequently, leveraging social change requires building effective alliances. The strategic issue that this team chose was to identify ways of building a network of progressive non-GLBT allies willing to work collaboratively toward realizing a comprehensive social justice agenda congruent with the Leadership Vision 2003.

- *Strategy movement planning.* It is difficult to create a collaborative social movement without a shared capacity for reflective action. The strategic issue this team chose was to define the preliminary design of a model for a think tank for Colorado's GLBT community.

- *Youth issues.* Strengthening the GLBT community clearly means being more inclusive. Youth are an important potential source of energy for the community, but often their voices are not heard. The strategic issue this team selected was to identify issues of concern to Colorado's GLBT youth and to examine ways that their concerns were and were not being addressed by existing organizations.

For the remainder of the year, each team engaged in research to develop a clearer idea of the challenges and opportunities available in their selected strategic area. For some teams, this research served to correct erroneous assumptions that they initially held; for other teams, it confirmed assumptions and led to the revision of project plans.

Simultaneously, individuals were challenged to employ principles of effective teamwork. This included addressing the challenges related to diversity without getting derailed by them. In a very real sense, the teams served as laboratories for collaboration.

At the end of the year, participants invited fifty community members to discuss their work and provide them with feedback. In general, responses to the work were positive and served to confirm that teams had identified areas that other community activists perceived as important.

## Year Three: Taking the Work into the Community

The goal of the final year of Leadership Challenge 2001 was for participants to be able to manage the challenges intrinsic to creating meaningful social change in the GLBT community. Although this year was expected to build directly on the work of teams up to this point, the Year Two teams were dissolved at the beginning of the third year, and participants were free to redefine the strategic focus of their work.

A central challenge for the year was to strike an effective balance between what decisions needed to be made by the management team and facilitators so that they could plan their work and what decisions participants needed to make regarding the work they would find meaningful. If the year was to be successful, then it would need to be more truly collaborative, with participants taking greater responsibility for defining their needs and facilitators and management team willing to share responsibility. Participants defined key leverage points, formed three new teams, and were assigned the task of convening the community to test their assumptions in three areas.

The Youth and Aging team defined its goal as seeking to create greater inclusivity by building bridges between youth and senior populations. Working in partnership with these populations, the team hoped to strengthen their links with the broader GLBT community in creating safe, supportive environments for dialogue, as articulated in this goal statement: "In all of our work, we are mindful that youth and senior populations comprise the full range of human diversity with regard to race, ethnicity, language, cultural heritage, national origin, political affiliations, religious tradition, physical ability, gender identity or expressions of sexual orientation, and many other categories, whether chosen or imposed."

A second team dealt with the issue of Power and Oppression, a focus clearly reflecting the ISMs work. Their goal statement was: "To develop tools and awareness that draw connections between individuals' belief systems on power and oppression and individuals' behaviors in their organizations to enable Leadership Challenge 2001 participants to become change agents in GLBT communities." This team expected to place a major focus of their work on how Leadership Challenge 2001 participants themselves were dealing with issues of power and oppression.

The third team dealt with the issue of increasing Access and Involvement in GLBT Organizations. The group's concern, in part, was focused on increasing access of different segments of the GLBT population to organizations, but a more central concern was to strengthen the ability of organizations serving the community to work with one another. The team's goal statement asked, "How do we lay to rest some of the in-fighting? It turns donors off. How can we make it clear to donors, volunteers, clients, and others that these organizations get along? Boards of directors should not be name-calling. Executive Directors should work together. We need to go through the process ourselves and then disseminate the model of how to engage community and doing things differently."

Participants then organized themselves into teams and developed strategic plans, based on the results of their convening community. Simultaneously, they explored how the work of all the teams could be integrated in support of the overall vision and goal that they identified for Leadership Challenge 2001.

## Outcomes

It is still too early to tell what the long-term, sustainable impacts of Leadership Challenge 2001 will be. In alignment with the desired results of the program, participants must now go back to their organizations, work to bring about change there, then work collaboratively with other organizations to meet the needs of the larger community more effectively. Realistically, significant systemic change could take years. Nevertheless, there are some early indications of success, as illustrated by the following example.

Toward the end of the second year of the program, its impacts on the leadership practices of participants were beginning to emerge. Some of this was evident in the ways that participants were working in the program itself, but other examples were occurring outside the training.

The application of collaborative practices to the work that participants were doing is illustrated by a second-year team project focusing on the issue of building alliances between GLBT and non-GLBT organizations around a shared interest in advancing social justice. The mission that the group defined for itself was "to clarify and build a network of progress allies that will work toward a comprehensive agenda congruent with the Leadership 2003 vision." The group believed that the GLBT community could not achieve its goal of effecting desired social change alone. It would need to leverage its capacity by building effective alliances.

The team began by surveying training participants, in part to identify non-GLBT organizations that they were involved with and in what ways. The survey revealed three significant findings:

- Thirty-nine responding participants were in some way working with or supporting a total of 145 different organizations.

- Respondents offer strong financial support to these organizations, but they were only infrequently members of their boards or staff.
- Respondents who were volunteering with organizations generally were not out to others in those organizations.

In order to understand how these organizations might be engaged as allies, the team conducted a second survey of three selected organizations. Based on information that they gathered on mission, membership, and activities, the team concluded that these organizations were very accepting of GLBT individuals and that it would be reasonable to expect them to become allies on social justice issues. Furthermore, the team concluded that if the contributions being made by GLBT individuals were more visible, such visibility alone could provide an important foundation for alliance building.

In contrast to this finding, it is important to acknowledge that a basic belief of the training participants was that the GLBT community needs to strengthen its own organizations first, before reaching out to form alliances with organizations outside the community. This team's research suggests a different way of building capacity: by reaching out early across organizational and community boundaries and building alliances.

An example of how principles of collaboration are being applied outside the training sessions also developed during the second year. A major fundraiser is conducted every February by the Denver chapter of the Human Rights Campaign (HRC), a gay and lesbian political action group that works primarily at the federal level.

The steering committee for the banquet planned to hold the event at a hotel owned by a major national chain. Two months before the event, a steering committee member ran into a fellow Leadership Challenge 2001 participant at a local bar. He asked where the HRC banquet was going to be held and was shocked to hear that it was to be at a hotel whose parent corporation was on the verge of being sued for racially discriminatory actions at another facility. Wasn't HRC aware of that fact? If not—having heard of it now—shouldn't the banquet steering committee move the event? This challenging set of questions was coming from a gay black activist with the ability to launch a boycott of the HRC dinner if that organization failed to respond in a manner that he felt was appropriate. For its part, HRC stood to lose a sizable deposit by pulling out of the hotel so close to the event, and it was not clear that an alternative venue was even available.

This situation could have easily flared up into a nasty confrontation between different factions of the local GLBT community. However, because the key individuals on both sides knew each other through Leadership Challenge 2001 and had developed a degree of trust, they agreed to take a couple of weeks to allow the banquet steering committee to investigate the charges and see if an alternative facility or course of action was available. In the end, HRC agreed to move the event. That decision demonstrated its solidarity with other major organizations protesting the hotel's discriminatory actions and showed the broader civil rights sympathies of a national GLBT organization often identified with more privileged, primarily white members.

Reflecting back on the incident, both of the Leadership Challenge 2001 participants felt that their training had positively affected their actions in several ways. It made them more sensitive to the importance of consensus building, including building buy-in among steering committee members and then between the local committee and the national organization. It also gave them an appreciation of the importance of "going to the balcony" and seeing things from another person's perspective—a practice that nationally recognized mediation expert Bill Ury had taught the group in a training session the first year.

In general, by the end of the second year of the program, it was clear that important networks were forming among participants. These networks were held together not simply by the personal contacts that people had made but by the trust that had been developed and the opportunities to share personal values and aspirations, providing the social capital necessary to address effectively the challenges of change in society.

## Key Learnings

Several other incidents, similar to the HRC banquet issue, provide early evidence that the skills learned through Leadership Challenge 2001 training are starting to affect the culture of collaboration in Colorado's GLBT community. Although the three-year training program has not yet concluded, some lessons can be drawn regarding efforts to create the training initiative itself:

• *Modeling the way.* Part of the challenge of creating a program in collaborative leadership is to be able to model that ethic in every aspect of the program, from design, to facilitation, to the training itself. The program was challenged to "walk its talk," and it has thus far met that challenge.

• *Reflective practice.* Individuals need theories of leadership but theory grounded in practice. Strengthening leadership capacity requires testing assumptions in the real world of organizations and community. In addition to traditional instruction, individuals being trained in leadership benefit from self-assessments and team coaching and mentoring.

• *Mutual construction.* Most leadership training programs make a clear distinction between trainers and trainees: one holds the knowledge, and the other is there to receive it. By contrast, Leadership Challenge 2001 has evolved in a process of mutual construction. This began with the initiating committee's defining the need and direction. As the program progressed, participants were expected to take increasing responsibility for its design, including identifying the focus of their projects in the community and being accountable for results. However, project work can be a distraction from the goals of leadership training if it is not perceived as being authentic and supporting useful learning for participants and the community.

• *Building trust and commitment.* Leadership Challenge 2001 required a major time commitment on the part of participants that had to be maintained along the way. In addition, the fact that this was a pilot program required that participants, facilitators, and management team trust the process, while at the same time they all were engaged in inventing and reinventing it. A major challenge in building trust is addressing the ISMs in ways that are authentic and empowering .

• *Dedicated and visible leadership.* Leadership Challenge 2001 resulted from the vision and commitment of one individual who served as the catalyst for development and implementation throughout. That individual constantly had to address challenges and redefine his role, as needed, to meet the demands of the program. Perhaps his greatest challenge, though, was simply knowing when to let go and turn the work back to the participants.

These and other lessons drawn from Leadership Challenge 2001 are applicable to leadership development in other socially emerging communities. All face challenges similar, if not identical, to the GLBT community. Some have a deeper history of efforts at organizing and training, but most are relatively new at it. Leadership Challenge 2001 offers one model for developing a form of collaborative leadership that can serve such communities. It is only a step, but an important one.

APPENDIX A

# LEARNING FROM RESEARCH AND EXPERIENCE

Collaboration attracts a broad spectrum of supporters and critics ranging from enthusiastic proponents, to lukewarm skeptics, to downright hostile opponents. Questions about it cover a gamut of perspectives. Is collaboration truly viable and valuable in the public arena? Can it replace or complement more traditional, ways of making public decisions? When collaboration fails, is the concept flawed, or does failure come from poor preparation and execution? Despite extensive experience with collaboration, relatively few studies and little in the way of reliable theory exist. What is known about collaboration tends to come from anecdotal evidence rather than from disciplined and rigorous research.

This appendix begins with an overview of the research methodology used to inform *Collaborative Leadership* (Chrislip and Larson, 1994), provides an assessment of this research incorporating new information from other researchers and practitioners, and presents an emerging agenda for future research on collaboration.

## Discovering the Keys to Successful Collaboration

The original research for *Collaborative Leadership* provided an understanding of collaboration in terms of why people choose to work together, the premises that inform their thinking about how public concerns should be addressed, the principles or practices that make for successful collaboration, and the form of leadership necessary to make it work. The research focused primarily on community and regional, ad hoc, multistakeholder collaborative initiatives rather than on partnerships between organizations. The research took place in 1992 and 1993 analyzing examples of collaboration occurring over several years from about 1985 to 1991.

Our research began with the assumption that working together on public concerns was both possible and practical. We quickly found a number of collaborative initiatives that achieved measurable and substantial results verifying this assumption. Since collaboration clearly worked, we wanted to know what made it work. We chose six cases as exemplars of collaboration and performed a detailed analysis of each one in order to develop tentative conclusions or hypotheses about the nature of successful collaboration.

We used the following criteria for selecting the cases:

- There were concrete, tangible results. That is, a fundamental impact on the root cause of a problem or situation was made. The effort produced more than simply a set of activities or some structure building with no real impact on the problem.
- The problem was sufficiently complex that collaboration across sector lines in the community was necessary in order to affect the problem or condition.
- Significant barriers or obstacles existed that had to be overcome in addressing the issue.
- There were many diverse stakeholders involved in the issue. It was not simply a collaboration of vested interests but went beyond to address concerns of the community as a whole.
- There was widespread acknowledgment and recognition of success in dealing with the issue.

The exemplary cases used to develop our hypothesis were the Phoenix Futures Forum, the Baltimore Commonwealth, the Newark Collaboration Group, Citizens for Denver's Future, Roanoke Vision, and the American Leadership Forum (Chrislip and Larson, 1994). A series of interviews with stakeholders and observers helped us identify a preliminary set of characteristics of successful collaboration. We tested these preliminary hypotheses on a larger sample of cases to develop the final list of the keys to successful collaboration

Ten characteristics of successful collaboration emerged from this analysis. At the time of the research, these characteristics were grouped into three broad categories:

- *Context.* The kinds of problems, the conditions surrounding the collaborative effort, and the broader context within which collaboration is more likely to succeed

- *Results.* The tangible results of the collaborative efforts, the less concrete results, and some noteworthy side effects associated with these cases
- *Process.* How it was done and what emerged as explanations or reasons for its success

Since completing the research, further experience suggests another way of organizing these characteristics that better reflects the way most collaborative processes unfold:

- *Getting to collaboration.* The contextual factors surrounding the initiation of a collaborative process, the motives for collaboration, and the role of leadership in getting started
- *Key elements.* The main organizing elements of a collaborative process and the dynamics of what happens when these elements are in place
- *Critical roles.* The roles that must be played in order for collaboration to work

These three categories provide a framework for describing our previous findings (Chrislip and Larson, 1994) and for incorporating new lessons from other research and experience.

## Evaluating the Keys to Successful Collaboration

Using the earlier findings as a starting point, new information from other research or experience either corroborates, negates, or extends our earlier conclusions. Where necessary, new topics not present or obvious in the earlier research have been added.

### Getting to Collaboration

Two characteristics influencing why people work together emerge from research and experience: contextual factors and convening leadership.

***Contextual Factors.*** One finding in the earlier research addressed contextual factors:

- *Good timing and clear need.* The initiation of the project was timely in that some stakeholders were ready to act in response to a clear need. There was a sense of urgency, which provided initial momentum to the effort.

Good timing and clear need help catalyze collaboration, especially when a sense of crisis exists. Others describe this as a favorable political and social climate (Mattessich and Monsey, 1992). Where these conditions do not exist, a sense of urgency must be created by leadership within the community or region. One report observes, "The only thing more challenging than a crisis may be its absence" (Peirce and Johnson, 1997, p. 16).

Other contextual factors that influence the possibility of collaboration include a history of similar efforts in the community (Mattessich and Monsey, 1992, p. 12). Previous success with collaboration helps encourage future collaboration. When gridlock or stalemate is present, collaboration becomes more likely. Snow describes this as "a perceived threat, major challenge, or new opportunity for a power shift felt by all stakeholders" (Snow, 1997, p. 36). The parties involved recognize collaboration as the only option. Unilateral action is no longer possible. A widespread awareness of collaborative alternatives and commensurate leadership capacity encourages working together.

*Convening Leadership.* The original research identified strong leadership of the process as a significant factor in sustaining collaboration but failed to emphasize its importance in the initiation of a collaborative process. In the absence of crisis, strong leaders "whose energy and vision mobilizes others to participate" are needed (Selin and Chavez, 1995, p. 191). Someone has to take the first step and be willing to take a risk to do something differently (Wondolleck and Yaffee, 2000). This convening and catalyzing role is essential for getting to collaboration (Mattessich and Monsey, 1992; Snow, 1997).

## Key Elements

In *Collaborative Leadership*, we identified what we called the collaborative premise. This premise captured a mind-set about how public issues could be addressed. These underlying beliefs contrast starkly with the usual ways of coping with these problems. Rather than a power struggle between opposing coalitions, collaboration relies on inclusion of diverse stakeholders, a constructive process for engaging them, and good information to inform their work to produce meaningful results. Several findings from our earlier research refer to these three key elements. Further research and experience corroborate and extend these findings.

*Inclusion.* Two characteristics identified in the earlier research refer to inclusion. Working together implies inclusion and, virtually all studies of collaboration verify its importance. In *Collaborative Leadership*, we described it as follows:

- *Broad-based involvement.* The effort involved many participants from several sectors—for example, government, business, and community groups—as opposed to few participants predominantly from one sector.

Others describe inclusion in a similar fashion: "The collaborative group includes representatives from each segment of the community who will be affected by its activities" (Mattessich and Monsey, 1992, p. 12). According to Susskind, "To be credible, a consensus building group must include participants representing the full range of interests and views relating to the issue or dispute" (Susskind, 1999b, p. 22). Another analyst observes that "the table gets larger—and rounder" (Peirce and Johnson, 1997, p. 10). Snow characterizes collaboration as "coalitions of the unalike" (Snow, 1997, p. 35).

Another aspect of inclusion reported in *Collaborative Leadership* needs refinement:

- *Strong stakeholders groups.* The city or region had strong stakeholder groups that represented many people or organizations. These groups were well organized and could speak and act credibly for the interests they represented. (For example, a strong chamber of commerce may broadly represent the business community; an association of neighborhood organizations may be able to speak credibly for its members.)

While collaborative initiatives should include members or representatives of well-organized groups, the capacity of these representatives to speak credibly for others is suspect. Selecting stakeholders reflecting the range of perspectives and experiences necessary to address the issue rather than selecting them as representatives of various interest groups works better. "It is important to de-couple the individual from his or her organizational label" (Wondolleck and Yaffee, 2000, p. 161). This is especially helpful when strong stakeholder groups do not exist or when the groups are too diffuse or hard to represent.

**Constructive Process.** An inclusive group of stakeholders inherently means diverse and conflicting perspectives on issues and the need for a constructive process. According to Susskind, deliberations must be pursued in a constructive fashion (Susskind, 1999b). Wondolleck and Yaffee defined this as "a meaningful and legitimate process for interaction" (Wondolleck and Yaffee, 2000, p. 101). *Collaborative Leadership* identified two types of findings related to process: characteristics of the process itself and specific results that emerge from the process. We described a constructive process in this way:

- *Credibility and openness of the process.* The process was seen as credible by the participating stakeholders: it was considered fair and was not seen as dominated by any
particular stakeholder group. In addition, the effort was seen as doing meaningful
work and not as simply rubber stamping; stakeholders participated in decision making or in providing input that influenced decisions. The process was open in that
stakeholders were free to participate as they felt necessary; important stakeholders were not purposefully excluded from the process. Norms or ground rules for
participation and meeting behavior were established (explicitly or implicitly) that
supported the credibility and openness of the process. The commitment of the participants was, at least in part, secured by the credibility and openness of the process.

Other research and experience confirms these elements. For example, when the
process is credible, members share a stake in both process and outcome (Mattessich
and Monsey, 1992; Wondolleck and Yaffee, 2000). Clearly defined roles and guidelines for working together influence success (Mattessich and Monsey, 1992; Susskind,
1999b). There is real, substantive involvement of stakeholders (Wondolleck and Yaffee,
2000). All stakeholders participate in decision making (Mattessich and Monsey, 1992).
This necessitates decision making by consensus (Wondolleck and Yaffee, 2000).
The process is flexible and adaptable (Mattessich and Monsey, 1992). Snow describes
the need for "a roughly equal power equation" where no one party can dominate the
process (Snow, 1997, p. 36).

Another finding relates to how collaborative efforts sustain momentum:

- *Interim successes.* The effort was characterized by interim successes along the way,
which built and sustained credibility and momentum. They provided encouragement that something was really happening and helped secure the commitment of the stakeholders to the process. These successes were acknowledged
and celebrated.

Wondolleck and Yaffee described this as "instilling hope by demonstrating success" (Wondolleck and Yaffee, 2000, p. 169).

Other research suggests deeper dimensions of a constructive process reflecting a capacity to address complex issues through adaptive work. Some words typically used to describe the process are *emergent, dynamic, interactive, exploratory,* and
*developmental* (see Gray, 1989). Snow defines collaborative efforts as "learning circles" seeking innovation ahead of compromise (Snow, 1997, p. 35). These characteristics foster deeper relationships, joint learning, fresh insights and perspectives,
and new, previously inconceivable visions, solutions, and strategies. In other words,
collaboration is a transforming experience.

This transformation is reflected in two of the findings described in *Collaborative Leadership* and substantiated by other research:

- *Overcoming mistrust and skepticism.* In the early phases of the project (perhaps when the participants were first learning about the idea behind the project or when the initial meetings were being planned or held), some or many participants were generally skeptical about whether anything significant would be accomplished. In some cases, there was some mistrust about the motives or objectives of those who had initiated the project; in other cases, there was a history of mistrust between different sectors or stakeholders. This skepticism or mistrust decreased over time.

"Successful collaborative efforts do not try to sidestep a lack of trust but instead begin taking steps to build trust" (Wondolleck and Yaffee, 2000, p. 163).

- *A shift to broader concerns.* As the effort evolved, the participants focused less on narrow parochial interests and more on the broader interests of the community. They seemed to recognize that their ability to do something about complex issues required them to collaborate as equal partners rather than as advocates of particular interests.

Wondolleck and Yaffee noted this transformation in their research and related it to unifying visions and goals, recognized interdependence, leading by example, and focusing on the problem, not who to blame (Wondolleck and Yaffee, 2000).

**Good Information.** A third element of successful collaboration is good information. Good information is essential in order for stakeholder groups to make good decisions. Although no specific finding in *Collaborative Leadership* validated it, others confirm the need for good information and joint fact finding, especially on highly technical issues (Susskind, 1999b; Ehrmann and Stinson, 1999, p. 376; McKinney, 2001). Others noted the need to "bound the problem with credible information" (Wondolleck and Yaffee, 2000, p. 134).

## Critical Roles

When collaboration works, several critical roles are played. Four prominent roles are the stakeholders who do the work, process experts who facilitate the engagement, content experts who provide knowledge and information, and strong leaders of the process from the community or region who help stakeholders work together. Several of the characteristics of successful collaboration defined in *Col-*

*laborative Leadership* referred to these roles. Other writers and researchers have expanded our understanding of these roles.

**Stakeholders.**  An earlier discussion described the need for an inclusive group of stakeholders that credibly reflects the broader community or region. This inclusive group of stakeholders plays an essential and well-defined role in collaboration. Stakeholders do the work of defining problems, solutions, visions, and strategies. In order for collaboration to work, this stakeholder group has to become a "constituency for change" (Chrislip and Larson, 1994). If the group succeeds in reaching agreement about what should be done, it also must have enough credibility or influence to hold formal bodies, such as city councils and implementing organizations, accountable for acting on its recommendations. This is not formal decision-making power but informal influence manifested in the inclusive nature of the stakeholder group and in the credibility of its work.

Two specific findings from the research refer to the idea of a constituency for change. The first identified the need for involvement or support from visible leaders:

- *Commitment and/or involvement of high-level, visible leaders.* The effort was characterized by the commitment or involvement of high-level, visible leaders such as mayors, city council members, chief executive officers, and executive directors. When these leaders were not directly involved, their commitment to the process was still obvious. When they were represented by other parties, they delegated decision-making power to the representatives. Their support brought credibility to the effort and was an essential aspect of the success of the endeavor.

Subsequent experience confirms that support from visible leaders is helpful. However, this should not be construed as needing visible leaders from all segments of the community in order to move ahead. Some are necessary to provide visual symbols of the importance of the collaborative effort (Wondolleck and Yaffee, 2000). Similarly, the presence of visible leaders in the stakeholder group should not be construed as wielding inordinate influence on decisions. They engage with other stakeholders as peers.

Visible leaders' delegating decision-making power to a representative poses problems for collaboration. Too many times, representatives who must check for approval with superiors stall a collaborative process. Reconceiving the stakeholder group as a credible reflection of the broader community rather than a select group of representatives of various interests or factions helps mitigate these problems. The credibility to hold others accountable for action on its recommendations comes more from the collective influence of the stakeholder group than from the delegates representing these organizations or interests.

The idea of a constituency for change is implied in one finding of the earlier research and in other research:

- *Support or acquiescence of established authorities or powers.* Established authorities or powers, such as city councils, mayors, and chambers of commerce, agreed to support and abide by the recommendations of the stakeholder groups arrived at through the collaborative process. They did not undermine the results of the project by refusing to live with the recommendations. Their ability to do this came, in part, because they or their constituencies were effectively represented in the process.

"Some collaborative partnerships build support for their efforts by working political channels to educate and influence key elected officials" (Wondolleck and Yaffee, 2000, p. 204). Similarly, Snow calls policy collaboratives "power circles" because they rearrange and confuse typical polarities to catalyze a power shift (Snow, 1997, p. 35).

**Process Experts.**  Most successful collaborative initiatives rely on process experts to help them achieve results. The more diverse the stakeholder group and the more complex the issue, the more imperative it is to have skilled, experienced facilitators (Elliott, 1999; Wondolleck and Yaffee, 2000). Process experts help stakeholders reach agreement on the issues that concern them but are impartial or neutral about content. Stakeholders do the work of gathering information, analyzing it, and defining problems, solutions, visions, and strategies.

**Content Experts.**  Good information is a key element of successful collaboration. Outside expertise can help stakeholders gather and understand this information (Ehrmann and Stinson, 1999; Wondolleck and Yaffee, 2000). Stakeholders have access to technical expertise while remaining in control of the information-gathering process. The information provided by content experts informs the deliberations of the stakeholder group but does not supplant its judgement.

**Strong, Facilitative Leaders.**  Like any other collective human endeavor, collaboration requires leadership, but it is leadership with a different focus. A singular characteristic of virtually all successful collaborative initiatives is the presence of a few strong facilitative leaders in the stakeholder group. Some writers have called this "mediative" or "collaborative" leadership (Snow, 1997, p. 36; McKinney, 2001, p. 40). In *Collaborative Leadership*, we defined this type of leadership as follows:

- *Strong leadership of the process.* The effort was characterized by at least a few (often many) examples of strong leadership of the process rather than strong leadership through advocacy of a particular point of view. Leadership of the process was exhibited in many ways, among them, keeping stakeholders at the table through periods of frustration and skepticism, acknowledging small successes along the way, helping stakeholders negotiate difficult points, and enforcing group norms and ground rules.

This type of leadership cannot be provided by those with strong agendas about what should be done because they might use their authority or influence to promote their own interests at the expense of others. Process experts or facilitators cannot provide this kind of leadership because they generally have little power or influence beyond their defined role. A few stakeholders with the credibility to encourage and support collaborative work without dominating or directing help catalyze, convene, facilitate, and sustain these efforts.

## Developing an Agenda for Future Inquiry

Collaboration offers an alternative approach to public concerns that works in some circumstances or conditions and not in others. It is not a panacea. Practitioners need to have the capacity to assess a particular situation and then help stakeholders decide whether collaboration is appropriate. When stakeholders choose to work together, the practitioner must have the skills to help them achieve results.

A long history of failed collaborations makes the choice to collaborate more difficult. These failures lead many to conclude that collaboration simply will not work. Rarely do these masters of hindsight take the time to look further.

Much of the literature on collaboration is anecdotal. While high-quality storytelling has great value, it cannot replace academic research. The reliance on anecdote reflects the recent emergence of collaboration as a social phenomenon and the paucity of rigorous studies of its principles and practices.

The shortage of good research also reflects the lack of a commonly held definition of what should be expected from collaboration. For example, researchers generally acknowledge that collaborative initiatives increase social capital. Building social capital may not be enough by itself to justify the expenditure of time and resources that collaboration demands. While many collaborative initiatives produce measurable short-term results, it is less clear that they produce deeper, longer-lasting, systemic responses to public issues. If deeper, substantive results are necessary, how can researchers identify and measure them? How should the quality of the decisions reached through collaboration be measured? Advocates make claims about the value of inclusion in terms of new perspectives and insights that lead to innovation, but others feel that collaboration leads only to compromise and the lowest common denominator. When the result is the lowest common denominator, is it because the concept is flawed or the execution? (See Kenney, 2000, for an extended discussion of these questions and the need for further research.)

If answering these questions would help build understanding of the importance of collaboration and what makes it work, a definition of successful collaboration can help focus future research and establish expectations for future collaborative initiatives. Such a definition of a successful collaborative endeavor might include these elements:

- The initiative builds social capital, that is, it builds relationships and skills for working together, increasing the capacity of the community or region to address future issues in constructive ways.
- The initiative produces short-term, perhaps symptomatic, responses to immediate presenting problems or areas of concern.
- The initiative produces longer-term, sustainable responses to deeper systemic problems or concerns.
- The initiative produces innovative responses to concerns that would not have occurred in the absence of adaptive work performed by a collaborative group.

Some examples of collaboration meet these standards, yet few serious efforts to find and study them in a rigorous way exist. The research that informed *Collaborative Leadership* was an early attempt, but understanding collaboration and satisfying skeptics needs more comprehensive efforts. Good theory and good practice must inform future efforts.

## An Emerging Agenda for the Study of Collaboration

1. *Getting to collaboration.* What provided the motivation to collaborate? What role did leadership play in getting to collaboration? Why was a collaborative strategy selected? Can collaborative strategies work in the absence of a crisis?
2. *How the process was initiated.* How was the process initiated? Who provided the credibility to convene or catalyze the process? What leadership practices were used to perform these tasks? How were participants and stakeholders selected? To what extent did the stakeholder group reflect the broader community? How was the process designed? What particular challenges was it designed to address? What was the process design? Why? Who provided the resources to support the process, and how were they obtained? How did this shape or otherwise affect the perceived credibility of the effort?
3. *How the process worked.* How did the stakeholder group become a constituency for change? How did the group's relationships evolve during the process? How

and why did these changes occur? How did the process build a series of agreements that could be implemented? What role did content experts play in informing the process? What role did process experts play in facilitating the process? Who played leadership roles in the process, and what practices did they use to help make the process work? What shifts occurred in terms of the stakeholders' perspectives on the issues? How and why did these shifts occur?

4. *How the initiative connected to the larger community.* How did the stakeholder group communicate its findings to the larger community? How did the community respond to these findings? Why? How credible was the stakeholder group in the eyes of the larger community? Why? What role did the media play?

5. *How the initiative connected with formal decision-making bodies and implementing organizations.* How did the stakeholder group work with, influence, or hold accountable formal decision-making bodies and implementing organizations? Why did implementing organizations accept or adopt the recommendations that came out of the stakeholder group?

6. *What results the process produced.* What specific short-term results or symptomatic responses to the presenting issues did the process produce? What deeper, longer-lasting, more systemic results did the process produce? What innovative responses clearly relate to the collaborative effort? What results in terms of building social capital did the process produce?

---

- For further reference, see the three studies of collaboration that informed this assessment along with the reflections of a number of skilled practitioners and analysts working with communities and regions: Barbara Gray, *Collaborating: Finding Common Ground for Multiparty Problems* (1989), one of the first attempts to provide a systematic framework for a theory of collaboration; Paul W. Mattessich and Barbara Monsey, *Collaboration: What Makes It Work* (1992), a review of research that summarizes findings from eighteen valid and relevant studies of collaboration and identifies a number of factors influencing success; and Julia M. Wondolleck and Steven L. Yaffee, *Making Collaboration Work* (2000), which uses thirty-five case studies to identify lessons of experience from collaboration in natural resource management.

- The lessons from experienced practitioners and analysts come from Philip Brick, Donald Snow, and Sarah Van de Wetering (Eds.), *Across the Great Divide: Explorations in Collaborative Conservation and the American West* (2001), and Lawrence Susskind, Sarah McKearnan, and Jennifer Thomas-Larmer (Eds.), *The Consensus-Building Handbook* (1999).

- For a further exploration of the emerging questions about collaboration relevant to future research needs, see Douglas S. Kenney, *Arguing About Consensus: Examining the Case Against Western Watershed Initiatives and Other Collaborative Groups in Natural Resources Management* (2000).

APPENDIX B

# INSTITUTE FOR CIVIC LEADERSHIP CURRICULUM AND AGENDA

## Overall Program

*Purpose:* Create a network of leaders who can act together on behalf of the shared concerns of the Portland region.

*Outcomes:* Participants will:

- Develop working relationships of trust and respect as diverse leaders and citizens in the region.
- Understand the challenge of leadership in organizations and communities in the Portland region.
- Learn the leadership skills, capacities, and behaviors that can create transformational change in organizations and communities.
- Explore and transform their understanding of themselves and their roles as leaders.
- Understand their roles and responsibilities as citizens and leaders in the region.
- Have an enhanced sense of public purpose and commitment to the well-being of the region.

## Orientation—1 Day

*Purpose:* Introduce participants to the program and to each other.
*Outcomes:* Participants will:

- Understand the scope and purpose of the program.
- Begin building working relationships of trust and respect.
- Explore the challenge of leadership in the Portland region.
- Agree on an initial set of ground rules for working together.

Agenda
    Introductions
    Scope and Purpose of Program
    Expectations
    Ground Rules for Working Together
    Teambuilding
    The Challenge of Leadership in the Portland Region

## The Role and Tasks of Leadership—1 Day

*Purpose:* Provide a framework for thinking about leadership and leadership development.
*Outcomes:* Participants will:

- Understand the challenge of leadership in the Portland region.
- Explore the role and tasks of collaborative leadership that can meet the challenges and transform communities and organizations.
- Have a framework for thinking about and working with leadership and leadership development.
- Have an understanding of the traditional and evolving paradigms of leadership.

Agenda
    The Challenge of Leadership in the Portland Region
        What Makes Leadership Difficult?
        Problem Types
    Implications for Leadership
        The Role and Tasks of Collaborative Leadership
        Leadership: Traditional and Evolving Paradigms
        The Role of Power and Vision in Collaborative Leadership

## Transforming Experience—4 Days

*Purpose:* Provide an experience that transforms how participants perceive themselves, their relationships with others, and their ability to work together as diverse individuals.

*Outcomes:* Participants will:

- Develop trust and respect for each other that transcends barriers of gender, race, class, and sector.
- Have experiences that expand perceptions about self; develop an understanding of the barriers to personal learning; and learn tools and strategies for self-renewal.
- Experientially explore the leadership capacities needed to foster collaboration.

Agenda (Outward Bound)
 Orientation
 Rock Climbing
 Group Initiatives
 Group Challenge (for example, peak climbing)
 Solo
 Reflection and Learning

## Collaborative Leadership—6 Days

*Purpose:* Develop skills and capacities to lead in collaborative ways in communities and organizations by working together on an action project(s) that engages the community in addressing an issue(s) of shared concern.

*Outcomes:* Participants will:

- Learn leadership and group skills and behaviors for working together effectively.
- Have tools for analyzing the leadership dynamics of complex community and organizational problems.
- Understand the lessons of experience about leadership and change in organizations and communities.
- Learn how to design and initiate collaborative initiatives in organizations and communities.
- Use collaborative approaches to leadership and change in communities to design and carry out an action project(s) that engages the community on an issue(s) of shared concern.

Agenda
    Working Together (2 days)
        Principles of Collaboration
        Consensus Building in Groups
        Decision Making
        Facilitative Behavior and Skills
        Selecting an Action Project
    Facilitative Leadership (2 days)
        The Facilitative Leader
           Role and Tasks
           Behavior and Skills
        Collaborative Problem Solving
        Designing the Action Project
    Creating Useful Change (2 days)
        Lessons of Experience from Communities and Organizations
        Understanding the Context for Collaboration
        Designing a Collaborative Intervention
           Process Design and Mapping
        Initiating the Action Project

# The Inner Side of Leadership—2 Days

*Purpose:* Provide an opportunity to explore, reflect on and develop oneself as a person and leader.

*Outcomes:* Participants will:

- Have concepts/frameworks for understanding the inner dimensions of leadership (including ethical leadership).
- Understand the need for and the lessons of experience about self-development and leadership development.
- Examine their own development as a person and a leader and identify ways to continue that development.

Agenda
    Introduction: The Inner Side of Leadership
    The Past as Prologue
    Personal Vision: Composing a Life
    Living the Vision: Obstacles and Openings
    Ethics and Leadership
    Developing the Self as Leader

## Integration and Celebration—1 Day

*Purpose:* Provide an opportunity to integrate the learnings from the year, establish ways to continue learning and working together, and celebrate successes.

*Outcomes:* Participants will:

- Explore the lessons of their experiences and how to carry them into the community.
- Identify ways to continue learning and working together.
- Celebrate!

Agenda
   The Lessons of Leadership
   Leadership Development: Lifelong Learning
      Self
      Group
      Organization and Community
   Leadership in Action
      Enhancing the Network
      Organization and Community
   Celebration

# REFERENCES

Association for Supervision and Curriculum Development. *How to Conduct an Effective Socratic Seminar.* Alexandria, Va.: Association for Supervision and Curriculum Development, 1999. Videotape.

Barber, B. *An Aristocracy of Everyone.* New York: Ballantine, 1992.

Berlin, I. *The Proper Study of Mankind.* (H. Hardy, ed.) New York: Farrar, Straus, Giroux, 1998.

Bernard, C. "Sitkans Collaborate On Waste Disposal." *Sitka Sentinel,* Dec. 12, 2000, p. 1.

Bolman, N. "Put Innovation, Creativity to Work in New Way: Make the Valley a Better Place to Live." *San Jose Mercury News,* Oct. 11, 1998, p. 7P.

Brick, P., Snow, D., and Van de Wetering (Eds.). *Across the Great Divide: Explorations in Collaborative Conservation and the American West.* Washington, D.C.: Island Press, 2001.

Burns, J. M. *Leadership.* New York: HarperCollins, 1978.

Chang, H. *Community Building and Diversity.* San Francisco: California Tomorrow, 1997.

Chrislip, D., and Larson, C. *Collaborative Leadership.* San Francisco: Jossey-Bass, 1994.

Clendinen, D., and Nagouney, A. *Out for Good: The Struggle to Build a Gay Rights Movement in America.* New York: Touchstone, 1999.

Cohen, J. *Defining the Systemic Nature of Leadership Change: The Issue, the Response, the Challenge in Greater Portland.* Portland, Me.: Institute for Civic Leadership, 1993.

Collins, P. H. "Toward A New Vision: Race, Class and Gender as Categories of Analysis and Connection." *Race, Sex and Class,* 1998, *1,* 23–35.

Cronin, T. E. *Direct Democracy: The Politics of Initiative, Referendum, and Recall.* Cambridge, Mass.: Harvard University Press, 1989.

Doyle, M., and Straus, D. *How to Make Meetings Work.* New York: Jove Press, 1976.

Drucker, P. "The Age of Social Transformation." *Atlantic Monthly,* Nov. 1994, pp. 53–71.

Du Bois, P. M., and Hutson, J. J. *Bridging the Racial Divide.* Brattleboro, Vt.: Center for Living Democracy, 1997.

Duberman, M. *Stonewall.* New York: Dutton, 1993.

Ehrmann, J. R., and Stinson, B. L. "Joint Fact-Finding and the Use of Technical Experts." In L. Susskind, S. McKearnan, and J. Thomas-Larmer (Eds.), *The Consensus Building Handbook.* Thousand Oaks, Calif.: Sage, 1999.

Elder, R. "Silicon Rally?" *San Jose Mercury News,* July 12, 1992, p. 7C.

Elliott, M.L.P. "The Role of Facilitators, Mediators, and Other Consensus Building Practitioners." In L. Susskind, S. McKearnan, and J. Thomas-Larmer (Eds.). *The Consensus Building Handbook.* Thousand Oaks, Calif.: Sage, 1999.

Etzioni, A. *The Spirit of Community.* New York: Crown Publishers, 1993.

Fahey, L., and Randall, R. M. (Eds.). *Learning from the Future.* New York: Wiley, 1998.

Foley, M., and Edwards, R. "The Paradox of Civil Society." *Journal of Democracy,* July 1996, pp. 38–52.

Frazier, C., and Imig, D. "Policies for Effective Teacher Education." Unpublished manuscript, 1999.

Fukuyama, F. *Trust.* New York: Free Press, 1995.

Gardner, J. *Leadership: A Sampler of the Wisdom of John Gardner.* Minneapolis: University of Minnesota Press, 1981.

Gardner, J. *On Leadership.* New York: Free Press, 1990.

Gardner, J. "Foreword." In N. Peirce and C. Johnson, *Boundary Crossers: Community Leadership for a Global Age.* College Park, Md.: Academy of Leadership Press, 1997.

Geertz, C. *Available Light.* Princeton, N.J.: Princeton University Press, 2000.

Gellner, E. *Conditions of Liberty: Civil Society and Its Rivals.* New York: Penguin Press, 1994.

Gerston, L. N. "Silicon Valley Survey Reveals Growing Dismay." *San Jose Mercury News,* June 28, 1992, p. 5C.

Goodlad, J. I. *A Place Called School.* New York: McGraw-Hill, 1984.

Goodlad, J. I. *Teachers For Our Nation's Schools.* San Francisco: Jossey-Bass, 1990.

Goodlad, J. I., Soder, R. and Sirotnik, K. A. (eds.). *The Moral Dimensions of Teaching.* San Francisco: Jossey-Bass, 1990.

Goodlad, J. I. *In Praise of Education.* New York: Teachers College Press, 1997.

Gray, B. *Collaborating: Finding Common Ground for Multiparty Problems.* San Francisco: Jossey-Bass, 1989.

Greider, W. *Who Will Tell the People: The Betrayal of American Democracy.* New York: Simon & Schuster, 1992.

Hall, D., and Ames, R. *Thinking Through Confucius.* Albany: State University of New York Press, 1987.

Harwood, R. *Citizens and Politics: A View from Main Street America.* Dayton, Ohio: Kettering Foundation, 1991.

Haugland, S. "Assembly Defines Role of Planning, Economic Panel." *Daily Sentinel,* Sept. 17, 1999, p. 1.

Heifetz, R. *Leadership Without Easy Answers.* Cambridge, Mass.: Belknap Press, 1994.

Henton, D. "A Profile of the Valley's Evolving Structure." In M. L. Chong, W. F. Miller, M.G. Hancock, and H. S. Rowen (Eds.), *The Silicon Valley Edge: A Habitat for Innovation and Entrepreneurship.* Stanford: Stanford University Press, 2000.

Henton, D., and Walesh, K. *Linking the New Economy to the Livable Community.* Palo Alto, Calif.: Collaborative Economics, Apr. 1998.

Henton, D., and Walesh, K. *Innovative Regions: The Importance of Place and Networks in the Innovative Economy.* Palo Alto, Calif.: Collaborative Economics, Oct. 1999.

Ignatieff, M. "On Civil Society: Why Eastern Europe's Revolutions Could Succeed." *Foreign Affairs,* March–April 1995, pp. 135–136.

Interaction Associates. *Facilitative Leadership.* San Francisco: Interaction Associates, 1991.

Jaspers, K. *The Question of German Guilt.* New York: Dial, 1947.

Joint Venture. *The Joint Venture Way: Lessons for Regional Rejuvenation.* San Jose, Calif.: Joint Venture: Silicon Valley Network, 1995.

Joint Venture. *Silicon Valley 2010: A Regional Framework for Growing Together.* San Jose, Calif.: Joint Venture: Silicon Valley Network, 1998.

Joint Venture. *The Joint Venture Way: Lessons for Regional Rejuvenation.* Vol. 2. San Jose, Calif.: Joint Venture: Silicon Valley Network, 2000.

Joint Venture. Statement by Dr. Martha Kanter. Press release, Joint Venture: Silicon Valley Network, May 1, 2001.

Kahane, A. *How to Change the World: Lessons for Entrepreneurs from Activists.* Emeryville, Calif.: Global Business Network, 2001.

Kaner, S. *Facilitator's Guide to Participatory Decision-Making.* Philadelphia: New Society, 1996.

Kaufman, S. "Valley Sliding: Area Outlook Dreary." *San Jose Mercury News,* June 24, 1992, p. 1F.

Kenney, D. S. *Arguing About Consensus: Examining the Case Against Western Watershed Initiatives and Other Collaborative Groups in Natural Resources Management.* Boulder, Colo.: Natural Resources Law Center, 2000.

Kids Count. Annie E. Casey Foundation. [www.aecf.org]. 1998.

Kleiner-Perkins. "Building Better Businesses." [http://www.kpcb.com/]. 2000.

Kretzmann, J., and McKnight, J. *Building Communities from the Inside Out.* Chicago: ACTA Publications, 1993.

Kuralt, C. *America.* New York: Putnam, 1995.

Levander, M. "Valley Execs Offer Schools $20 Million 'Venture' Deal." *San Jose Mercury News,* Jan. 19, 1995, p. 1A.

Lundy Foundation. "Leadership Challenge 2001." Unpublished manuscript. Denver, Colo., 1998.

Mathews, D. *Politics for People: Finding a Responsible Public Voice.* Urbana: University of Illinois Press, 1994.

Mattessich, P. W., and Monsey, B. R. *Collaboration: What Makes It Work.* St. Paul, Minn.: Wilder Foundation, 1992.

McKearnan, S., and Fairman, D. "Producing Consensus." In L. Susskind, S. McKearnan, and J. Thomas-Larmer (Eds.), *The Consensus Building Handbook.* Thousand Oaks, Calif.: Sage, 1999.

McKinney, M. J. "What Do We Mean by Consensus? Some Defining Principles." In P. Brick, D. Snow, and S. Van de Wetering (Eds.), *Across the Great Divide: Explorations in Collaborative Conservation and the American West.* Washington, D.C.: Island Press, 2001.

"Meeting Race Relations Head On." *USA Today,* June 22, 1993, p. 11A.

Mitchell, J. "Joint Venture Must Transform Assent into Action." *San Jose Mercury News,* Jan. 24, 1993a, p. 1E.

Mitchell, J. "Hiring Morgan a Risk Worth Taking." *San Jose Mercury News,* July 10, 1993b, p. 10D.

Mitchell, J. "Joint Venture: Perfect? No. Worthwhile? Yes!" *San Jose Mercury News,* Aug. 22, 1993c, p. 1E.

Moore, C., Longo, G., and Palmer, P. "Visioning." In L. Susskind, S. McKearnan, and J. Thomas-Larmer (Eds.), *The Consensus Building Handbook.* Thousand Oaks, Calif.: Sage, 1999.

Morgan, R. Q. "Joint Venture's Vision: Collaborating to Compete." *San Jose Mercury News,* Jan. 30, 1994, p. 7C.

Okubo, D. *Governance and Diversity.* Denver: National Civic League Press, 1994.

Osborne, D., and Gaebler T. *Reinventing Government: How the Entrepreneurial Spirit Is Transforming the Public Sector.* Reading, Mass.: Addison-Wesley, 1992.

Peirce, N. "John Gardner: Legacy of a Civic Olympian." Press release, Washington Post Writers Group, Mar. 3, 2002.

Peirce, N., and Johnson, C. *Boundary Crossers: Community Leadership for a Global Age.* College Park, Md.: Academy of Leadership Press, 1997.

Philanthropic Initiative. Confidential briefing paper. 1992.

Putnam, R. *Making Democracy Work: Civic Traditions in Modern Italy.* Princeton, N.J.: Princeton University Press, 1993.

Putnam, R. "Bowling Alone." *Journal of Democracy,* 1995, *6* (1), pp. 65–73.

Putnam, R. *Bowling Alone.* New York: Simon & Schuster, 2000.

Saguaro Seminar: Civic Engagement in America. *The Social Capital Community Benchmark Survey.* [http://www.cfsv.org/communitysurvey/]. 2001.

San Jose Mercury News. "The State of the City and the County: We Will Fight to Change Hard Times." *San Jose Mercury News,* Jan. 28, 1993, p. 7B.

San Jose Mercury News. "Doom and Boom: Social Networks Give Silicon Valley a Competitive Edge." *San Jose Mercury News,* June 22, 1994, p. 10B.

San Jose Mercury News. "President Hails Valley Education Alliance." *San Jose Mercury News,* Aug. 8, 1996, p. 14A.

San Jose Mercury News. "Silicon Valley: Victim of Its Own Success." *San Jose Mercury News,* Jan. 13, 1997, p. 1E.

San Jose Mercury News. "Boom Leaves Many Behind." *San Jose Mercury News,* Jan. 13, 1998a, p. 1C.

San Jose Mercury News. "Vision of the Valley." *San Jose Mercury News,* Oct. 7, 1998b, p. 6B.

San Jose Mercury News. "Joint Venture's New Leader Has a Tough Act to Follow." *San Jose Mercury News,* Nov. 30, 1998c, p. 6B.

San Jose Mercury News. "Silicon Valley Quality of Life Gets Low Marks." *San Jose Mercury News,* June 20, 1999, p. 1E.

Sandel, M. "America's Search for a New Public Philosophy." *Atlantic Monthly,* Mar. 1996, pp. 57–70.

Saxenian, A. *Regional Advantage: Culture and Competition in Silicon Valley and Route 128.* Cambridge, Mass.: Harvard University Press, 1994.

Schwanhausser, M. "Uniform Building Rules Set for the Valley." *San Jose Mercury News,* Aug. 31, 1995, p. 1A.

Schwartz, P. *The Art of the Long View.* New York: Currency Doubleday, 1991.

Schwarz, R. *The Skilled Facilitator.* San Francisco: Jossey-Bass, 1994.

Selin, S., and Chavez, D. "Developing a Collaborative Model for Environmental Planning and Management." *Environmental Management,* 1995, *19,* 189–195.

Senge, P. *The Fifth Discipline.* New York: Currency Doubleday, 1990.

Senge, P. *The Fifth Discipline Fieldbook.* New York: Currency Doubleday, 1994.

Sepulveda, J. "The Common Enterprise: A Report from San Antonio, Texas." *National Civic Review,* 2000, *89,* pp. 39–46.

Servid, C. *Of Landscape and Longing.* Minneapolis: Milkweed Editions, 2000.

Shilts, R. *And the Band Played On: Politics, People, and the AIDS Epidemic.* New York: St. Martin's Press, 1987.

Sirotnik, K. A., and Goodlad, J. I. (eds.). *School-University Partnerships in Action.* New York: Teachers College Press, 1988.

Smolar, A. "From Opposition to Atomization." *Journal of Democracy,* Jan. 1996, pp. 24–38.

Snow, D. "What Are We Talking About?" *Chronicle of Community.* 1999, *3*(3), 33–37.

Straus, D. "Designing a Consensus Building Process Using a Graphic Road Map." In L. Susskind, S. McKearnan, and J. Thomas-Larmer (Eds.), *The Consensus Building Handbook.* Thousand Oaks, Calif.: Sage, 1999a.

Straus, D. "Managing Meetings to Build Consensus." In L. Susskind, S. McKearnan, and J. Thomas-Larmer (Eds.), *The Consensus Building Handbook.* Thousand Oaks, Calif.: Sage, 1999b.

Straus, D., and Doyle, M. *How to Make Meetings Work.* New York: Jove Press, 1976.

Strong, M. *The Habit of Thought.* Chapel Hill, N.C.: New View, 1997.

Study Circles. *The Study Circle Handbook.* Pomfret, Conn.: Topsfield Foundation, 1993.

Susskind, L. "Introduction." In L. Susskind, S. McKearnan, and J. Thomas-Larmer (Eds.), *The Consensus Building Handbook.* Thousand Oaks, Calif.: Sage, 1999a.

Susskind, L. "An Alternative to Robert's Rules of Order for Groups, Organizations, and Ad Hoc Assemblies That Want to Operate by Consensus." In L. Susskind, S. McKearnan, and J. Thomas-Larmer (Eds.), *The Consensus Building Handbook.* Thousand Oaks, Calif.: Sage, 1999b.

Taylor, B. "Board Ends Honors-Class Discussion." *Daily Camera,* Dec. 9, 1994a, p. 1.

Taylor, B. "School Board Tensions Erupt." *Daily Camera,* Dec. 10, 1994b, p. 1.

Vaid, U. *Virtual Equality: The Mainstreaming of Gay and Lesbian Liberation.* New York: Anchor Books, 1996.

van der Heijden, K. *Scenarios: The Art of Strategic Conversation.* New York: Wiley, 1996.

Vroman, B. "Joint Venture Will Try to Fly Local Ideas." *San Jose Mercury News,* Jan. 17, 1993, p. 7C.

Wondolleck, J. M., and Yaffee, S. L. *Making Collaboration Work.* Washington, D.C.: Island Press, 2000.

WuDunn, S., and Kristoff, N. D. *China Wakes: The Struggle for the Soul of a Rising Power.* New York: Times Books, 1994.

Zimmerman-Oster, K., and Burkhardt, J. *Leadership in the Making.* Battle Creek, Mich.: W. K. Kellogg Foundation, 2000.

# Index

## A

*Across the Great Divide:* (Brick, Snow, and Van de Wetering), 257
Action plans, 118–119
Activity tracks, 83
"Acts of God," 104
Adaptive work: collaborative, 44–45; providing environment for, 45–46
Adversarial politics: Boulder's legacy of, 8–9; civil society's ability to confront, 22; new civic engagement standards to avoid, 10–12; social capital and mitigating, 24–25; of U.S. interest groups, 27
*The Agenda for Education in a Democracy,* 189
AIDS, 232
Alaska Marine Conservation Culture, 169
ALF (American Leadership Forum), 223
Alliance of Regional Stewardship, 158

American Economic Association, 137
American Electronics Association, 139
American Institute of Architects, 156
American Leadership Forum, 247
AmericaSpeaks, 172–173, 174
Ames, R. T., 200
Angier, J., 225
Applied Materials, 136
*Arguing about Consensus* (Kenney), 257
*The Art of the Long View* (Schwartz), 106
*The Art of Strategic Conversation* (van der Heijden), 106
"As Good As It Gets" scenario, 205
AT Kearney, 154, 156

## B

Ballot initiatives, 13–14
Baltimore Commonwealth, 247
Baranof Island (Alaska), 160, 165. *See also* Sitkan civic culture

Barber, B., 31
Barrales, R., 153–154, 156, 157
Barry, M., 171
Bernard, C., 167
*Blueprint for a 21st Century Community* (JVSV), 142–143, 145
Bolger, B., 134, 136
Bollman, N., 151
Bonding social capital, 24–25
Boston Foundation, 211
Boston region: "City of Villages" scenario, 212; Devil-ution of, 213–214; future of nonprofit sector in, 210–212; "Tea Party II" scenario, 213; "To Hell in a Handbasket" scenario, 214–216
Boulder (Colorado): controversial political activities of, 8–9; debate over honors classes in, 8
*Boundary Crossers,* 151
*Bowling Alone* (Putnam), 7
Brick, P., 257
Bridging social capital, 24–25
Budget, 91

*Building Communities from the Inside Out: A Path Toward Finding and Mobilizing a Community's Assets* (Kretzmann and McKnight), 112
Building and Construction Trades Council, 139
Burkhardt, J., 33
Burns, J. M., 113
Bush, G. W., 153, 156

**C**

California Proposition 187, 13, 14
Call Center, 178
Campaign reform, 12–13
Carolina's Partnership, 203
Carr Center for Human Rights (Harvard University), 25
The Center for Living Democracy, 1
Center for Public Leadership (Harvard University), 45
Central Carolinas Region scenarios, 203–206
Central Oklahoma 2020, 35
Centre for Continuing Study of the California Economy, 137
Centre National de la Recherche Scientifique (Paris), 22
CEO Advisory Board, 139, 140–141
Challenge 2000 Multimedia Project (Joint Venture), 146, 154, 157
Chang, H., 1
Charismatic leadership, 16–17
*Charlotte Observer*, 203
Chavez, D., 249
Chen, W., 139
China, 25, 26
Chrislip, D., 42, 50, 223, 247, 248, 253
Citizen Summit I (Washington, D.C.), 173
Citizen Summit II (Washington, D.C.), 184–185
Citizens: direct democracy/ballot initiatives and, 13–14; entrepreneurial government role by, 15–16; forums for civic engagement for, 34–35; ideal democratic role of, 21–22; judgment of civic leadership by, 113; new

civic engagement standards for, 10–11; understanding public concerns of, 65–68. *See also* Public participation; Stakeholders
Citizens for Denver's Future, 247
The City Is Mine: Youth Summit 2000, 182–183
City of San Jose, 137
"City of Villages" scenario, 212
Citywide Strategic Planning Process (Washington, D.C.), 174
Civic associations: mitigating conflicts function of, 24–25; resisting oppression function of, 23–24
Civic capacities, 30
Civic challenges: campaign reform as, 12–13; charismatic/heroic leadership as, 16–17; communitarian movement as, 17–18; direct democracy/ballot initiatives as, 13–14; evaluating alternative responses to, 12–18; implications for democracy/civic engagement by, 18; legacy of nonviolent approach to, 18–19; public participation as, 14–15; reinventing government as, 15–16; of U.S. Society, 9–10
Civic community: building social capital investment by, 33–34; building the, 129; defining civic capacities of, 30; democratic benefits of, 29–30; developing civic leadership investment by, 32–33; educating for democracy investment by, 31–32; forums for civic engagement investment by, 34–35; investing in the, 31–37; networks of responsibility investment by, 35–36; public decisions responding to, 43; scenarios used by, 202–204*fig*; understanding political dynamics of, 65–66; working with diverse, 1, 122; working together investment by, 36–37
Civic community SWOT analysis of, 102–105
Civic culture. *See* Sitkan civic culture
Civic engagement: civic challenges

requiring, 9–10; implications of civic challenges for, 18; investing in forums for, 34–35; new standards for, 10–12; quality of public decisions and, 43
Civic leadership: civic challenge of charismatic, 16–17; collaborative strong and facilitative, 54, 88, 254–255; convening collaborative, 50; determining collaboration feasibility, 68–70; developing shared responsibility networks with, 35–36; investment in developing civic, 32–33; production measurement of, 113; working with diversity, 122
Civic leadership development program: description/faculty of, 125–128; designing, 123–124; initiating, 122–123; on leadership capacity, 122; outcomes of, 124; participants and evaluation of, 128–129; working premises of, 121–123
Civil rights movement (1950s and 1960s), 23
Civil society: advocating for inclusion into, 23–24; civic challenges of, 9–10; collaboration for sustaining, 5; debate over health of United States, 7; democracy and resisting oppression role of, 22–23; evolution of democracy and, 25–27, 26*fig*; for filling human needs, 2; ideal vision of democracy and, 21–22; mitigating conflicts function of, 24–25; political practices congruent with, 42
Clark, S., 224
CLCO (Citizens League of Central Oklahoma), 35
Clendinen, D., 231
Clinton, B., 149
Cohen, J., 219, 222, 223, 224, 228
Cole, R., 224, 225
*Collaborating Finding Common Ground for Multiparty Problems* (Gray), 257
*Collaboration: What Makes It Work* (Mattessich and Monsey), 257
Collaboration: for building social capital, 5; community invest-

ment in, 36–37; contextual factors of, 248–249; critical roles of, 252–255; defining, 41–42; defining purpose, scope, focus of, 70; determining feasibility of, 68–70; developing agenda for future inquiry into, 255–256; discovering keys to successful, 246–248; emerging agenda for study of, 256–257; evaluating keys to successful, 248–255; getting to, 49–50; incentive for, 50; inclusion element of, 249–250; realizing promise of, 47–48, 119; recent initiatives demonstrating, 2–3; shared understanding required for, 43; stakeholder engagement during, 1–2

Collaboration framework: constituency for change requirement of, 52–53; content experts requirement of, 53; four critical requirements of, 52–54; premise and elements of, 50–51; process expertise requirement of, 53; strong/facilitative leadership requirement of, 54, 88

Collaboration resources, 91

Collaboration strategies: adaptive work of, 44–45; adaptive work structure provided by, 45–46; basic concepts of, 44–47; consensus-based decision making using, 47; deciding on, 68; emergence of, 41; facilitation through, 46–47; role of experts in, 53, 85, 88, 254; working assumptions of, 42–44

*Collaborative Leadership* (Chrislip and Larson), 41, 50, 249, 250, 252

Collaborative premise, 50–51

Collaborative problem solving, 107–108

Collaborative process: budgeting/funding, 91; constructive, 250–252; defining work flow/activity tracks/process map for, 82–83, 84*fig*; designing, 81–83; documenting the, 90–91; four phases of, 54–55, 56*fig*; getting started, 55,

56*fig*, 57, 63–70; initiating, 70; management of, 88–91; moving to action, 56*fig*, 58–59, 113–119; setting up for success, 56*fig*, 57, 71–92; working together, 56*fig*, 57–58, 93–112

Collaborative resources, 91

Collins, P. H., 239

Colorado Educator Licensing Act (1991), 190, 192

CommerceNet, 147

Common Enterprise (TCE), 34

Communitarian movement, 17–18

*Community Building and Diversity*, 1

Community Trusteeship (SLI), 33

Consensus-based decision making, 47

*The Consensus-Building Handbook* (Susskind, McKearnan, and Thomas-Larmer), 257

Constructive process design: for collaborative process, 81–83; defining decision-making method for, 79–80; establishing ground rules and, 80; important role of, 78–79

Content experts, 53, 85, 88, 254

CoPER (Colorado Partnership for Educational Renewal): connections between community and, 192–197; Diversity Cadre formed for, 196–197; educational collaboration by, 187–188; layers of collaboration involved in, 190–192; leadership/professional development and, 197; lessons learned from, 197–199; origins of, 188–190; partner schools involved with, 195–196; teacher recruitment/retention and, 196

Council of Co-Chairs, 139, 141

Courtise, K., 139

Cronin, T., 14

CSI (Customer Service Initiative), 178

Culture: bridging boundaries between participating, 43–44; Sitkan civic, 159–169

Cuneo, T., 156

Cypress Semiconductor, 134

**D**

Dalai Lama, 18

DCPS (District of Columbia Public Schools), 176

Decision makers/making: collaborative and consensus-based, 47; defining method of, 79–80; engaging with, 117–118

Defense/Space Consortium, 144

Del Prado, Y., 139

Deloitte & Touche, 156

Democracy: ballot initiatives and direct, 13–14; civic community education investment in, 31–32; civil society and evolution, 25–27, 26*fig*; civil society and ideal vision of, 21–22; as evolutionary process, 20; implications of civic challenges for, 18; inclusion into civil society and, 23–24; political practices congruent with, 42; resisting oppression as necessary for, 22–23; strategies for deeper U.S., 27–28

Denver Foundation, 194

"Devil-ution" scenario, 213–214

Dewey, J., 31, 189

Dialogue: community building through, 1; debate vs., 97*fig*; engaging through, 96–97; learning skills of, 97–99

Diverse community: challenges of engaging, 1; Colorado GLBT, 230–244; leadership working with, 122

Diversity Cadre (CoPER), 196–197

Documentation, of collaborative process, 90–91

Doyle, M., 46, 96, 107, 108

Drucker, P., 9, 27

Du Bois,, 1

Dukay, V., 232, 234, 236

**E**

Economic Development Roundtable, 156

Economic Prosperity Council, 146, 147

*An Economy at Risk* (SRI report), 137, 138

Education collaboration. *See* CoPER (Colorado Partnership for Educational Renewal)

Education needs, 84

Edwards, B., 23, 25

Ehrmann, J. R., 102, 252, 254

Elder, R., 137

Elliott, M.L.P., 254

Ellison, L., 155

Enterprise Network, 144, 145

Entrepreneurial government model, 15–16

Environmental Partnership, 142, 144, 147

Etzioni,, 17

Experts: content, 53, 85, 88, 254; process, 53, 85, 88, 254

**F**

Facilitation, 46–47

*Facilitator's Guide to Participatory Decision-Making* (Kaner), 46, 79, 96, 108

Fahey, L., 106

Fairman,, 79

Family Violence Prevention Programs conference (2000), 226–227

"Field of Dreams" scenario, 207

*The Fifth Discipline Fieldbook* (Senge), 98, 110

Finding Democracy in Standards-Based Education Initiative (CoPER), 197

"Flight of the Flamingoes" scenario, 201

Focus groups: assessment using, 66; developing protocol for, 66–67

Foley, M., 23, 25

Foundation for the Carolinas, 203

Frazier, C., 188, 193, 195

Fukuyama, F., 31

Future of Boston Area Nonprofits Seminar, 211

**G**

Gaebler, T., 15

Gandhi,, 18

Gardner, J., 1, 35, 117, 120, 151, 199, 258

Gellener, E., 22

Gerston,, 134

Gerzon, M., 80, 97

Getting started phase: analyzing context for collaboration, 63, 65; deciding on collaborative strategy during, 68; defining purpose, scope, focus during, 70; described, 55, 56*fig*, 57; determining collaboration feasibility during, 68–70; guide to practices of successful, 64*fig*; initiating collaborative process during, 70; understanding political dynamics and, 65–66; understanding public concerns of citizens, 65–68

Gilder, G., 139

GLBT (gay, lesbian, bisexual, and transgender) community (Colorado): building leadership problem of, 231–232; diverse nature of, 230; key players in, 232–234; Leadership Challenge 2001 goal of, 230–231; Leadership Challenge 2001 outcomes and, 242–244; Leadership Challenge 20001 implementation by, 234–242

The Global Business Network, 105

Global Trading Center, 144, 145, 147

GMTF (Missoula's Growth Management Task Force), 37, 207, 210

Goldberg Seminars, 203, 211

Goodlad, J. I., 31, 32, 187, 188–189, 190, 191, 198

Government: civil society and democratic, 21–22; Entrepreneurial model of, 15–16; Progressive political model of, 44–45

"Grapes of Missoula" scenario, 207

Gray, B., 251, 257

Greene, C., 147

Gregory, L., 226, 227

Greider, W., 14

Ground rules establishment, 80

Guardino, C., 155

**H**

*The Habit of Thought: From Socratic Seminars to Socratic Practice* (Strong), 100

Hall, D. L., 200

Hammer, S., 137, 139, 140, 142, 149

Hanson, J., 165, 167, 169

Harris, J., 145, 155

Hart, T., 168

Harvard University's John F. Kennedy School of Government, 8, 25, 45

Harwood, R., 11

Haugland, S., 164

Hayes, T., 136, 137, 142, 143

Heifetz, R., 45

Henton, D., 134, 135, 139, 144, 146, 149, 154, 155

Heroic leadership, 16–17

HIV/AIDS, 232

*How to Conduct Effective Socratic Seminars* (Strong videotape), 100

*How to Make Meetings Work* (Doyle and Straus), 46, 96, 108

HRC (Human Rights Campaign) [Denver chapter], 243–244

Human needs, creating society which fills, 2

Hutson, J. J., 1

**I**

IBM, 136

"Icarus" scenario, 201

ICL (Institute for Civic Leadership): curriculum and agenda of, 258–262; initiating collaborative effort of, 220–221; lessons learned from, 228–229; networks of responsibility for, 35–36; origins of, 219–220; outcomes of collaboration, 214, 224–228. *See also* Portland (Maine)

"If Not for Bad Luck" scenario, 205

Ignatieff, M., 25

Imig, D., 193, 195

*In Praise of Education* (Goodlad), 31

Inclusion principle/practice, 74–76

*Index of Silicon Valley* (1995), 144,
   145, 148–149, 150, 158
Indoor Air Forum, 225
Information needs: assessing,
   83–84; defining, 101–103; of
   stakeholders, 100–101
Institute for Educational Inquiry's
   Leadership Associates Program,
   197
IntelliQuest, 154
*Internet Cluster Analysis* (JVSV and
   AT Kearney), 156
Interviews: assessment using, 66;
   setting protocol for, 66–67
Island Institute (Sitka), 160, 163,
   169

**J**

Jaspers, K., 16
Johnson, C., 151, 249, 250
"Joint Fact-Finding and the Use of
   Technical Experts" (Ehrmann
   and Stinson), 102
Joint Venture's Challenge 2000,
   146, 154, 157
Joint Venture's Economic Develop-
   ment Team, 146
Joint Venture's Leadership Council,
   140, 141, 145
Joint Venture's *Lessons for Regional
   Rejuvenation*, 151–152, 153
Joint Venture's Regulatory Streamlining Council, 147
Joint Venture's *Silicon Valley 2010*,
   150–151, 152*t*, 153
Joint Venture's Smart Permit, 154
JVSV (Joint Venture Silicon
   Valley): background of,
   133–135; *Blueprint for a 21st Century Community* recommendations
   by, 142–143, 145; changing
   leadership at, 153–158; concept
   of champions and, 138–140;
   making the case for collaboration of, 135–138; MOUs (memorandums of understanding)
   used by, 142, 145; results generated by, 146–148; shaping of,
   140–143; sustaining collaboration by, 143–146; sustaining
   momentum of, 148–153

**K**

Kahane, A., 202
Kaner, S., 79, 96, 108
Kaufman, S., 134
Kemmis, D., 37
Kennedy, J. F., 170
Kennett, J., 135, 136, 140, 147–148
Kenney, D. S., 257
Kettering Foundation, 12
Kimsham landfill debate (Sitka),
   163–165, 167–168
King, M. L., Jr., 18, 170
Kretzmann, J., 112
Kuralt, C., 214

**L**

"Lame Duck" scenario, 201
Larson, C., 41, 42, 50, 232–233,
   247, 248, 253
Leadership Challenge 2001:
   Connecting, Communicating,
   Collaborating (Colorado):
   curriculum/faculty/participants
   in, 235–237; GLBT commu-
   nity's goal for, 231; GLBT com-
   munity's implementation of,
   234–242; lessons of, 244–245;
   outcomes of, 242–244; year one
   of, 237–238; year three of,
   241–242; year two of, 238–241
Leadership Council (Joint Venture),
   140, 141, 145
Leadership. *See* Civic leadership
*Learning from the Future* (Fahey and
   Randall), 106
*Lessons for Regional Rejuvenation*
   (JVSV), 151–152, 153
Locatelli, P., 139
Longo, G., 110
LRPEDC (Long Range Planning
   and Economic Development
   Commission), 163, 164–165
Lukensmeyer, C. J., 173, 175
Lundy Foundation (Colorado), 234,
   235, 236

**M**

McCracken, E., 139, 143, 155
McKearnan, S., 79, 257

McKinney, M. J., 252, 254
McKnight, J., 112
Maine Environmental Priorities
   Project, 2
*Making Collaboration Work* (Wondol-
   leck and Yaffee), 257
Martinez, C., 153
Mattessich, P. W., 249, 250, 251,
   257
Matthews, D., 12
Meciar, V., 27
MEPP (Maine Environmental Pri-
   orities Project), 225–226
Mills, P., 144
Missoula (Montana), 37
Missoula, Montana scenarios proj-
   ect, 206–210, 208*fig*–209*fig*
Mitchell, J., 140, 143
Monsey, B., 249, 250, 251, 257
Mont Fleur scenarios, 201–202*fig*
Moore, C., 110
*The Moral Dimensions of Teaching*
   (Goodlad, Soder, and Sirotnik),
   189
Morgan, J., 136, 137, 138, 139,
   142, 143, 155
Morgan, R., 143, 144, 145, 148,
   153, 155
MOUs (memorandums of under-
   standing) [JVSV], 142, 145
Moving to action process: de-
   scribed, 56*fig*, 58–59; facilitating
   public forum during, 116–118;
   guide to successful, 114*fig*; importance of, 113, 115; management of, 118–119; reaching out
   during, 115–116

**N**

Nader, R., 14
Nagouney, A., 231
National Civic League, 1, 223
National Semiconductor, 226
Neece, J., 139
Neighborhood Action Forum
   (follow-up), 185
Neighborhood Action Forum
   (January 29), 176
Neighborhood Action Web page,
   175
Networks of responsibility: building

civic community and, 129; civic leadership development and, 121–129; described, 35–36; new role of, 120–121; working leadership premises of, 121–123

Newark Collaboration Group, 247

NGOs (nongovernmental organizations), 27

NLS (National Leadership Symposium), 33

NNER (National Network for Educational Renewal), 32, 188, 189, 190, 193, 198. *See also* CoPER (Colorado Partnership for Educational Renewal)

Nonviolent politics legacy, 18–19

Norton, J., 139

"A Not-So-Grimm Fairy Tale" scenario, 207

NSI (Neighborhood Action Initiative): Citizen Summit I organized by, 174–176; Citizen Summit II organized by, 184–185; core teams developed by, 178–179; focus/functions served by, 177–178; future of, 185–186; implementation/ actions taken by, 176–177; model development of, 180; origins of, 172–173; scope of, 181; SNAP (Strategic Neighborhood Action Plan) of, 181, 185; strategic management cycle of, 183–184; strategic planning/ citizen engagement goals of, 173–174; successful collaboration by, 170; week in life of Ward 1 services under, 179–180. *See also* Washington, D.C.

**O**

Okubo, D., 1

Orr, J., 220, 222, 228

Osborne, D., 15

"Ostrich" scenario, 201

**P**

Packard, D., 155

Palmer, P., 110

Peirce, N., 151, 249, 250

"The People's Republic of Boulder," 8

Peters, T., 139

Pew Charitable Trusts, 173

Phoenix Futures Forum, 247

Platt, L., 138, 155

Political dynamics: adversarial, 8–12, 22, 24–25, 27; understanding the, 65–66

Portland (Maine): cruise ships visiting harbor of, 224–225; described, 214–215; Family Violence Prevention Programs conference (2000) held in, 226–227; MEPP implementation in, 225–226; National Semiconductor's expansion in, 226; political leadership problem of, 219; TPI (The Philanthropic Initiative) of, 220–224; youth need developmental assets study in, 227. *See also* ICL (Institute for Civic Leadership)

Pringle, A., 228

Process experts, 53, 85, 88, 254

Process maps: defining, 83; example of, 86*fig*–87*fig*; symbols used for, 84*fig*

Professional Standards Boards (Colorado), 192, 193

Progressive political model, 44–45

Proposition 187 (California), 13, 14

PRx, 136

Public decisions: engaging with makers of, 117–118; quality of engagement and, 43; responding to community needs, 43

Public forums: facilitating, 116–118; scenarios used in the, 202–204*fig*

Public issues: how citizens think about, 65–68; spectrum of strategies for addressing, 69*fig*

Public participation: as civic challenge, 14–15; civil society function ensuring, 21–22; as equal peers, 44; forums on engagement in, 34–35. *See also* Citizens; Stakeholders

Public Sector Roundtable, 140, 141

Putnam, R., 7, 11, 24, 29, 30, 31, 228

**Q**

*Queen Elizabeth II,* 225

**R**

*Race Matters* (West), 11

Randall, R. M., 106

Referendum process, 13–14

*Reinventing Government: How the Entrepreneurial Spirit Is Transforming the Public Sector* (Osborne and Gaebler), 15

Rice, C., 153

Roanoke Vision, 247

Rodgers, T. J., 134

Rogers, T. J., 137

Romer, R., 231

Rose Community Foundation, 194

Royal Dutch Shell, 105

**S**

*San Jose Mercury News,* 133, 140, 145, 148, 150, 151, 157

San Jose Real Estate Board, 136

Sandel, M., 24, 27

Santa Clara County Manufacturing Group, 136

Santa Clara University, 139

Sawyer, D., 228

Saxenian, A., 134, 148

*Scenarios: The Art of Strategic Conversation* (van der Heijden), 112

Scenarios: used in Boston region, 210–216; Central Carolinas project using, 203–206; used in the civic arena, 202–204*fig*; development of, 103–106; enhancing strategic planning/visioning through, 200; Missoula, Montana project using, 206–210, 208*fig*–209*fig*; Mont Fleur, 201–202*fig*; value of, 216–217

Schirmer, J., 226

Schmidt, L., 226

Schwanhausser,, 147

Schwartz, P., 106

Schwarz, R., 46

Search Institute (Minnesota), 227

Selin, S., 249

SEMATECH, 134

Semiconductor Industry Association, 136

Senge, P., 98, 110

September 11th, 185

Sepulveda, J., 34

Setting up for success phase: defining critical roles during, 84–85, 88; defining information needs during, 83–84; described, 56*fig*, 57, 71; designing constructive process during, 78–83; guide for successful, 72*fig*; identifying/convening stakeholders during, 74–78; initiating time line for, 73*fig*; managing process during, 88–91; principle and practice of inclusion during, 74–76; stakeholder map used during, 75*fig*, 77*fig*

Shared responsibility: defining work flow as part of, 82–83; described, 17; developing networks of, 35–36

Shilts, R., 232

Shoos, J., 227

Silicon Graphics, 139

*Silicon Valley 2010* (Joint Venture), 150–151, 152*t*, 153

Silicon Valley Environmental Partnership, 147

Silicon Valley Manufacturing Group, 155, 158

Silicon Valley Technology Fast 50, 156

Sirotnik, 189

Sitka municipal waste collaboration, 166*fig*

Sitkan civic culture: background on, 160–161; building civic capacity of, 161, 163; Kimsham landfill debate and, 163–165, 167–168; legacy of solid waste strategies development and, 169; "the strategy of first resort" plan and, 167–168; successful collaboration incorporated in, 159; understanding, 161, 162*fig*

*The Skilled Facilitator* (Schwarz), 46

SLI (Student Leadership Institute) [University of Colorado], 33

Slovakia, 25, 26–27

Smart Growth, 156, 225

Smart Permit project (Joint Venture), 154

Smart Valley, 144, 145, 146, 147

Smolar, A., 22, 23

SNAP (Strategic Neighborhood Action Plan) [NSI], 181, 185

Snow, D., 249, 250, 251, 254, 257

Social capital: bonding and bridging, 24–25; building community, 33–34; collaboration for building, 5

Social Capital Community Benchmark Survey (Saguaro Seminar), 8

Social virtues, 17–18

"Society-first" strategy, 22

Socratic inquiry, 99*fig*–100

Socratic Seminar workshops, 197

Soder, 189

Software Industry Coalition, 146

Solectron, 136, 139

Solidarity trade union (Poland), 22

Solow, R., 149

South African Mont Fleur project, 201–202*fig*

South Bay AFL-CIO Central Labor Council, 150

SRI International, 134

SRI report, 137, 138

Stakeholder map: expanding the, 77*fig*; illustration of, 75*fig*

Stakeholders: building broader constituency among, 115–116; building relationships among, 95–96; challenges of engaging diverse, 1; collaboration for engaging, 1–2; collaborative process roles by, 55–59; as constituency for change, 52–53; critical collaboration role by, 253–254; dialogue between, 96–97; establishing ground rules for, 80; identifying/convening, 74–76; information needs of, 83–84, 100–103; methods for identifying, 76–78;

perception of collaboration by, 51; principle and practice of inclusion and, 74–76; visioning/shared vision created by, 108–110. *See also* Citizens; Public participation

"Status Quo Vadis" scenario, 37, 207

Steering committee: establishing, 89; management functions of, 118; staffing to support, 89–90

Steffen, J. "Stef," 169

Stinson, B. L., 102, 252, 254

Stonewall uprising (1969), 232

Strategic planning, 110–112*fig*, 111*fig*

Straus, D., 79, 81, 96, 107, 108

Strong, M., 100

*The Study Circle Handbook* (Study Circles), 98

Susskind, L., 47, 250, 251, 252, 257

SV-CAN (Silicon Valley Civic Action Network), 154, 155, 156

Swardlick, D., 225

Swardlick, D., 225

SWOT (strengths, weaknesses, opportunities, and threats) analysis, 102–105

**T**

Tandem Corp., 139

Tandem Corporation, 136

Tax and Fiscal Council, 156

Taylor, T., 8, 137

TCE (Texas Common Enterprise), 34

"Tea Party II" scenario, 213

Teacher Leadership Initiative (CoPER), 197

Teacher and Special Services Professional Standards Board (Colorado), 192

TechNet, 158

Thomas-Larner, J., 257

Thompson, M-T., 165

Title I CARE Act, 232

Tlingit Indian community, 161. *See also* Sitka civic culture

"To Hell in a Handbasket" scenario, 214–216

Toffler, A., 139

TPI (The Philanthropic Initiative): first test of collaborative acumen of, 222–224; formation of, 220–221

*Trust* (Fukuyama), 31

Turning Point, 169

21st Century Education initiative, 142, 146

**U**

United States: political background between interest groups in, 27; strategies for deeper democracy in, 27–28

United Way, 227

UNUM Foundation, 223

UNUM Insurance, 220

Urban Institute (University of North Carolina Charlotte), 203

Ury, B., 244

*USA Today*, 11

USDC (U.S. Display Consortium), 144

**V**

Vaid, U., 232

Vallaeu, T., 225

Van de Wetering, S., 257

van der Heijden, K., 106

Verstovia Elementary School (Sitka), 163

Vision Leadership Team, 150

"Visioning" (Moore, Longo, and Palmer), 110

Visioning/shared vision, 108–110

Voices & Choices, 203–206

Vroman, B., 140

**W**

Walesh, 149

Washington, D.C.: The City Is Mine: Youth Summit 2000 held in, 182–183; powerful images of, 170–171; transforming governance of, 172–176; Williams recruited to run for mayor of, 171–172; Youth Advisory Council of, 183.*See also* NSI (Neighborhood Action Initiative)

Washington, D.C. Control Board, 171

*Washington Post*, 175

*Washington Times*, 175

Water Monitoring Project, 225

West, C., 11

"Whatever Will Be, Will Be" scenario, 205

Williams, A., 170, 171–172, 173, 186

Wondolleck, J. M., 249, 250, 251, 252, 253, 254, 257

Work flow agreement, 82–83

The Workforce Working Group, 145, 146

Working Group on Physical Infrastructure, 139

Working together phase: building capacity during, 93; building relationships/skills during, 95–96; collaborative problem solving during, 107–108; deciding what needs to be done during, 106–107; described, 56*fig*, 57–58; developing scenarios during, 103–106; developing ways of engaging during, 96–97; guide for successful, 94*fig*; informing stakeholders during, 100–103; strategic planning during, 110–112*fig*, 111*fig*; SWOT analysis during, 102–105; visioning/shared vision during, 108–110

World Bank, 174

WuDunn, S., 26

**Y**

Yaffee, S. L., 249, 250, 251, 252, 253, 254, 257

Young, J., 138

Youth Advisory Council (Washington, D.C.), 183

**Z**

Zimmerman-Oster, K., 33